Melvin B. Tolson's
Harlem Gallery
A Literary Analysis

Melvin B. Tolson's
Harlem Gallery
A Literary Analysis

Mariann Russell

University of Missouri Press
Columbia & London, 1980

University of Missouri Press, Columbia, Missouri 65211
Library of Congress Catalog Card Number 80-50306
Printed and bound in the United States of America

Library of Congress Cataloging in Publication Data

Russell, Mariann, 1935–

    Melvin B. Tolson's *Harlem Gallery:* A Literary Analysis
    Bibliography: p.. 124
    Includes index.
    1. Tolson, Melvin Beaunorus. Harlem gallery. 2. Afro-Americans in literature.
    3. Harlem, New York (City), in literature. I. Title.
    PS3539.0334H337   811'.52   80-50306
    ISBN 0-8262-0309-4

Passages from *Harlem Gallery* by Melvin B. Tolson, copyright 1965 by Twayne Publishers, Inc., are reprinted with the permission of Twayne Publishers, A Division of G. K. Hall & Co., Boston.

Chapter 9 appeared previously in Mariann Russell, "Ghetto Laughter," *Obsidian* 5 (Spring–Summer 1979): 7–16. Reprinted by permission of the editor.

To Miss Jeannetta and Mrs. R.

Acknowledgments

I am indebted to the National Endowment for the Humanities for a fellowship to enable me to do research on and write about Melvin Tolson's *Harlem Gallery*. I am also indebted to Sister Eugene Gottimer and Sister Anne Courtney who read and commented on the manuscript. I am further indebted to the Tolson family, especially the late Ruth Marie Tolson, and to the late James Cannon who answered many questions about life in Harlem. I am also indebted to relatives and friends who encouraged me throughout the preparation of the book.

M. R.
Mount Vernon, N.Y.

Contents

1. Introduction, 1
2. Harlem, the Double Image, 12
3. Harlem and the Literary Artist, 27
4. Tolson's Harlem Portraits, 40
5. The Harlem Milieu, 55
6. Characters, 69
7. Personae, 82
8. Some Thematic Elements, 94
9. Ghetto Laughter, 104
Notes, 112
Bibliography, 124
Index, 138

1

Introduction

Melvin B. Tolson once described himself and his varied activities: "shoeshine boy, stevedore, soldier, janitor, packinghouse worker, cook on a railroad, waiter in a beachfront hotel, boxer, actor, football coach, director of drama, lecturer for the NAACP, organizer of sharecroppers' unions, teacher, father of Ph.D's, poet laureate of a foreign country, painter, newspaper columnist, four-time mayor of a town, facer of mobs."[1] These many activities reflected the multifaceted talents and interests of the small, muscular black man from the West who was almost exactly as old as the twentieth century. But the backbone of his lifework was provided by his teaching career of over forty years at Texas (Wiley) and Oklahoma (Langston) colleges. During this career, the Missouri-born son of a Methodist Episcopal minister spent himself not only in teaching chores and cocurricular activities, but also in the lonely task of forging a poetic expression suitable to himself and to his audience.

Melvin B. Tolson's first great literary success came after the publication of *Harlem Gallery (HG)* in 1965, the year before he died. The literal beginning of his writing career was the publication of one of his poems in an Oscaloosa, Iowa, newspaper in 1912. He continued to write poetry, drama, and fiction with some interruption for most of his life. Little of his early work was published. During the thirties, except for an occasional article or poem and a regular newspaper column in the *Washington Tribune*, Tolson's work — including his series of poems on Harlem — went unpublished. In 1940, however, Tolson was invited to submit an entry to the National Poetry Contest sponsored by the American Negro Exposition in Chicago. His poem, "Dark Symphony," won first place, was exhibited in the Hall of Literature in Chicago, and was later printed in the September 1941 edition of the *Atlantic Monthly*. The publication of the poem eventuated in publication of Tolson's first book of poetry — *Rendezvous with America* — in 1944.

Tolson continued to publish in periodicals, but his appointment in 1947 as poet laureate of Liberia, with a commission to write a poem for the Liberian centennial, led to the creation of a book-length ode that was later published as *Libretto for the Republic of Liberia*. Recognition of Tolson's poetic merits slowly began to accrue. He had won the Bess Hokim award in 1952 for "E. & O. E.," a poem published in *Poetry: A Magazine of Verse*. After the publication of *Libretto*, the Liberian government held a literary tea at its embassy in Washington, D. C., and bestowed a significant honor: Knighthood of the Liberian Order of the Star of Africa. He was also an invited guest at the inauguration of Liberian President William Tubman.

In 1955 Tolson was designated permanent fellow in poetry and drama at Breadloaf, Vermont. However, recognition on a much wider scale eluded him for ten years.

Following the publication of *HG*, Tolson received an invitation to present the book to President Lyndon Johnson at a White House ceremony, an opportunity to deliver a Gertrude Clarke Whittall Poetry and Literature Fund Lecture at the Library of Congress, an invitation to serve as the first poet-in-residence and the first appointee to the Avalon Chair in the Humanities at Tuskegee Institute, and the annual poetry award of the American Academy of Arts and Letters.

What indeed is the nature of the book that brought such previously elusive fame to a black professor at a small, predominantly black Oklahoma college? The ode, written in a style so brilliant and difficult as to lead to Tolson's being compared to T. S. Eliot and Hart Crane, is grounded in the life of Harlem from the twenties on. *Harlem Gallery* is about Harlem, some fictional and typical characters who dwelt there, their talk and activities. This book is, in one sense, Harlem approached through talk — talk and such talk! The words flowing from the Harlem background reveal an approach to Harlem and black America that is, in the best sense, idiosyncratic. And the talk itself becomes a symbolic reenactment of what Tolson saw as the significance of the lives of black folk.

The intention of this study is to examine the book from the focus of its relationship to the Harlem community. This community, with its double image of cultural capital and ghetto, will be examined, as well as those aesthetic movements associated with or touching upon the Harlem experience. Then, the progression from a representational attempt to capture the Harlem experience in *A Gallery of Harlem Portraits* (*Portraits*) to a symbolic reenactment of the significance of that experience in *Harlem Gallery* will be treated. Finally, *Harlem Gallery*'s evocation of Harlem and its life from literal to symbolic levels will be considered. The approach is not primarily aesthetic or epistemological or sociological; it is an attempt to move from the actuality of the Harlem community to those symbolic meanings that Tolson saw therein. What is particularly focused upon is the ambiguity of Harlem and its image, which Tolson incorporates into his artistic performance.

A former colleague of Melvin Beaunorus Tolson once described the man: "'He is an aggressive leader. He is a pacing, pounding man, a shouting, screaming man.'"[2] The energy, which even the most casual observer could note, was a vital aspect of the character of the man. A brilliant teacher, speaker, debate coach, theater director, and poet, Tolson brought to each of these activities a store of creative and physical energy that perhaps overshadowed the intellectual discipline accompanying it. The man Tolson, who responded uniquely to the challenges he met in his life, displayed throughout a mental discipline, an intellectual discipline, and a bedrock integrity that made him a "superbly successful human being."[3]

Dr. Hobart Jarrett provides a picture of Tolson as teacher and speaker during the thirties. On the Wiley campus, Tolson was the teacher, the professor, whom people "held in awe." His classes, especially in grammar, were exposed to a strict intellectual discipline. In the actual conduct of the class, however, there was the give-and-take of Socratic dialogue. The pacing Tolson, frequently with yardstick anchored under his arms, held the class's attention as he illustrated his points, sometimes humorously, and challenged his students to test their own thought and expression. In his role of public speaker, Tolson — a small, cigar-smoking, athletic man, without regard for the niceties of personal appearance — evoked the histrionic tradition of his preacher father; the vigor and fire of Tolson's speaking presence recalled the dynamism of the preacher. Tolson combined in his speeches energy of delivery, of intellectual content, and of language to render a total orchestration of meaning and style.[4]

Although Tolson had written poetry since he had been a boy, and continued to write to some degree for the rest of his life, during the thirties his creative energies were largely directed to the coaching of his debate teams. His extraordinarily successful teams had a ten-year winning streak, defeating two national champions as well as debaters from Oxford University.[5] These teams were "absolutely secure" because their coach had drilled them in all possible arguments to a position, and the debaters had incorporated these arguments into speeches delivered until letter perfect. Good speakers already, they were honed to an intellectual and verbal proficiency by debating with their coach and colleagues. The energy, inventiveness, and tenacity so characteristic of Tolson were exhibited in the polish of these teams from a small black college in the East Texas Black Belt.

When interest in debate waned in the late thirties, Tolson turned his energy to drama, an interest he maintained into the fifties. Again, Tolson's great energy was thrown into helping students achieve in an area of communication.[6] He had founded the Log Cabin Theatre in 1925 and, with his deepened interest in drama in the late thirties, he helped found and served as an official of the Southern Association of Dramatics and Speech Arts. His enthusiasm for this task is indicated by his comments: "That's [drama] as much a part of the college as holding classes. These presidents are finally getting that thru (*sic*) their befogged minds. I am sure we'll have a great time. It will inspire your students as nothing else."[7]

Still, regardless of the dispersal of his energy and talents, Tolson had always been a poet.[8] Like the man himself, Tolson's poetic career was constantly evolving. Sparked by Crane's *The Bridge* and other classics of modern poetry, Tolson set about fashioning the style that he felt challenged to attain, the style of his later poetry. It seems clear from Tolson's comments in *Anger, and Beyond,* and in his notebooks and papers,[9] that he conceived a style of poetry associated with Eliot, Pound, Crane, Carlos Williams, and others as the preeminent school of modern poetry. He evidently began to emulate at least the techniques of such poetry.

The intellectual, the witty, the allusive on the one hand accorded with the bent of Tolson's mind; on the other hand, the style of such poetry was distinctly not easy and natural for a young man reared on Dunbar and Longfellow and nurtured on Tennyson and Spenser. Tolson was thus stimulated by the techniques and achievements of modern poetry as he had been excited by the achievements possible in debate and drama. In a field nearest to his creative wellsprings, he found a new challenge to which he characteristically responded. Tolson worked out for himself, with only books and magazines as guides, the rudiments of his later characteristic style. There is a measure of truth in the perception of Dr. Jarrett: "My point is that the great teacher that Tolson was was not enough for Tolson. He went into debate strenuously because of the need for self-expression, desire to do things for his students in a different way. Then he began developing an increased interest in theater. . . . It seems pretty clear to me that the next phase for Tolson was to concentrate on poetry."[10]

Tolson's activities, however, followed no narrow channel. He was intensely interested in many things, from tennis to jazz. One area of continuing development and commitment was his interest in the underdog in general and blacks in particular. In the beginning of the Depression, he was instrumental in attempts to organize sharecroppers in the South. He was also involved in talks aimed at unionizing workers in a coal company during the thirties. Often called upon to speak, he frequently touched upon black-white relations and the disastrous effects of the prevailing system. Outspoken, frank, and committed, he was considered in the South of his day a controversial figure, and on at least two occasions was fortunate to escape a mob.[11] His central theme was the dignity of the individual of whatever race, and he nurtured in his students a pride in themselves and their abilities. Tolson displayed and communicated what he was to see in another generation: "a hard-bitten, undaunted hopefulness about man" (Notebooks).

A former student recalls a story that, as a result of an altercation between a white townsman and a Wiley College faculty member, the white man and his supporters came to "get" the faculty member. According to the story, the only person who said that no harm was to come to the black was Melvin Tolson. Whether exaggerated or not, the story illustrates the kind of courage and commitment that Tolson characteristically displayed. Like Oliver Cox, his colleague at Wiley, he tended to stress the socioeconomic foundations of discrimination; nevertheless, his commitment to practical efforts at betterment was no less real. Tolson worked for the NAACP in a place where speakers for the organization were "taking their lives into their hands" by such work in a time when the NAACP was branded as a communist organization and many blacks refused to have the *Crisis* come into their homes. Like the NAACP organization, Tolson advocated the black man's enjoyment of all rights pertaining to American citizens. In a milieu in which this notion was revolutionary, Tolson did not go beyond it to discuss nuances of assimilation and black identity. Simply and often controversially, he stressed his own personal commitment to the dignity of every man: "I lived 25 years in the Black Belt. I had to learn to live with 'Crackers' and yet retain my vision of Man" (Notebooks).

As might be expected of his time and place, Tolson saw achievement as a blow for racial equality. The Wiley College debaters' triumph over white opponents and the black poet's mastery of mainstream techniques seemed to illustrate the native ability of the Afro-American. At the same time, demands that poetry be used to impress whites or be unartistic propaganda were anathema to Tolson. He evolved his own idea of what the black scholar and the black poet should be.

Tolson saw scholarship as a way of affirming one's existence. In a characteristic image, he declared: "Like a fish, I shall grow and grow [continue to grow] until the day I die."[12] He saw the genuine scholar as a kind of Columbus, sighting new discoveries. Opposed to the freedom that sustains the life of the scholar are the forces of social oppression. Drawing his images from Bacon's idols of the tribe, theater, cave, and marketplace in the *Novum Organum*, Tolson saw these idols as social forces standing between the individual and truth. Especially imprisoning were the idols of the tribe that embody racial prejudice. The scholar, therefore, is forced into the social arena and can become one of the leaders of the people against "imperialism in Africa and Asia." The black scholar is particularly important since "a minority demands more involvement on the part of its intellectuals and artists than a ruling majority." The black scholar is then "promethean"; on him rests the responsibility to see through the traps of conventional thinking and to act as a kind of prophet as he leads his people through the wilderness.

> The Negro scholar must uproot the lies
> Of ermine classes, puncture sophistries,
> Break through dilemmas, rip the fallacies
> Between his people and the Bill of Rights.[13]

Examination of Tolson's concept of the poet shows that he hold similar views for poet and scholar, especially in regard to their place in society. Both scholar and artist demolish the stereotypes of conventional thinking. The poet is opposed to "conformity, bureaucracy, routine, stereotype . . ., status-seeking, etc." (Notebooks). Noting that once the poet and the priest had been the same man, Tolson outlined a concept of poet as akin to the seer. Although the poet is also the maker, the craftsman, his individual vision has a wider, social implication even though that greater relevance may not make him popular. The notion of the poet as an iconoclastic figure resulted from the poet's pursuit of his vision despite lack of appreciation.

"The Poet" sums up Tolson's view in poetic form:

> . . . this lapidary
> Endures the wormwood of anonymous years:
> He shapes and polishes chaos without a fee,
> The bones of silence fit no pedigree.
>
> ....
>
> Gives not a tinker's dam
> For those who flatter or deride
> His epic or epigram:
> The potboy, not the connoisseur, toadies for a dram.[14]

Calling the poet an Ishmaelite whose "lien exempts the Many nor the Few,"

Tolson concludes by calling the poet:

A champion of the People versus Kings —

....

A hater of the hierarchy of things —
Freedom's need is his necessity.
The poet flings upon the winds blueprints of Springs:
A bright new world where he alone will know work's
    menacings.

(Rend., p. 29)

Thus, Tolson's concept of the poet in his social role is similar to that of the scholar's role. Added to that is the notion of the poet's absolute integrity as he ignores the silence of his peers and continues his lonely but necessary task. In this as in so much else, one can see the imprint of Tolson's own life and experience — his characteristic response to challenge, toughness of mind, and unshakeable optimism — transformed into poetry.[15]

"He talked of Harlem as though it were the omega and by omega I mean the ultimate, not death, the ultimate achievement of Negro life. He thrilled to it."[16] Tolson's experience in New York City, and particularly Harlem, was fundamental to his development as a man and as a poet.

The date of Tolson's first visit to Harlem is uncertain. In *Anger, and Beyond*, Tolson remarked that he "was in the middle of this literary revolution before the panic of 1929" ("A Poet's Odyssey," p. 194). While he was a student at Lincoln University in Pennsylvania (1920–1923), he had worked as a waiter in the Breakers Hotel in Atlantic City during "the heyday of Capone."[17] Since Tolson's notes indicate that he was offered a job with the Cause of African Redemption by Marcus Garvey, who was imprisoned in 1925 and deported in 1927, it seems likely that Tolson's acquaintance with Harlem began early in the twenties.

However, Tolson's most prolonged period of residence in New York was during the 1931–1932 academic year when he was studying for his master's degree at Columbia University under a Rockefeller Foundation Fellowship.[18] He lived in Harlem at 326 W. 118th Street where he had an opportunity to become familiar with community life during the Scottsboro year. According to rumor at Wiley College, the reason for the delay in the awarding of Tolson's degree was that instead of studying at Columbia he was walking the streets of Harlem. This apocryphal story may have been based on Tolson's descriptions of the particularities of the Harlem he observed and in which he participated. As one Wiley faculty member said: "I can't understand how Tolson sees all those things in Harlem. I've been to Harlem. I didn't see all those things."[19]

Tolson was becoming acquainted with the tempo of Harlem life and, through his study of the Harlem Renaissance writers, with such writers as Langston Hughes, Wallace Thurman, Dr. Rudolph Fisher, Charles S. Johnson, and probably Countee Cullen and others. He had the opportunity to read some of the letters and scrapbooks of the Harlem writers — as well as to meet and talk with the masters. Tolson indicated that this period marked his first intimate acquaintanceship with celebrities (Notebooks). In fact, such Harlem encounters seemed to form the base of a pyramid of intellectual and cultural relationships.

Tolson's study at the time was conducted at Columbia under Edward Thorndike and others. Tolson said that he discovered the true meaning of race — that race in America was a biological myth but a sociological and psychological fact — through Melville Herskovitz's work ("C.and C.," 26 August 1939). The notion of "the world's cultural fabric," the interrelatedness of various cultures, came to Tolson through Arthur Christy, a favorite teacher at Columbia.[20] Changes in Tolson's literary concerns occurred when a fellow student suggested that he read contemporary writers, such as Sandburg, Masters, Frost, and Robinson ("Odyssey," p. 7). In the process of writing his master's essay, Tolson got in touch with Zona Gale and Harriet Monroe. These writers, with their varying emphases on the common man, their shifting ironic responses to the temper of society, their estrangement from conventional outlooks, and their search for liberating verse forms, appealed to Tolson and laid the groundwork for the kind of poetry he was to write during the thirties.

After the Columbia period, Tolson became acquainted with V.F. Calverton, Marxist critic, author, and editor, whom Tolson was to regard as closer than a brother, a "sort of mentor."[21] When Tolson visited New York, he spent time with Calverton and his Greenwich Village friends in discussions that the poet was to find extremely fruitful.[22] Tolson maintained that his real education was a matter of interaction with "certain books" and "certain men" ("C. and C.," 30 November 1940).

Alfred Kazin described Calverton as a man of eclectic interests, capable of citing in speech and writing authorities, both traditional and esoteric, in a wide variety of fields.[23] Calverton believed that humanity was at a crossroad, but that Marxism and such modern disciplines as sociology, psychology, and anthropology would lead man to triumph. With his eclectic approach, Calverton represented an essentially hopeful view of life and people. Kazin noted "the positive, hopeful glance he turned on every old subject and every new person."[24] His home, like his magazine, was a gathering place for radicals of every sort who were not doctrinaire Stalinists. There one could meet Norman Thomas, Max Eastman, Sidney Hook, and Eugene Lyons.

Into this atmosphere came Tolson, who was later to say: "After all, I received my education in Greenwich Village in the thirties" (Notebooks). Calverton suggested books not included in the university curriculum and introduced him to men and ideas previously unknown to him. It may have been through Calverton that Tolson met Joel Spingarn and Franz Boas, and it may have been through Calverton that Tolson became acquainted with some of Calverton's black friends: Alain Locke, Abraham Harris, George Schuyler, Walter White, and Sterling Brown. At Calverton's "Saturday Night Clusters," Tolson was exposed to ideas and persons who could provide a theoretical basis for his natural iconoclasm.

Tolson also shared with Calverton a Marxist explanation of mankind's failure in general and of discrimination in particular. Richard H. Barksdale has commented: "I should also add that Tolson knew Wright and Ellison when he was in Harlem around the late 1930s and all three involved in radical politics."25 In a letter to Tolson, Calverton lightly chided Tolson for Stalinism (Notebooks). Tolson's colleague at Wiley, Oliver Cox, had also proposed a Marxist explanation of racial prejudice and discrimination.26 This viewpoint can also be seen in the "C. and C." columns that Tolson wrote from 1937 to 1945. Tolson could say as late as the sixties: "I guess I'm the only Marxist poet Here and Now."27 He also commented: "A poet can be a Marxist without being a Communist or Socialist" (Notebooks). What Tolson seems to have done was to eschew all party politics but retain the Marxist worldview, modified by his own experience.

Tolson continued to visit New York. He did not receive his degree until 1940, so he may have had to keep in touch with the graduate faculties. In the thirties, he seems to have divided his time between Greenwich Village and Harlem. After the thirties, one can find Tolson in New York on various occasions: attending a Columbia commencement, spending holidays in New York, discussing poetry with white intellectuals, and visiting International House.28 For the rest of his life, Tolson continued to visit New York and Harlem for various reasons, including lectures and visits to publishers. As closely as he could, Tolson observed the changes in Harlem during his long acquaintanceship with New York and its black community.

The range of Melvin B. Tolson's interests — "My catholicity of taste and interest takes in the Charleston and the ballet, Mr. Jelly Roll and Stravinsky, the Congolese sculptor and Phidias, the scop and the classicist" ("A Poet's Odyessy," p. 184) — is evidenced in the poems of *Harlem Gallery*. This study of *Harlem Gallery* is concerned chiefly with those elements of Tolson's tastes and interests that had their roots in the black community. However, a brief look at some modern American poets whom Tolson had studied, and the tradition from which they derive, will indicate that somewhat similar attempts have been made to capture the spirit of place in poetry.

Crane's *The Bridge,* Pound's *Cantos,* and Eliot's *The Waste Land* and *Four Quartets* all combine exploration of inner depths and symbolic landscapes. These poems can be seen as records of the individual poets' discovery of self; they are also attempts by the poets to recapture the actuality of contemporary civilization. The point of intersection between self and community is often the poetic examination of a particular locality or localities that have been mythologized. While the poems of Pound and Eliot do not use one geographical place as a controlling image, they do encompass the use of specific localities to evoke the quality of Western civilization, especially as manifest in contemporary Anglo-American experience. Crane (*The Bridge*) and Williams (*Paterson*) begin with specific urban American localities: through poetic voyaging they make the particular place the occasion for attempting to seize the reality of the American experience.

In similar fashion, Tolson's *Harlem Gallery* contains an exploration of the inner lives of his black artists and the symbolic Harlem landscape. As in the earlier poems, the significance of the self in Tolson's poem is rooted in the meaning of a community figured by a landscape that has been mythologized through symbolic extension. Tolson is exploring the values of the life of the black man in America and of the creative endeavor of poetry, including the very act of poetic creation by which he attempts to embody these values. At the same time, like these representative modern poets, he is projecting the epic significance of this material.

Two poems, *The Bridge* and *Paterson*, illustrate this modern American approach to the continuing theme of the seizure of the American experience through poetic definition. The poems contain two elements: a self-reflective movement as the poet attempts to fix the spirit of the country of which he is a citizen, and an outward movement as the poet attempts to locate that spirit in outer reality — "No ideas but in things — " Despite subjective elements, an epic intention underlies both *The Bridge* and *Paterson*. Starting with the urban reality of Brooklyn Bridge, Crane moves westward in space and back and forth in time as he grasps and embodies the continuum of the American experience. "Using the city as a microcosm of the United States, Williams attempts to discover, in specifically American terms, the nature of the American experience, attempts to embody the whole knowable world about him."[29]

Tolson, in a similar vein, envisioned his *Harlem Gallery* as the beginning of an epic, intended to convey the reality of the black man's experience in America. Tolson saw his creative act as one way of fixing a changing ethnic experience that might disappear altogether: "The Gallery is an attempt to picture the Negro in America before he becomes the giant auk of the melting-pot in the dawn of the twenty-second century" (Notebooks). Since integration for Tolson meant the end of the Negro race as such, "Literature is all-important. The spirituals, Jazz, Negro art and Literature will outlast the Negro as a racial group" (Notebooks). The *Harlem Gallery* not only expresses the reality of the experience of a people; it also captures in some permanent form an experience, impermanent though nonetheless valuable. The artist is therefore attempting to seize the past and the present and to outwit the future as the artist's endeavor becomes itself a medium for a people's spirit.

Even without a detailed discussion of Tolson's literary forebears, one can see that the idea of the city itself has been a continuing one in Western tradition from Plato to the present.[30]

The idea of the city has been given impetus by the rise of cities in modern times. The landscape of river, mountain, and tree has been replaced by an urban landscape, neon lights, and city waste. As city is a counterpart of technology, and as technology is the central language of our society, the city has become an easy and natural metaphor for society, and values seen in society have been read into the city.

In Dickens, for instance, whose creation was inspired by both the fact of industralization and the reality of London and other rising cities, the city is ambiguous in its values. On the one hand, it is the locus of communal values, such as the familial love and support found in Tom Pinch and his sister and their housekeeping, the housekeeping of the Maylies, and the housekeeping of Miss Esther Summerson. But it is also the locus of the evils of Fagin, of the activities of the detective who owns Tom's house, and of the mores of the Dedlock townhouse. Even specific ills, such as child abuse, wife-beating, thievery, and murder, spring naturally from the landscape of the city. On the other hand, familial love and sacrifice also flourish in the blighted or flourishing city.

In Baudelaire, however, such virtues seem muted as the city is associated with flowers of evil. Lamppost, cadaver, garbage, and prostitute are realities and metaphors for a quality of the modern city that is life-destroying rather than life-affirming. More strongly, one finds the city an image of the infernal city in Eliot, the Waste Land, as urban images are used to figure an inner desert. Whether a final salvation is read into *The Waste Land* or not, most specifically modern city imagery is associated with an inner waste land. In effect, where Dickens reads values into an existent location, Eliot uses an existent location — the same city, London — to symbolize an already given value system. Therefore, the tradition of the city, in both modern and earlier times, encompasses an abstract, symbolic city — nexus and locus of values — and, usually, a real city, a physical location that embodies, captures, or holds such values. These two cities — the real and the symbolic, with both destructive and affirmative connotations — are the essential components of Harlem as it is developed by Tolson.

Western tradition encompasses the city as urban apocalypse, either literally or figuratively. In the material of Williams and Tolson, individual and communal distress are finally to be worked out in terms of events that occur in the city. The city is the place of blood and burning (future), but also of renewal, new geography, the new man. For Tolson, this is worked out in terms of political and aesthetic revelation of the destiny of the black man, seen as pivotal in American life and to the destiny of the world.

The immediate starting point of Tolson's attempt to capture the spirit of a people through the examination of a place was Edgar Lee Masters's *Spoon River Anthology.* The book was the model for *A Gallery of Harlem Portraits,* the first version of *Harlem Gallery.*[31] In *Spoon River,* through a series of autobiographical monologues delivered from the cemetery, the poet limns the portrait of a small American town in all its variety. Masters's book includes portraits of characters, interactions among characters, the sociology of the town itself and its past participation in the nation's history, discussions of the meaning of life, visions of life and its meaning, and an appeal to the Delphic Apollo. Spoon River thus becomes a microcosm: "The germ of the book was the idea of telling the story of an American country town so as to make it the story of the world."[32]

Tolson saw his projected epic of Harlem portraits as a microcosm of black America: "It is a poem similar to Masters' *Spoon River Anthology,* with Harlem as a magnet drawing characters of diversified types from all corners of the world. It gives, I think, Negro America, its comedy and tragedy, in prismatic epitome" (Notebooks). In Tolson's final plan, *Harlem Gallery: Book I, The Curator* was to be followed by four books that would present the historical reality of the black man in America, beginning with his African origins. Tolson expressed his intention to "analogize the history of the Hebrew people in the episodes of the Old Testament as regards persons, places, and events. The dominant idea of the *Harlem Gallery* will be manifest" (Notebooks). This mythologizing would involve a dramatization of the 350-year history of the black man in America. Book II, Egypt Land, was to be an analogy for the Slave Trade and Southern Bondage; Book III, The Red Sea, an analogy for the Civil War; Book IV, The Wilderness, an analogy for Reconstruction; and Book V, The Promised Land, "a gallery of highbrows and middlebrows and lowbrows against the ethnological panorama of contemporary America" (Notebooks). Harlem, then, is viewed as the gateway to and the nucleus of the special experience of the Afro-American. In a fashion not unknown in contemporary American literature, Tolson envisioned a poem in which a place is required to serve as the means of revelation of the spirit of a people.

Finally, in *The Bridge* and *Paterson*, Crane and Williams share with Whitman the desire to express, and ultimately celebrate, the American spirit. The ugliness, coarseness, and devitalization of the American experience are noted, but the poet in each case is working toward affirmation. There are parallels between *Paterson* and *The Bridge* and Tolson's last work besides the obvious one of poetic idiom. A more significant parallel is the attempt to capture the spirit of a people through the examination of a place. Another related parallel is the maintenance, despite disillusionment, of a final, hard-won optimism. It would seem that both these elements — the desire to encompass and express the spirit of a whole people and the ultimate assertion of the value of that spirit — are peculiarly American in a Whitmanesque sense. As his *Rendezvous with America* as a whole, and its title poem in particular, aptly illustrate, the black American, Melvin B. Tolson, professed this Whitmanesque brand of American optimism. Variously developed and maintained throughout the years, this finally resulted in the complex, ironic optimism of the ode, *Harlem Gallery*.

2

Harlem, the Double Image

The Harlem where Melvin B. Tolson lived during the 1931–1932 academic year was still regarded as a focal point of black life in America.[1] This Janus-faced Harlem looked back to the glamorous days of the twenties and forward to the intensely somber days of the Depression. But in 1930, and for some time longer, the image of Harlem as the capital of urban black America lingered. The *New York Times* could describe Harlem in 1928 as "the cosmopolis of colored culture, of gaiety, of art, and the capital of Negro cookery."[2] In 1930 James Weldon Johnson, and in 1932 Vernon Kiser, described the community as "the black metropolis." In 1940 Claude McKay described the New York black community as "more than the Negro capital of the nation. It is the Negro capital of the world." Roi Ottley, described Harlem in 1943 as the "nerve center of advancing black America," and in 1968 Allon Schoener, an outsider, could still nostalgically describe Harlem as the "capital of urban black culture."[3]

A surface view of Harlem of 1931–1932 reveals many elements of an autonomous black city.[4] Harlem duplicated many of the customary features of American cities everywhere, but with a distinctive racial note. Harlem had its tourist attraction, the Harlem nightlife, and its institutions: churches, political clubs, benevolent organizations, social service agencies, schools, hospitals, library, and Ys. Harlem had its movements, groups, personalities, and newspapers to chronicle them. Of Harlem of the late thirties, it could be said: "To whites seeking amusement, it is an exuberant, original and unconventional entertainment center; to Negro college graduates it is an opportunity to practice a profession among their own people; to those aspiring to racial leadership it is a domain where they may advocate their theories unmolested; to artists, writers, and sociologists it is a mine of rich material; to the masses of Negro people it is the spiritual capital of Black America."[5] Harlem wore several masks, its particular image depending on the viewer's desires.

Perhaps the most widely celebrated aspect of Harlem life in the twenties and early thirties was the nightlife that led to Harlem's designation as the playground of the city. From after the closing of the Broadway theater to three or four o'clock in the morning, visiting whites could be entertained by black performers at Harlem nightclubs where various genres of exoticism were featured. Eleven high-class clubs catered almost exclusively to white patrons. The Cotton Club, Connie's Inn, and Small's Paradise were the best-known of these clubs. At the Cotton Club during the twenties, Duke Ellington and his "Jungle" band held forth, as at a later date did Cab Calloway, "Prince of 'Hi-de-ho,'" and, still later, Jimmie Lunceford. Connie's

Inn, which had featured such dancers as Earl "Snakehips" Tucker, closed in 1933. Later, at the same address, the Ubangi Club spotlighted Gladys Bentley in male attire, accompanied by a male chorus in female attire.[6] For a time, Small's had been the Harlem rendezvous of white novelist Carl Van Vechten during his Harlem phase, and, as Black Venus, appeared in *Nigger Heaven.* Some clubs featured a plantation decor, as did the Cotton Club, the Sugar Cane, and the Second Part of the Night.[7] Obviously, the attraction of this kind of entertainment lay in its novelty, and much of the novelty lay not so much in the jazz but in the supposed exoticism of the blacks. One white observer reacted violently to the exoticism of a Harlem nightclub: "Then we were at it, again, Whites down on Negro level, Negroes down to Whites' level, darkness, red-flashing lights, insurgent, bombastious, idolatrous trombones and horns, euphonium twinkling like the eyes of the obscene, baleful red center star glowing as if patterned in hell to give the club its due astral influence."[8]

Harlemites patronizing most of the five hundred cabarets, theaters, and dance halls were seeking not the exotic but the entertaining. Most clubs provided standard nightclub fare — dancing, floor show, band, and M.C. — in a gay and intimate atmosphere. At theaters and dance halls, visiting performers such as Louis Armstrong, Bessie Smith, and Jelly Roll Morton entertained. The most popular of the theaters was the Lafayette, Seventh Avenue and 131st Street, where the regular fare included a jazz orchestra, female dancing acts, monologues by black-faced comedians, clog dancing, male quartets, and soloists.[9] Dance halls featured both public and private affairs. Although few dances could match the novelty of the annual masked, integrated drag balls of the Hamilton Lodge of Odd Fellows at Rockland Palace, the dancing and the music at Harlem dance halls were outstanding. The Savoy, the most popular although not the largest dance hall, often featured a "battle of the bands" between two or more of Harlem's ten to fifteen big bands. From such ballrooms and black shows organized in New York came dances like the Truck, the Lindy Hop, the Charleston, the Camel Walk, the Black Bottom, the Susie Q, and the Big Apple.[10]

But Harlem nightlife was not confined to public entertainment. One much publicized institution was the rent party, variously known as "whist," "tea-cup," or "rent-raising" parties. Originally designed to provide money for rent, the parties were soon divorced from their original purpose and became fundraising devices for individuals and clubs: "a distinctively Harlem innovation, that became the vogue in other Black Belts of the country."[11] At these parties, the fifteen-cents admission provided the opportunity to purchase bootleg liquor at twenty-five cents a drink, such delicacies as fried fish, chitterlings, black-eyed peas, and collards, and to enjoy music by a guitarist, pianist, or even saxophonist and drummer. Home entertainment ranged from the prestigious house parties featuring pianists, Willie "The Lion" Smith, James P. Johnson, Willie Gant, or Fats Waller, to the merely commercial sale of liquor at apartment speakeasies, also known as buffet flats or hooch joints.[12]

Among the simpler pleasures of Harlem life was socializing by "visiting around" and promenading. Lenox and Seventh avenues and 135th Street were thronged with pedestrians, especially in the evenings and on Sunday when "one puts on one's best clothes and fares forth to pass the time pleasantly with the friends and acquaintances and, most important of all, the strangers he is sure of meeting."[13] On these occasions there was much joking, small talk, and gossip. The sight of gaily clad strollers estimated at not less than 25,000 per hour from morning to theater time led observers to call these avenues and streets the "Gay Black Way."[14]

Another form of public engagement, and sometimes entertainment, was provided by the street speakers. In 1917, along Lenox and Seventh avenues, "dozens of speakers could be heard explaining to listening groups the principles of socialism and the more revolutionary doctrines; trying to show them how these principles applied to their conditions; hammering away at traditional attitudes of caution."[15] Among the well-known street orators were Marcus Garvey, Hubert Harrison, Richard B. Moore, A. Philip Randolph, St. John Grant, Sufi Abdul Hamid, Arthur Reid, and Frank Crosswaith. Street speakers were still in evidence during the early thirties. Along Lenox, Fifth, and Seventh avenues, street orators, usually perched on ladders, lashed away at problems evolving from the life of the black man in New York.

While the oddities of Harlem nightlife and streetlife attracted the eyes of journalists,[16] there were other institutions serving the social and cultural needs of the community. Clyde Vernon Kiser pointed out that the central role in Harlem was not played by the cabarets but the church. It has been estimated that there were 209 churches in Harlem, with a membership of 75,695 in 1930.[17] Most of these churches were housed in storefronts, apartments, and rooms, but most members belonged to the more conventional, established churches. Besides non-Christian religious groups like the Divinites and Commandment Keepers, there were, especially during the Depression, hundreds of cultists. Some were mere "jackleg" preachers; others were merely glorified herb doctors. "Perhaps nowhere in America except in California is religion so extensively and variously developed. Cults of every description abound, while tenement houses, apartments, store-fronts, rooms and even street corners are converted into places of worship."[18]

While the less formal churches generally provided occasion for their members to pray and sing, the established churches provided a number of social services not necessarily connected with religion. "Such interests dominate church life under the title of 'institutional work.' The spiritual side except on Sundays is left to shift for itself."[19] Abyssinian Baptist Church, 132 W. 138th Street, with the largest Baptist congregation in the world, was a typical institutional church. In 1931, Abyssinian could boast of fifty-five clubs, thirty-two paid workers, a summer camp, a missionary to Africa, and a chair of religious education at a southern college. Almost any large church had twenty-five to forty clubs attached to it. Offering these services to a black congregation, the church was a means of raising black consciousness as well as caring for the extrareligious needs of the people.[20]

Besides the usual activities for boys, the YMCA at 135th Street promoted activities of a cultural and educational nature. The Y sponsored a group of players, a radio club, the Harlem String Trio, and the Little Symphony

Orchestra, led by Juilliard student Dean Dixon in 1934. The Y's Hunton School gave classes in arts and crafts, black history, music, theater, and radio. Serving on its various committees were such community leaders as Aaron Douglas, Arthur Schomburg, and Augusta Savage for art; William E. Kelly, Dr. Rudolph Fisher, Elmer Carter, Countee Cullen, and Ernestine Rose for literature; and Adam C. Powell, Frank Wilson, and Carlton Moss for theater. Music lectures were given by Harry T. Burleigh, W.C. Handy, Will Grant Still, and others.[21] Engaged in the YMCA activities were some leaders of the Harlem community who were known beyond that community. The burgeoning black culture in which these leaders participated could be filtered down to the level of the ordinary, interested citizen.

Even more of a center of cultural activity was the 135th Street branch of the New York Public Library. Housed at 103 W. 135th Street in 1931, the branch included three floors, with the top floor housing the seven thousand books, pamphlets, and other materials of the Schomburg Collection. The fourfold aim of the collection was to provide "a historical record of people of African descent, stimulate race consciousness and encourage race pride, inspire writers and students, and give information about the Negro."[22] The library augmented its collection by sponsoring or providing room for other activities. There were lectures by Franz Boas, W.E.B. Du Bois, Carl Van Doren, James Weldon Johnson, Carter Woodson, Kelly Miller, Melville J. Herskovitz, R.R. Moton, and Arthur Schomburg.[23] The branch provided a center for cultural activities of all sorts by sponsoring, or providing a base for, artistic, theatrical, and, of course, literary functions. The library staff made conscious efforts to serve the surrounding black community in all these activities.[24]

A glance at a list of meetings held during 1931 will illustrate the manner in which the library served to disseminate the emergent black culture. On 6 January there was a lecture on Liberia delivered by Charles S. Johnson. On 31 January a reception and literary program for the International Club of Columbia University had James Weldon Johnson, Ira De A. Reid and Jessie Fauset Harris as speakers with music by the Jubilee Singers. On 17 February there was a lecture by Mary White Ovington, "Early Negro Writers." On 19 February Wallace Thurman led a discussion of George Schuyler's *Black No More*. On 4 March W.C. Handy, James E. Harris, Arna Bontemps, and Dr. Rudolph Fisher were speakers at a program for library school students. On 16 March Dr. Alain Locke delivered a lecture, "Negro Art." The March book club discussion of Arna Bontemps's *God Sends Sunday* was led by Countee Cullen, and discussion of James Weldon Johnson's *New Book of American Negro Poetry* by Gwendolyn Bennett. Other speakers and discussants during the year included Dr. George Haynes, Regina Andrews, and Dr. J.A. Rogers. There were visits by eleven different groups, many from outside the community. At the same time, the branch was conducting an adult education program as well as providing space for various community groups including the Harlem Players.[25]

With the development of Harlem as a distinctive black community, there came an increase in race consciousness.[26] "In the period between the First and the Second World Wars, the emphasis upon racial pride became a mass phenomenon among the Negroes in large urban communities."[27] A number of movements developed in Harlem that reflected various responses to this race consciousness, this "defensive racialism." Marcus Garvey and Father Divine led mass movements and there were more selective movements addressing the black man's condition led by such widely differing personalities as Dr. W.E.B. Du Bois and Sufi Abdul Hamid.

Marcus Garvey came to Harlem in 1916, drawn by the ideas of Booker T. Washington, whose notions of black economic development had appealed to Garvey. In New York, Garvey quickly attracted followers, such as Hubert Harrison, developed an American-based organization of the United Negro Improvement Association at 56 W. 135th Street, and published a newspaper, *Negro World*, which disseminated his ideas. He acquired several laundries, a factory, and Liberty Hall.[28] Garvey also sponsored other all-black organizations, such as the African Legion, the Black Cross Nurses, the Black Star Line, and the African Orthodox Church. Garvey's program eventually involved a scheme for racial independence: the idea that American expatriates and native Africans, in cooperation with Liberia, could found a colony that would be a nucleus of a great African state. Beginning in 1920, Garvey organized New York conventions of blacks from all over the world who met to forward his plans.

At one time Garvey claimed a following of six million, two million dues-paying members and four million sympathizers. Although the actual figure was probably less than that, it is impossible to deny the massive appeal of the man and the movement. In his parades, Garvey dressed in a uniform of purple, green, and black, topped by his white plumes. His dress and the colorful uniforms of his followers, the resounding titles of members of the organization — Duke of Nigeria, Overlord of Uganda, for instance — the mass meetings with the cry, "Up, you mighty race, you can accomplish what you will," accounted for a large measure of his success. But the heart of the appeal that Garvey dramatized was his appeal to racial pride and his dream of racial self-sufficiency.[29] Although Garvey moved from schemes of economic independence to schemes of African nationhood, his appeal was essentially the same: "Only when we strike out toward empire on our own account, and by our own achievement build up a permanent culture and civilization of our own, will the world say to itself that the Negro is a man and will accept him as such."[30]

According to Claude McKay, a combination of black intellectuals and white liberals were ultimately instrumental in Garvey's downfall. Some critics assailed the flamboyance of Garvey's personality, some objected to the spectacle he created, and others regarded him as a megalomaniac. Opposition was aroused not only by his personal flair but by his program, which was considered utopian at best, fraudulent at worst.[31] However, a very real cause of resistance to Garveyism was its analysis of the position of the black man in America. Garvey had given up all hope of assimilation into white American society. His analysis of the relationship between white and black gave little credit to constant moral appeals: "The white man is becoming so vile that today we cannot afford to convert him with moral, ethical, and physical truths alone, but with that which is more effective

— instruments of destruction."32

Considered equally utopian by some, Father Divine was the next mass leader in Harlem. Major J. Divine had operated in Sayville, Long Island, from 1919 to 1931 when he was arrested and convicted. His conviction was reversed on appeal, and on 21 June 1932, the day after his release, Father Divine arrived in triumph at Harlem's Rockland Palace. This appearance marked the beginning of Father Divine's great Harlem popularity, which grew steadily during the thirties: "Since Marcus Garvey's time no Negro has achieved a larger following among the masses of Harlem."33

What did Divine have to offer Harlemites? In his fifteen restaurants, he provided the general public with meals at low cost: ten cents a meal and fifteen cents for a chicken dinner. He also provided lodging for one or two dollars a week. In one Depression year, it was estimated, he fed three thousand destitutes daily.34 A number of his Kingdom Halls functioned as dormitories, restaurants, bakeries, barbershops, and temples where all the material aspects of life were communally dispersed. In addition to meals, shelter, and necessities, Divine gave an all-encompassing program that redirected the lives of his followers.

Father Divine's program was based on his followers' assumption of his divinity, with complete control over the lives of these followers, or angels. Illustrative of this belief was the chant: "He has the world in a jug and the stopper in his hand."35 Father Divine and his teachings became the central reality of the angels' lives. Money, sex, and race were banished from their concerns. The new communal way of life assumed by the angels was manifested by their assumption of such names as "Glorious Illumination," "Heavenly Dove," and "Pleasing Joy."36 The followers received spiritual sustenance from the practice of Father Divine's teachings and from his appearance at one or another of the Kingdoms. Father Divine appropriated biblical phrases to himself in public speeches that articulated the spiritual solace he provided. In private banquets lasting three hours or more, he continued his teachings. Even a boat outing became a religious experience, as Pollard indicated in her account of the trip of the Gospel Ship up the Hudson to the Promised Land, Divine's Krum Elbow Estate.37 Roi Ottley could therefore argue that, "Like Garvey before him, he is a Utopian seeker: unable to gain recognition in a white-dominated world; he creates his own world."38

A leader who was even more of a Depression phenomenon than Father Divine was Sufi Abdul Hamid. Called a "crude, racketeering giant" and a "Harlem Hitler," Sufi helped initiate a movement for jobs that was later taken up by more respected members of the community. Unlike the Garveyites and Divinites, this movement did not promise a radical departure from the American way of life. But the movement did attack a basic cause of discontent in the black community — what has been called the "job ceiling."39 A movement was started to ensure that blacks would be employed in white-owned stores in the black community at levels other than the most menial. Such a movement had already been started in Chicago in 1930. Abdul Hamid (a man of many names) had been one of those active in the successful Chicago campaigns. Coming to New York, he attempted to organize similar picket and boycott campaigns, aimed finally at the large 125th Street merchants. With headquarters at the Hotel Dumas, 135th Street near Seventh Avenue, the Sufi and his followers took their campaign to the streets as they urged the masses to join in the campaign early in 1933.[40] The Sufi's campaign precipitated other actions on other levels.

The fact that so many community leaders, including Rev. Adam Clayton Powell, Jr., eventually joined the jobs movement indicates that the movement addressed itself to a condition that symbolized the plight of the community. The 1935 riot, whose target was the same white-owned stores in Harlem, was a more spectacular response to the same condition. During the thirties, "Harlemites in increasing numbers attend street meetings protesting evictions; picket stores to compel the hiring of Negroes, or WPA offices to indicate disapproval of cuts in pay or personnel; parade against the subjection of colonial peoples, or to celebrate some new civic improvement; and march many miles in May Day demonstrations."[41]

The year 1934 marked the end of Dr. W.E.B. Du Bois's editorship of *Crisis* magazine, the organ of the NAACP.[42] During his long tenure, Du Bois, an extraordinarily complex man, had been associated with the kind of protest carried on by the NAACP and similar organizations. From its inception in 1910, the NAACP envisioned the cooperation of enlightened whites and blacks to achieve its aim, saw racial equality as its basic goal, and, despite mass appeals, tended to be regarded as an elitist group. Blacks who had joined Du Bois in the Niagara Movement, and whites summoned by Mary White Ovington in 1909, joined to form in 1910 the NAACP, committed to the tradition of protest exemplified by Douglass and the Abolitionists. In 1906, Dr. Du Bois stated what was to become the ultimate aim of the later organization: "We will not be satisfied to take one jot or one tittle less than our full manhood rights. We claim for ourselves every single right that belongs to a freeborn American, political, civil, and social, and until we get these rights we will never cease to protest and assail the ears of America."[43] The means was primarily a moral assault based on ideals read into the American form of government. The basic premise of both white and black reformers was that the system and individuals would ultimately respond to the moral challenge.

Although the NAACP was a national organization, it was essentially based in New York,[44] and such black members as Du Bois, James Weldon Johnson, Walter White, and Roy Wilkins lived in Harlem. Another national organization, the Urban League, had leaders — Eugene Kinckle Jones and Charles S. Johnson — who contributed to the cultural life of Harlem. As leaders of national organizations, and as writers and activists in their own rights, they exercised influence but had no massive appeal in Harlem. Nathan Huggins summed up their position: "It [Harlem leadership] had no grass-roots attachments. Its success depended on its strategic placement, not its power."[45]

Like any community, Harlem had groups and lists of notables. A glance at two representative theatrical and artistic groups in Harlem, and a random sampling of personalities, might help illuminate the tenor of the community's cultural life.

A number of black shows had been mounted on Broadway during the twenties. Much of the talent had received training in the cabarets and theaters of Harlem, but there had been efforts by blacks to produce theater for black audiences. Loften Mitchell noted that during the 1930s there were "glorious attempts to build a permanent Negro theater."[46] A number of little theater groups flourished in Harlem in the late twenties and thirties. There were the Krigwa Players ("About Us, . . . By Us, . . . Near Us"), founded by Du Bois, the Harlem Experimental Theatre,[47] the Negro Art Theatre of Abyssinian Baptist Church, the Harlem Community Players, who performed in the auditorium of the 135th Street library, and the Dunbar Garden Players, who performed at St. Mark's Church. Other little theater groups were the Harlem Suitcase Theatre and the Campbell Rose McClendon Players. The Negro Unit of the Federal Theatre Project, while not considered "little theater" strictly speaking, did operate out of the Lafayette Theatre from 1935 to 1939. The unit employed blacks and the plays were sometimes written by blacks, as in *Run Together Chillun* and *Conjure Man Dies*, or had black themes, as *Haiti*, or, like the 1936 Orson Welles and John Houseman production of *Macbeth*, were given a racial slant.

Unlike the writers whose fame was associated with the twenties, the artists flourished during the thirties. Romare Bearden was one of a number of artists who formed a fairly cohesive group. Bearden recalls that prior to the thirties, black artists tended to work in isolation. Even Harlem Renaissance figures, such as Richmond Barthé, Palmer Hayden, Malvin Gray Johnson, William H. Johnson, and Augusta Savage, failed to comprise a distinctive group. With the advent of the thirties, however, "meaningful contacts" among the black artists in New York began. The Federal Art Project was one group focus, the Harlem Artists Guild with Aaron Douglas as president was another, and the Charles Alston and Henry Bannarn studios at 306 W. 141st Street were a third group focus. With these foci, the artists became better acquainted with each other and with other members of the cultural community: Langston Hughes, Claude McKay, Ted Ward, and other writers and actors from the Federal Theatre Project, and the entertainers at the Savoy. "We actually became so well established in our community that whenever any Black person in the arts came to New York, they were likely to show up at 306."[48]

The artists' work on the WPA project also fostered a social consciousness and political commitment typical of the thirties. From such practicalities as demonstrations to protect jobs, the artists moved on to large-scale consideration of economic and political problems. "An overall result of this struggling, studying and self-searching was not to make us effete exponents of 'art for arts (*sic*) sake' on the one hand, nor unartistic political hacks on the other."[49] So far as Bearden is concerned, the artists' activities in the thirties were another expression of a tradition of "community oriented art among Black people here in the United States."[50]

Among the community figures who suffered a decline during the thirties, but whose legend remained, was Casper Holstein, the numbers king: "He is Harlem's favored hero, because of his wealth, his sporting proclivities and his philanthropies among the people of his race."[51] Holstein's wealth pyramided after he devised a new scheme of selecting numbers.[52] In a year's time he had acquired three of the finest apartment houses in Harlem, cars, a home on Long Island, and several thousand acres in Virginia. Holstein became a leading figure in black society: he was owner and president of the Turf Club, "the rendezvous of Harlem's fastest set," and exalted ruler of one of the best lodges of Negro Elkdom. Holstein was also a philanthropist: he gave relief to quake victims, fed and clothed the needy, donated to black colleges and charitable institutions, and provided money to *Opportunity* for its second and third literary contests. He also made contributions to Marcus Garvey and his enterprises. All in all, Casper Holstein was *"persona grata* among Harlem's élite."[53]

Holstein's decline began in 1928 when he was kidnapped by white underworld figures. After the Seabury Investigation turned the spotlight on the black "kings" and "queens" of the numbers racket in 1931, the racket was taken over by whites who formed a syndicate headed by Dutch Schultz. "The numbers game in Harlem now came under the undisputed control of the white booze raiders. . . . And the éclat in the atmosphere, which formerly made Harlem hum like a beehive, went out of the game forever."[54]

Another prominent figure of the twenties, whose legend remained in the thirties, was Mrs. L. A'Lelia Walker Robinson, daughter of America's wealthiest black woman, Madame C.J. Walker. Madame Walker, who made a fortune with a hair-straightening process, established herself in New York. She purchased Villa Lewaro at Irvington-on-Hudson, which was luxuriously furnished with such items as a twenty-four-carat gold piano and phonograph. Madame Walker also had a townhouse at 108 West 136th Street. At her death, the estate as well as the social position passed to her daughter, who established herself as a social dictator of sorts: "Assisted by Sari Price-Patton, a Harlem Elsa Maxwell, she entertained the black literati, many influential white people and visiting royalty, and in the process evolved a new and more daring society."[55]

Her parties and her role have been described roughly in Carl Van Vechten's *Nigger Heaven*, where she figures as Adora Boniface; Langston Hughes described her as the "joy-goddess of Harlem's 1920's."[56] Long remembered were her at-homes, attended from time to time by Countee Cullen, James W. Johnson, Zora Neale Hurston, Langston Hughes, Florence Mills, Charles Gilpin, Bruce Nugent, Aaron Douglas, Jean Toomer, and Rudolph Fisher. In 1930, A'Lelia Walker Robinson gave up her townhouse in Harlem. She died in 1931 and was buried at a funeral attended by invitation only.

Walter White was active in the Negro Renaissance and in the national campaign of the NAACP, which he served as assistant secretary and executive secretary. White was possibly best known for his documentation of white mob violence. A voluntary Negro, White was able to gather firsthand information about lynchings and could relay many an interesting tale of his exploits. He was also a creative writer, having published *Fire in the Flint* and *Flight,* and winning a Guggenheim Fellowship for creative writing in 1927. White, although not one of the deans of the Harlem Renaissance, was especially active in fostering the New Negro movement in the arts, and he acted as a catalyst to the production of black literature. It was White who introduced Carl Van Vechten to many of Harlem's leading citizens; thus began the intercourse between Van Vechten's group of downtown intellectuals and bohemians and the Harlem group. "White was able to help many of the young Black writers — Fisher, Hughes, McKay, Cullen, and others — get published; his contacts with whites like Carl Van Doren and publishers like Alfred Knopf enabled him to bring the attention of these men to the burgeoning poets and novelists of the nineteen-twenties."[57] White, entertaining generously at his Harlem apartment, was on one level a quickener of the cultural life of Harlem.

A Harlem personality more familiar to the other end of the social scale was the Harlem cultist, the Barefoot Prophet. Elder Claybourne Martin wore a homespun white robe, had long, mixed gray, later white, hair, and walked barefoot through the Harlem streets. Reported to be nearly seven feet tall, he was known as a preacher with a repertoire of sermons, such as the one about the fox gnawing off his foot to survive.[58] Until his death in 1937, the Barefoot Prophet was a frequent house-party visitor: "This giant carried the 'Word' to gin mill, cabaret, tavern, and poolroom" in a career as preacher that spanned fifty years.[59]

Another Harlem personality more familiar to the masses than to the elite was Earl "Snakehips" Tucker. The names of dancers Bojangles, Bill Bailey, Peg Leg Bates, and Buck and Bubbles are still familiar though fading, but Tucker is relatively unknown. He was identified with his specialty, the Snakehips dance, "one in which the anatomy rather than the feet did the work. The dance created a sensation, and even today there are many imitators."[60] There were, however, no successful imitators because the dance depended on the acrobatics of the dancer who could do splits, somersaults, and shimmies while shaking various parts of his body. Tucker, dressed in white satin shirt and black satin pants and sash, would dance under the colored lights, a shimmering, shifting spectacle, a Harlem original.[61]

Exhibiting some of the flamboyance of a showman was Adam Clayton Powell, Jr.: "He is an incredible combination of showman, black parson, and Tammany Hall. He is at once a salvationist and a politician, an economic messiah and a super-opportunist, an important mass leader and a light-hearted playboy."[62] Powell's later reputation as a congressman is familiar, but in the thirties Powell was just finding his direction as a black spokesman. He began by helping direct activities at his father's church, Abyssinian Baptist, and by taking an active part in community activities. He extended his scope by leading a mass demonstration to city hall in 1931. After 1935, he acted as a community spokesman in his column in the *Amsterdam News*. In 1938, with Imes and A. Philip Randolph, he joined the New York Coordinating Committee for the Employment of Negroes, and eventually he organized massive picketing with Consolidated Edison and New York Telephone as particular targets. Powell was extending the role of activist pastor to include wider community affairs, and he went on eventually to play the role of community spokesman in the political arena as the pastor became the politician.

A different kind of spokesman for the race was Countee Cullen, "younger brother to Houseman."[63] Living in Harlem at the home of his adoptive father, the Reverend Frederick Cullen, pastor of Salem Methodist Episcopal Church, Cullen obtained early fame as a poet in college, where he published his first book of poems, *Color*, in 1925. He became one of the group of artistic figures in Harlem of the twenties; was, in fact, one of the regular group, with Harold Jackman, Mac Stinette, Jules Bledsoe, Carl Van Vechten, and Langston Hughes, that met frequently in Harlem.[64] Cullen grew into a kind of elder statesman of black verse. He had published five books of original verse by 1935; he had won prizes from the Witter Bynner award to a Guggenheim Fellowship. "As an examplar, he could point the way to others, he could be a symbol of possibility, and he could turn other black boys' eyes to poetry and art so that the muse might allow them to transcend their condition as he had."[65]

As widely varying as these personalities were, to some extent they all depended on an exploitation of the special condition of blacks in America to give them scope, and they were tied to that community psychologically if not always physically.

With this separate community life, Harlem was, in many respects, a city within a city. E. Franklin Frazier has commented: "It appears that, where a racial or cultural group is stringently segregated and carries on a more or less independent community life, such local communities may develop the same pattern of zones as the larger urban community."[66] The white and black populations of the cities come to regard black neighborhoods as black communities. As Robert Weaver indicated, "Development of 'their' areas offered compensation for exclusion from the larger phases of the city's life. Community pride dictated such an adjustment to the situation."[67] However, St. Claire Drake and Horace Cayton have remarked on the ambivalence of the community's feeling toward the black neighborhood: "they see a gain in political strength and group solidarity, but they resent being compelled to live in a Black Belt."[68] Underlying the pride in the separate black community are feelings of resentment at the economic powerlessness and the racial patterns that have defined its existence.

In 1940, McKay asserted that "Harlem is like the glorified servant quarter of a vast estate."[69] He was referring to the fact that, regardless of its seeming autonomy on the cultural and institutional levels, economically the community was not so much a city as a colony. Its business life was to a large extent white dominated, and its citizens were chiefly wage earners in other parts of the city. Harlem, despite its surface autonomy, was not, during the Depression nor since, an economically viable community. Beneath the surface lay the economic reality: marginal employment and unemployment were the most outstanding features of Harlem's economic life. Living conditions reflected the lack of economic power; housing was largely substandard, and concomitant services — education, recreation, health, and police — were also inadequate.

The most successful businesses in Harlem were owned by whites. The largest group of black-owned businesses were those dealing with personal services for the most part, businesses with little or no competition from whites in Harlem. White-owned businesses in the black community were chiefly pawnshops, coal and ice, supermarkets, meat stores, department stores, furniture stores, and grocery stores: " . . . 36.3 percent of the businesses controlled by whites as compared with 18.4 percent of the Negro businesses provided for the basic needs of the Negro community."[70] Although the number of black owned and white owned business establishments was roughly the same, most of the significant trade was done by whites.

Most blacks in Harlem were wage earners in businesses where the job ceiling obtained. In semipublic companies, such as Fifth Avenue Coach, Consolidated Gas Company, New York Edison, New York Telephone, New York Railways Company, and Western Union, blacks were almost totally shut out.[71] Other private businesses would hire blacks, but chiefly for low-paying positions. Although the job ceiling was slowly rising during the period between the wars, skilled, clerical, managerial, and supervisory positions were reserved for white workers. The mass of black workers were confined to marginal jobs especially susceptible to Depression slowdowns. Although the American Federation of Labor paid lip service to the concept of equal opportunity, in practice blacks were virtually excluded from all but certain unions, such as the Brotherhood of Sleeping Car Porters and the American Federation of Musicians, Local 802. In 1930, black males were employed chiefly in mechanical and manufacturing operations, principally as laborers, while black women were still employed mainly in domestic work and personal services.

If the participation of employed blacks in the city's economy was fitful at best, the economic condition of the unemployed was even more negligible. By 1934, 43.2 percent of the families in the Harlem area were on relief.[72] Even in WPA jobs, blacks met some forms of discrimination: there were almost no skilled jobs for blacks in the WPA. One estimate was that "the Negro quota is never above 6 percent" on all works projects except snow jobs.[73] When one adds the partially employed to the unemployed and marginally employed, Harlem's economic position was one of powerlessness.

An analysis of the economic situation in the black community reveals a condition that has become a sad cliché. Although the black man in general earned less than his white fellow citizen, for the same accommodation he paid more rent. "These things are possible in Harlem because the people are without economic power and are thereby unable to resist the landlords."[74] Like falling dominoes, other ills follow.

Harlem, originally a desirable place to live (and still regarded as such by James W. Johnson in 1930), had been "built for another race, another economic level, different family composition."[75] As a result, brownstones were converted to kitchenettes and rented to roomers. Families were forced to accept lodgers, many of them strangers. In some instances, beds were rented by day and by night (the "hot bed" system), or bathtubs were boarded over and rented as beds. The Mayor's Commission reported that the density of population was 150 to 450 persons per acre in some areas. The area between 138th and 139th streets between Lenox and Seventh avenues was estimated to have 620 persons per acre.[76]

Overcrowding, landlord neglect, and tenant abuse contributed to the deterioration of buildings that were already old. Even better homes and residential areas were subject to the same process as residents were increasingly unable to maintain better dwellings without resort to lodgers and doubling up: "The fashionable set cannot keep it [Sugar Hill] exclusive, for it is infinitesimal. Families double up in apartments as elsewhere in Harlem. And racketeers of clandestine professions also set the pace."[77] Although the economic status of the black man can account in part for the conditions of housing in the black community, a part of it is attributable to racism. "The economic and residential mobility permitted white people in the city was, and would continue to be, largely denied Negroes."[78] The black community remained and became ghettoized while residents of other ethnic communities were dispersed under the pressure of Americanization.

Comparing Harlem schools of the 1960s with those of an earlier date, Kenneth Clark stated that "children attending Harlem schools in the 1920's and 1930's had average academic achievement close to, if not equal to, the white norms."[79] It seems clear that certain problems beset the schools at that time also. The Mayor's Commission Report deplored the conditions of many of the Harlem schools that it found overcrowded, antiquated, and plagued by students who carried weapons and menaced others.[80] "One of the most serious charges . . . is that today they [the schools in Harlem] lack the personnel and the equipment which modern schools have at their disposal for handling intelligently and efficiently the social problems of the pupils."[81]

In the early 1930s, the public health situation in Harlem was the worst in the city. The figure for overall deaths for blacks was 19.7 per 1,000 compared to 13.8 for whites. Figures for heart disease and pneumonia were comparatively higher, while figures for deaths from tuberculosis were nearly five times as great for blacks. One block — Lenox to Seventh Avenue, 142nd to 143rd streets — became known as Lung Block. "In the Harlem area as in the country at large the Negro death rate is exorbitantly high in the very diseases where lack of sanitation and medical care and poverty are important factors."[82]

The chief medical resource was Harlem Hospital, a storm center of racial controversy. The problem of the admission of black doctors and nurses was solved, at least in principle, by the reorganization of Harlem Hospital in 1930, with Negro physicians "on a full footing of equality with the whites so far as representation on the medical board and opportunity for hospital training and experience are concerned."[83] But there remained the problem of the quality of medical care dispensed at the hospital. "Because of overcrowding, there are double rows of beds in the middle of wards, and at times even in corridors."[84] In 1932 the hospital had the lowest average length of stay of patients of all municipal general hospitals except Coney Island, and a consistently higher mortality rate. Such conditions contributed to the image of Harlem Hospital as the "morgue" or "butcher shop" to which other hospitals sent their black patients.

Charges of police brutality led increasingly to unrest during the thirties. An incident of alleged police brutality, later proved to be untrue, set off an explosion of the Harlem community in the 1935 riots, an explosion that led to the reevaluation of the image of the black community.[85] The riot was judged to be a "spontaneous and unpremeditated" outbreak brought about by a "highly emotional situation" due to "various strains of unemployment and insecurity."[86] The riot, directed against property not people, was regarded as protest: "Among all classes, there was a feeling that the outbreak was justified and that it represented a protest against discrimination and privation resulting from unemployment."[87]

It would seem then that the latter-day description of Harlem, as a "philanthropic, economic, business, and industrial colony of New York City," has some basis in fact. [88] The economic control was effective to some extent on all levels. McKay has pointed out that even the entertainment world was subject to the economics of prejudice. On a cultural level, the Harmon Foundation, Guggenhoim, Spelman, and Rockefeller awards helped to subsidize creative efforts, as did such publishers as Boni, Viking, Knopf, and magazines such as *The Century* and *Harper's*. Even politically, the colonial status obtains since Harlemites, for the most part during the thirties, were represented by politicians who were represented by whites in Tammany Hall. The autonomy of Harlem seemed illusory to Langston Hughes: "I soon learned that it was seemingly impossible for black Harlem to live without white downtown. My youthful illusion that Harlem was a world unto itself did not last long. . . . White downtown pulling all the strings in Harlem. Moe Gale, Moe Gale, Moe Gale, Lew Leslie, Lew Leslie, Lew Leslie, Harper's, Knopf, the *Survey Graphic*, the Harmon Foundation, the racketeers who kidnapped Casper Holstein and began to take over the numbers for whites."[89]

The pattern of a segregated but dependent black community has continued. Mary White Ovington noted as a "new and important factor of their [blacks'] New York life" the crowding of the black population into well-defined areas.[90] The development of separate institutions within a physically separate community, whose economic life was controlled by whites, continued to be outlined in descriptions of Harlem during the twenties, thirties, and forties.[91] Commentators, noting similarity between the pattern of life developed in Harlem and that developed in other urban black communities, saw segregated black urban communities as a product of modern, urban, industrialized America. New York's Harlem and Chicago's Bronzeville, in their time the fabulous black communities, have written in larger letters the story of black urban development throughout the country.

Harlem can be seen as a community representative of the dilemma of the black man in America. Opinions range from James W. Johnson's essentially hopeful view, "But Harlem is more than a community; it is a large-scale laboratory experiment in the race-problem . . . "[92] to Richard Wright's fairly pessimistic: "The question of what will ultimately happen to the Negro in New York is bound up with the question of what will happen to the Negro in America. It has been said that the Negro embodies the 'romance of American life'; if that is true, the romance is one whose glamor is overlaid with shadows of tragic premonitions."[93] Both saw Harlem as intrinsically bound to the fate of black America. Drake and Cayton have summed up the "possibility" inherent in the urban black community: "Negroes in America are becoming a city people, and it is in the cities that the problem of the Negro in American life appears in its sharpest and most dramatic form. It may be, too, that the cities will be the arena in which the 'Negro problem' will be finally settled."[94] In all these cases, the observer is looking beyond the specific community to wider implications arising from the special status of the black man in America, as the black community is seen as microcosmic of black America.

Harlem, a very special community with its own tone and its own pace, has fired the imaginations not just of the Sea-Islander plowing his field but of black Americans on all levels. Harlem, reflecting the best and worst of Afro-America's life, Harlem, with its historical double image of cultural capital and ghetto or vast slum, is never precisely defined. Through the years the actual life of the community has been imbued with "possibility," so that to define Harlem is to define both a reality and one's own evaluation of the dream contained in the reality.

3

Harlem and the Literary Artist

As a cultural capital, Harlem was involved in the continuing process of definition of self and group by those black artists, especially literary artists, who responded to its call.[1] The literary movement of the twenties, the Harlem Renaissance, was Harlem-based and subsequent trends in black artistic developments, although not so firmly anchored to Harlem, can be related to their Harlem manifestations. A continuing problem of these literary artists was that of shaping the language in the widest sense of the term: the finding of an appropriate vehicle for the experience of the black American.

The 1925 edition of *Survey Graphic* had as its title, "Harlem: The Mecca of the New Negro." The New Negro, a term used at least as early as 1916, implied a black man who was responding to new conditions with an altered attitude: "from the old to the new Negro: from the patient, unquestioning, devoted semi-slave to the self-conscious, aspiring, proud young man."[2] This young, self-conscious, probably urbanized young man was considered emblematic of the latest advance of the black man in America and symbolic of the progressivist faith in awakening black potential. "He stands today on the threshold of a renaissance of civilization and culture after four hundred years of interruption by captivity, slavery and oppression."[3]When the *Survey Graphic* used the phrase, "Mecca of the New Negro," it was figuring the more than accidental confluence of three currents: the awakening race consciousness of the New Negro, the cultural awakening of the twenties, and Harlem, the focal point of these movements.

Harlem drew black writers from all over the United States and beyond its borders. Hughes, Hurston, Larsen, McKay, Thurman, Toomer, Bontemps, Fisher, and Walrond, as well as such older men as Johnson and Du Bois, responded to New York's call. They were known to each other through common participation in Harlem's literary and social life. *Opportunity* and *Crisis* gave them a chance to publish; magazine award dinners gave them the opportunity for literary contacts, white and black; magazine reviews and criticism discussed the new works and sketched the often contradictory elements of a black aesthetic as Charles S. Johnson, Jessie Fauset, and Du Bois, and other editors sought to encourage the new movement.[4] Typical of this common participation was the public debut of the younger black writers at the dinner meeting of the Civic Club held 21 March 1924, when the younger generation — Countee Cullen, Walter White, Eric Walrond, Jessie Fauset, Gwendolyn Bennett, Alain Locke, and others — chatted with the established generation — Du Bois, James W. Johnson, and Georgia Douglas Johnson — and met representatives of *The Century, Harper's,*

Scribner's, World Tomorrow, The Nation, and *Survey Graphic,* among others.[5] Socially, Locke, Cullen, Bontemps, McKay, S. Redding, Fauset, Charles Johnson, or James W. Johnson, might meet on the whist-party circuit or at Walker parties. "On Saturday nights, nearly everyone either gave parties or went to parties, including Thurman and other members of the Harlem literati."[6] Of course, Harlem was small enough so that the writers and the artists might meet.

Although artists as varied as these were far from presenting a united front on any single question, there were certain questions to which one or another of the writers returned again and again. Such questions were frequently bound up with the broad concept of "Negro Literature." The self-consciousness of the movement led to a questioning of the premises on which the movement was based. What was the function of the black artist? What should be the artist's attitude toward his audience? What should be the content of black literary art? What was the role of the black artist? In one form or another, these questions were the recurrent foci of discussion. The actual works produced constituted one and, in the last analysis, the most definitive answer to these questions. Nevertheless, consideration of this probing will indicate the shape of the Harlem-oriented creation of a "Negro literature" and sketch a burgeoning, though rudimentary, black aesthetic.

"'A renaissance of American Negro literature is due; the material about us in the strange, heart-rending race tangle is rich beyond dream and only we can tell the tale and sing the song from the heart.'"[7] With these words, Du Bois called for a distinctive American Negro literature based on the ethnic experience of the group. The possibility that there could be a body of "Negro literature" was new and, to most, exciting. Du Bois and Locke saw the new black art in terms of the phenomenon of Irish literature, in which a national group was able to express its "soul" by using the dominant group's language altered by the special experience of the less powerful group.[8]

Leaders, seeing the potentiality of the arts being developed by activities of the New Negro, began to explore possible uses of this new literature. Alain Locke's references in *The New Negro* to nationalist movements, such as those in India, China, Ireland, and Russia, indicate that he considered the Harlem Renaissance as a cultural arm of the movement toward a heightened racial consciousness. Du Bois, whose emphasis on the function of art differed somewhat from Locke's, also envisioned the possibility of a Negro school in which the individual, consciously or unconsciously, would find the proper artistic form for the group experience.[9] Even Claude McKay was fascinated at least by the idea of a group art: "talented persons of an ethnic or national group working individually or collectively in a common purpose and creating things that would be typical of their group."[10]

The function of the art was not confined to this kind of racebuilding; it also had a relationship to the larger white world. Du Bois and others argued that the New Negro art should be used quite deliberately as propaganda, as an illustration of the innate ability and equality of the black man: "but the point today is that until the art of the black folks compels

[sic] recognition they will not be rated as human."[11] Since all art is propaganda, according to Du Bois, the black artist should use his art to help him achieve his racial goals: "The apostle of Beauty thus becomes the apostle of Truth and Right." Locke wished to achieve the same kind of recognition of the black man's ability through its manifestation in the arts, but he attempted to subordinate the propaganda to a more subtle aesthetic of being racial "purely for the sake of art." In this aesthetic approach to art, "the social promise of our recent art is as great as the artistic," and "free" art is seen to bear a social burden.[12]

A third function of New Negro art was to provide a bridge between the races. Interracial parties in Harlem cabarets and Village apartments were supposed harbingers of the new day that some Harlemites saw dawning. "Some of them even expressed the opinion that Negro art would solve the centuries-old social problem of the Negro."[13] McKay found a vague hint of this approach in Locke's introduction to The New Negro. Something of the NAACP approach to interracial cooperation was transferred to the field of art: the culturally elite of each race was supposed to be able and willing to provide the foundations for a coming social rapprochement.[14] As Hughes remarked: "They thought the race problem had at last been solved. Art plus Gladys Bentley. They were sure the New Negro would lead a new life from then on in green pastures of tolerance created by Countee Cullen, Ethel Waters, Claude McKay, Duke Ellington, Bojangles and Alain Locke."[15]

The new art was also seen as making a distinctive contribution to American civilization and culture. As a whole, the shaping of a distinctive racial art was to lead to a cultural democracy in which each group would add its distinctive flavor to the melting pot. There was, of course, disagreement about the distinctive racial note of the Negro. Charles S. Johnson asked whether race was merely an idiom or a distinctive endowment; E. Franklin Frazier wondered whether the Negro was simply following the tradition of American nationalist groups; and Du Bois traced the roots of Negro art to centuries of slavery and oppression.[16] Some white critics apparently found little difficulty in defining the Negro gift as a kind of primitivism. Some indeed appeared to view black art and its Harlem home as a kind of lost Eden.[17] However the gift was to be interpreted, it is evident that the founders of the Renaissance regarded the distinctive, group-oriented art, not as antagonistic to the dominant culture, although they realized such possibilities, but as contributory to a shared culture.

The question of audience for black art was itself troubling to some members of the Renaissance group. Neither those who viewed art as propagandistic nor those who saw it as free or indifferent could be sure of its audience. The black audience was small and chiefly middle class, as Du Bois's attempt to organize a bookbuying club attests. The white audience was dominant and, regardless of goodwill or lack of it, profoundly ignorant of the reality of the black experience. The black writer frequently found himself caught in a crossfire between the two groups since the black press often condemned books that the whites endorsed. "The Negro artist works against an undertow of sharp criticism and misunderstanding from his own group and unintentional bribes from the white."[18]

To some white critics, viewing black literature from the standpoint of prevailing European and American literature, "Negro material" fulfilled a particular white cultural need. Some, in keeping with the spirit of the Jazz Age, seemed to be looking for traces of a prepuritanical age in the literature of the Afro-American. Albert Barnes saw in the Negro, "this mystic," a life of poetry that "our prosaic civilization needs most." Carl Van Doren thought that "what American literature most needs at the moment is color, music, gusto: the free expression of gay or desperate moods. If the Negroes are not in a position to contribute these items, I do not know what Americans are." Carl Van Vechten advised: "The squalor of Negro life, the vice of Negro life, offer a wealth of novel, exotic, picturesque material to the artist."[19]

Some black critics were also seeking the fulfillment of a particular need: the need to project an acceptable image. Du Bois wrestled with the problem and came to the theoretical solution that when the artist could make beautiful art out of sordid conditions, then the art was acceptable.[20] However, a list of questions he proposed in the symposium, "The Negro in Art: How Shall He Be Portrayed," indicates that Du Bois was much concerned with the propagandistic aspects of the artist's portrayal of the Afro-American.[21] Some of the questions focus on whether Negroes "at their worst" were to be frequently portrayed. The symposium produced varying replies, from Hughes's comment that "the true artist is going to write about what he chooses anyway regardless of outside opinions," to Georgia Johnson's admonition to "let the artist cease to capitalize the frailties of the struggling or apathetic mass — and portray the best that offers." Writing in *Opportunity*, Countee Cullen emphatically concluded: "*Put forward your best foot*," after he observed that "American life is so constituted, the wealth of power is so unequally distributed, that, whether we relish the situation or not, Negroes should be concerned with making a good impression."[22]

Blacks, and some whites, agreed when it came to music, that here was a distinct contribution in spirituals, blues, jazz, and shouts. In seeking the literary counterpart, some black artists turned to folk material or Africa. Claude McKay in his novels and James Weldon Johnson and Langston Hughes in their poetry turned to the folk. Hughes indicated that Washington's Seventh Street residents were a welcome relief from the intense snobbery and color-consciousness of the Washington Negro elite. "But gay or sad, you kept on living and you kept on going. Their songs — that of Seventh Street — had the pulse beat of the people who keep on goin'."[23] The denizens of Seventh Street, of Lenox Avenue, of South Street in Chicago, were found in Hughes's books during the period. James Weldon Johnson turned to the sermons of black preachers: "I should take the primitive stuff of the old-time Negro sermon and through art-governed expression, make it into poetry."[24] McKay turned to the "lowdown Negro," whom he knew intimately, for the "primitive vitality, the pure stamina, the simple unswaggering strength of the Jakes of the Negro race."[25] Although each of these writers wrote about the folk whom he had honestly known and lived among, not from an exotic but from an honest point of view, the assumptions that these authors. especially McKay, made — that the black masses possessed a vitality that countermanded the machine culture of the whites — rested on decidedly sophisticated premises.

Other black artists turned to Africa. Locke urged the "conscious and deliberate threading back of the historic sense of group tradition to the cultural background of Africa."[26] On a literary level, poets like Cullen sought to define themselves in relationship to Africa. As Locke and Frazier indicated, the black American had few direct unreconstructed cultural links to the African "motherland," so his invocation of Africa was all too often colored by prevailing notions of African civilization. Although the Trader Horn view of Africa too frequently prevailed, there was a genuine movement toward Africa as a focus of self-definition, if only as a counterbalance to the denial of black selfhood found in the American context.

The question of the role of the black artist too often resolved itself to the question of whether or not to be a Negro writer. Some black writers attempted to escape the label of "Negro writer," just as other professionals sought to escape labels of "Negro teacher," "Negro doctor," or "Negro lawyer." Behind the label was the specter of the minstrel show, the Octavus Roy Cohen tradition of Negro material as a special area of American literature. George Schuyler presented this view when he asserted that to characterize the Negro as different was to imply that he was inferior.[27]

Perhaps Countee Cullen articulated most forcefully and most often the position of the black writer who wanted to be regarded as writer, not black writer. Cullen wrote of himself: "He has said perhaps with a reiteration sickening to some of his friends, that he wishes any merit that may be in his work to flow from it solely as the expression of a poet — with no racial consideration to bolster it up." Cullen in effect denied the possibility of "Negro poetry" in his time and in this country;[28] he himself did not intend to subordinate his individual talent to any racial commitment. Perhaps Cullen's concept of poetry "that good poetry is lofty thought beautifully expressed,"[29] perhaps his commitment to the traditional forms of English poetry, perhaps his devotion to Keats and Millay, help to explain his ideal of raceless poetry.[30] Although McKay's literary identification with blackness was more direct, he too exalted the individual above the racial impulse: "'but there is a vast chasm between the artist's personal expression of himself and his making himself the instrument of a group or a body of opinion.'"[31] For some black writers, the desire to escape classification as a black artist was not always an attempt to escape the label of inferiority, but was sometimes a desire to disentangle the aesthetic impulse from any sociological burden.

On the other hand, some poets disagreed with Cullen's view. Hughes stated flatly: "Most of my own poems are racial in theme and treatment derived from the life I know." Eschewing propaganda, he still perceived his black identity as expressing itself in poetry, and he considered the black poet who wished to be simply a poet as desiring to "run away spiritually from his race" in a manner of the black bourgeoisie.[32] Wallace Thurman also regarded the Cullen position as escape — escape from reality into literary tradition: "fleeing from the stigma of being called a *Negro* poet . . . by ignoring folk material and writing of such abstractions as love and death."[33]

Although an element of the "to be or not to be a Negro" writer debate was traceable to an "attempt to break through racial barriers that bridge in even art in the United States"[34] (a desire to escape racial provincialism, another element was traceable to the contemporary aesthetic. According to this aesthetic, great literature was universal; literature that spoke too crudely of its specific local origins failed to attain the highest rank. Therefore, black artists seeking to create an authentic racial literature with the kind of greatness that other literature had attained must simultaneously represent and transcend the group. James Weldon Johnson expressed this ideal when he saw the black artist as standing on "his racial foundation, he strives to fashion something that rises above mere race and reaches out to the universal in truth and beauty."[35] Race was the starting point; universality the goal. Universality was an element of belles lettres that had been received from the Western tradition in terms of the Western tradition, and this belletristic ideal dictated that any special province of literature be justified in terms of transcending its origins.

There were social changes during the Depression that led to different answers to questions raised in a black aesthetic. The deans of the Renaissance left Harlem for academic posts: Locke remained at Howard University where he had been during the Renaissance; James Weldon Johnson and Charles S. Johnson accepted posts at Fisk University; Du Bois returned to Atlanta University. Of the well-known Harlem writers, McKay, Hughes, and Hurston spent time, especially during the early thirties, traveling abroad or in the United States. Hughes and Hurston visited New York from time to time, and McKay settled there in 1934, the year when both Wallace Thurman and Rudolph Fisher died. Cullen and Fauset settled down to teaching posts in the New York City system; Cullen produced his last book of verse in 1935, Jessie Fauset's last novel was published in 1933. Although Harlem remained a cultural center, as evidenced by the visual artists, the Harlem Renaissance surge was over.

With the changed milieu came a reassessment of the Harlem Renaissance by many who had been included in it. Wallace Thurman, as his *Infants of the Spring* illustrated, felt that excessive race consciousness had spoiled the Harlem Renaissance authors, had somehow crippled their talents, and had left them a choice between propaganda and decadence. Du Bois traced the failure of the movement to its pandering to whites and to its lacking a true black constituency and roots in the black experience.[36] Hughes felt that as a vogue or fad the movement had lost its impetus when whites tired of their enthusiasm for blacks.[37] McKay also saw the movement as artificial, with its artificial Harlem consciousness induced by the interest of whites.

However varied the criticism, Depression conditions brought criticisms that the movement had been inadequately rooted in the experience of the black community, and had therefore failed to find an appropriate literary vehicle for its experience. Alain Locke, writing in the *Survey Graphic*, eleven years after its Harlem issue, found that the movement had lacked "sound economic underpinnings" and that "no emerging elite — artistic, professional or mercantile — can suspend itself in the air over the abyss of a mass of unemployed stranded in an over-expensive, disease-and-crime-ridden slum."[38] According to Locke, the 1935 riot made apparent what some had known all along: that besides the gay cabaret scenes, there was another, more somber reality in Harlem. Just as Depression and riot had turned the consciousness of Harlem dwellers to bread-and-butter issues, so the artists had directed their attention from racial self-consciousness to social and economic issues.[39]

With the change in mood came a redefinition of what "Negro literature" was, and there were new definers of the term. In New York as elsewhere, the Communist party and the Left were influential in directing opinion, and a group focus was the Federal Writers Project; a Harlem-based magazine, *Challenge*, attempted to give new direction to the arts movement.

In Harlem, Benjamin Davis and James Ford were active; James Ford, the premier black Communist, had been the Communist vice-presidential nominee in 1932. Langston Hughes and Countee Cullen both supported his candidacy: Hughes served as president of the Communist League of Struggle for Negro Rights in 1933. Later attracted to the Party through the John Reed Club was Richard Wright; the Party in some ways influenced McKay and Ellison as well. As McKay was later to see it, the Communists, through their influence on Federal One projects and through the United Front, were able to penetrate many black organizations and gain influence among the younger intellectuals.[40] The Communist program for black creative artists envisioned their striving to prepare the way for the "nationalist consciousness" necessary to implant a policy of black self-determination. What was proposed was an "aesthetic extension of Stalin's definition of a nation, as applied to the American Negro by the Sixth World Congress of the Comintern."[41]

The Federal Writers Project (1935-1939) was another force for social commitment and interracial cooperation. Many writers on the project "began to believe that the detested values of middle-class Americans could be counteracted, and even cancelled, by a class of Americans that commanded their attention as never before . . . the so-called common people whose lives were already vividly interwoven into the fabric of the national character."[42] One of the subjects under scrutiny was ethnic groups, and the Afro-American in particular. Under Sterling Brown's general directorship, the Negro projects throughout the country produced "the first objective description of the Negro's participation in American life."[43]

In New York, Roi Ottley was the head of the Negro unit; under him as editors at various times were Ralph Ellison, Claude McKay, Richard Nugent, Carlton Moss, Ted Poston, Waring Cuney, J.A. Rogers, Abram Hill, and Carl Offord among others. Wright contributed to the Harlem section in the Federal Writers Project's *New York Panorama* and *New York City Guide*. The project writers had the opportunity to do research on the New York black community and to engage in activist roles through the frequent demonstrations and other union activities.

The development of the Harlem-based literary magazine, *Challenge*, illustrates some preoccupations of the decade. The first issue of the magazine (March 1934) contained an introductory article by James Weldon Johnson, in which he said of the Harlem Renaissance, "we expected much; perhaps too much." He then outlined the task for younger writers: to destroy old stereotypes and create a "higher and more enlightened opinion about the race" without being propagandistic, by being "sincere artists, disdaining all cheap applause and remaining always true to themselves."[44] It seems evident that Johnson was proposing an extension of the Harlem Renaissance without its pitfalls. Subsequent publication of work by Bontemps, McKay, Cullen, and Hurston seemed to indicate some sort of continuum. Although new writers — Attaway, Yerby, Cuney, and Dodson — appeared, the magazine remained a "pale pink" version of Renaissance hopes. However, in the fall of 1937, Wright and others of the Chicago school were represented, and the *New Challenge* appeared, still under the editorship of Dorothy West, but with Richard Wright as associate editor. *New Challenge* was no longer an attempt to develop the Renaissance concerns (built on "false foundations"), but an attempt to "point out social directives." The newly named magazine, which was hailed but not sponsored by the *Daily Worker*, had developed a social consciousness and a social commitment.

Despite the turn to realism, social consciousness, and interracial cooperation, black writers of the day still had to wrestle with the ongoing problem of finding an appropriate literary vehicle for the black experience. The essential question of the function of the artist, the nature of the audience, the content of "Negro literature," and the role of the black writer, remained. Although not all writers swung to the left, a considerable number did exhibit an awakened social consciousness.

According to Wright, "Negro literature" had been previously an instrument for the black bourgeoisie who regarded it either as a hallmark of achievement or as the voice of the educated Negro pleading for justice — functions external to the lives of the writers and their black audience.[45] However, writing in the thirties was to be tied more closely to the actual lives of the masses of the people. The writer was "called upon to do no less than create values by which his race is to struggle, live, and die." Although the function of the writer was still, as Locke expressed it, to evoke the group soul, the racial identity was to be redefined according to the Marxist view of the class struggle and its relation to the black man. The writer must "reflect the epoch, the movement of social forces, the struggle of classes, the political motives, the hopes and fears of his own people." The function of the artist definitely involved implanting the seeds of social consciousness in the minds of the people. According to Wright: "Every first rate novel, poem, or play lifts the level of consciousness higher."[46]

The audience of the artist was not strictly defined, but conflicting demands from black and white reading publics were replaced by imperatives derived from heightened social consciousness. Wright deplored what he saw as the Harlem Renaissance's addressing itself to white audiences: "Rarely was the best of the writing addressed to the Negro himself, his needs, his sufferings, his aspirations."[47] Supposedly, the new literature would be addressed to blacks, with the presumption that whites would follow where they pleased. However, the necessity for literature that would raise the consciousness of the masses and proselytize the middle class resulted in the kind of polemics found in Max's speech in *Native Son*, in such proletarian novels as Conroy's *The Disinherited*, or in outright agitprop techniques. Proletarian literature of the thirties, like the black and white audiences of the twenties, dictated artistic images to a certain extent. Just as the twenties' audience could not be expected to know the details of black life without explicit comment, so the thirties audience must be educated to the reality of the class struggle.

The content of art should be proletarian. Although Locke said that the new art need not be explicitly proletarian, most of these artists were attempting to find the identity of the Afro-American in the masses of the people. According to Wright, since the identity of the black American is deposited in his folklore (as in his church), the writer should attempt to continue and deepen the folk tradition. Folklore and legendary heroes were to be the stuff from which literature was to be derived: "legends, myths, and ballads in which Negroes immortalized folk heroes for elements of universality."[48] Writers such as Bontemps, Dodson, and Davis become praiseworthy because they turned to the past of the race. A great contemporary subject was the unmonied class. The black writer could find sources in the "soil folk and the industrial masses."[49] Sterling Brown, who wrote of sharecroppers, and Langston Hughes, who wrote of steelworkers, were also deemed praiseworthy. A later observer, LeRoi Jones, described the literary results of this reinterpretation of content: "Even in the thirties, when Langston Hughes and what we call the Harlem school began to focus and describe what was really around them and to create that place as an instrument of feeling — they turned out a literature about poverty, a literature of violence, a literature about the seamier side of the so-called American dream."[50]

Especially for Wright, the Communist ideology played a liberating function by assuring the artist of a worldwide perspective that valued the experience of the Afro-American. "It seemed to me that here at last in the realm of revolutionary expression, Negro experience could find a home, a functioning value and role." The Communist ideology also imparted a sense of dignity to the Afro-American. "With the exception of the church and its myths and legends, there was no agency in the world so capable of making men feel the earth and the people upon it as the Communist Party."[51] Thus the universality of the twenties was reinterpreted in terms of a Marxist universality of a worldwide proletariat. The black group and its life were not seen in isolation, nor in terms of the American dream, but "against the background of the total configuration of world-wide human emotions, ideals and struggles." The "consciousness of the interaction of people in modern society" was the universality for which the writers strove. A group work was to be accomplished through the "ideological unity of Negro writers and its alliance of that unity with all the progressive ideas of our day."[52]

Only one issue of *New Challenge* appeared. Harold Cruse saw this failure as symptomatic of the failure of radical thinkers to come to terms with the reality of the black American's experience. He also believed that the trends of the thirties seduced black thought from the direction glimpsed, but not articulated, in the twenties: "Unable to arrive at any philosophical conclusion of their own as a *black intelligensia*, the leading literary lights of the 1920s substituted the Communist leftwing philosophy of the 1930s and thus were intellectually sidetracked for the remainder of their productive years."[53] Despite the co-optation by Marxist ideology, there was a genuine impulse during the thirties toward coming to terms with the Afro-American experience as lived by the majority of black people.

The artistic movements of the twenties and thirties most strongly affected M.B. Tolson because these decades constituted the formative period of his life and thought. But Tolson, never a static person, lived beyond the thirties into the sixties. The generation of the sixties addressed itself to the black urban masses and the ghetto world, concerns of Tolson since the thirties. The later generation could, like Tolson himself, see possibilities in the ghetto condition.[54]

New forces were again sweeping the black community by the sixties.[55] Although many such forces were part of broader forces operating throughout the nation, there were significant local manifestations. Muhammed's Mosque No. 7, led by Minister Malcolm X Shabazz, and the Yoruba religion were indicative of one new wave. A renewed Harlem consciousness in the arts was evidenced in the 1963 *Freedomways* issue dedicated to Harlem, and the emergence of the Harlem Writers' Guild. The LeRoi Jones/Imamu Amiri Baraka spiritual quest paralleled a movement of black cultural history. In the course of his career, Jones moved from the integrationist fifties to the cultural nationalism of the sixties. Eventually, Jones left the Villiage for Harlem and Newark, and his philosophy eventually became a metaphysic of blackness.[56] Without attempting to detail the many movements and personalities at work during the sixties, one can say that in Harlem, as in other black communities, there was a renewed interest in the *possibilities* inherent in ghetto living.

One of the new organizations operating for change was the Harlem Youth Opportunities Unlimited (HARYOU), "an experiment in community psychiatry." Perceiving the Harlem community to be a "monument of human cruelty, injustice and insensitivity which spawns human casualties," Dr. Kenneth Clark, HARYOU's director, asserted that "the ghetto is a compound of despair, inertia, apathy, seething frustration and turbulence and chronically covert and, occasionally, overt violence."[57] The aim of various activities conceived and sponsored by the organization was to give young Harlemites an opportunity to learn how to work for social change. By working with youngsters, HARYOU hoped eventually to work a social change in the community at large. Although the director saw this social change as a "contribution to strengthing of American democracy," the operation was conceived as an attempt from within the community to solve the peculiar problems of the separate black community.

The program, active on the economic and social fronts, evolved no explicitly cultural arm until 1964 when LeRoi Jones, Charles Patterson, Clarence Reed, Johnny Moore, and others opened the Black Arts Repertoire Theatre/School (BART/S) with some funding from the federal government's Office of Economic Opportunity (OEO) through HARYOU.[58] Besides featuring drama and other cultural activities, this short-lived project provided about eighty children with instruction in remedial reading, mathematics, and "Hardcore nationalism." Jones saw in this project the "realization of an idea — the involvement of the masses of black people in viable cultural experiences, his job being, basically, to put on a play a week, utilizing the community's human resources and talents."[59] Among the plays produced were *Experimental Death Unit #1, Black Mass, J-E-L-L-O,* and *Dutchman.* For three months, poetry readings and concerts played to the citizens of the streets. When Jones moved in his career from his and his country's integrationist fifties to the cultural nationalism of the sixties, he changed his name to Imamu Amiri Baraka.

Jones was attempting to establish cultural institutions that could implement change in the ghetto. He founded BART/S in order "'to re-educate the nearly half a million Harlem Negroes to find a new pride in their color.'" Baraka was later to recognize the project, despite its apparent failure, as a forerunner of the Spirit House he founded in Newark. BART/S served as a prototype "for the type of community-theatre-workshop-school that sprang up in black neighborhoods in other cities in the United States."[60] The movement was seen by one of its founders as "the flowering of a cultural nationalism that has been suppressed since the 1920's. I mean the 'Harlem Renaissance' which was essentially a failure." According to Neal, the Renaissance failed because it did not address itself to "the mythology, and the life styles of the Black community."[61]

Black communities throughout the country sensed a cultural awakening. New names, new magazines, and new groups became evident, and though the groups were diverse, certain common ingredients could be observed. Many of the new writers saw Baraka as their mentor, and the Black Arts Movement as a crystallization of goals that might be applicable to themselves. Underlying much of the activity was a redirection toward the black community. It was believed that the new art should be ghetto-oriented — an art growing out of the experience of the mass of Afro-Americans, especially those in urban centers. A constant of much of the quickened consciousness was the perception of the ghetto as a colony. Ideas of cultural liberation, like those of Franz Fanon, could be relevant here. Thus, the establishment of an appropriate literary vehicle for the black experience would involve the "decolonization" of "Negro literature" since creative activity was seen as a confrontation between black and white over control of the image: "For to manipulate an image is to control a peoplehood."[62]

The chief function of the new art was to aid in the rebirth of black people by substituting a constructive "blackness" for internalized white, middle-class values. According to Baraka, white American society is sterile, deathdealing, "a madhouse." Harlem, typical of Afro-American communities, "is a community of nonconformists, since any black American, simply by virtue of his blackness is weird, a nonconformist in this society." But, according to this early essay, Harlem is also "a colony of old-line Americans, who can hold out, even if it is a great deal of the time in misery and ignorance, but still hold out against the hypocrisy and sterility of big-time America."[63] Borrowing from Wittgenstein the insight that ethics and aesthetics are one, Baraka felt that the artist must spearhead the community's rejection of the prevailing white culture. As Baraka said in a later essay, "State/meant," "The Black Artist's role in America is to aid in the destruction of America as he knows it."[64]

However, the artist was not to confine himself to the rejection of white American values; he was also to help in the effort to construct a black nation. "The Black Artist must draw out of his soul the correct image of the world."[65] He must help weld the community into a nation with its own values. His art then becomes a "literature of ideas, literature for social change."[66] This redirection of effort is to be revolutionary: "The Black Aesthetic, for those trying to create today is necessarily the business of making revolution, for we have tried everything else."[67] Whether the revolution was to be literally bombs and burning, or whether words were to be the chief weapon, is open to question,[68] but the intention is revolutionary in either case. "The function of black authors, then, according to most recent essays in *Negro Digest* should be to build psychological peace within the black community while carrying psychological war across the color line."[69]

The audience of the new black art was to be primarily the black masses, so much so as to earn its designation as "black populist cultural nationalism." But the black artist did, at least in Baraka's earlier work, address himself to the white and black middle-class audiences. This artist was to convey to the "white-eyes" the death of their world, and perhaps quite literally of themselves: "The Revolutionary Theatre must teach them their deaths."[70] The Afro-American artist was to destroy what was perceived as black middle-class shame at their blackness. For the masses, the black artist is recorder, voice, and celebrator: he recorded the substance of life as it was lived by the masses, usually ghetto inhabitants; he was the voice of present and future values inherent in the community, and he celebrated the essential beauty to be found in their lives. The black masses thus become both the sources and critics of the new art.

The content of the new art was to be derived from the life experience of the community; the new folk often defined as the ghetto dweller raised to the heroic — his mores, music, outlook, and language were to form the substance of art. "For he [Baraka] would find in the Black ghetto the contemporary form of an ancient archetype."[71] There was also a concentration on heroes necessary for the evolution of a new culture; heroes such as Crazy Horse, Vesey, and Lumumba became symbols of rebellion. The past and present yielded heroes suitable for literary exploitation. Africa also became a subject; not an exotic Africa, but Africa viewed as a repository of ethnic values. Then Clyde Taylor can substantially agree with a tenet of Richard Wright's literary faith: "The underlying function of Black literature is to move the process of Black folk art to a further stage of development."[72]

Some techniques associated with the Black Arts Movement are those linked to making that art more available or relevant to the masses. Baraka's techniques for this were "the prose-poetry declarative statement, the breezy and slangy street idiom, the nonsense lines, and the aural (or nonverbal) line."[73] Techniques derived from street life and soul music were incorporated into poetry. Baraka posited: "The language would be anybody's, but tightened by the poet's backbone."[74] The techniques are part of an attempt to create a distinctive vehicle for the Afro-American experience: "It proposes a separate symbolism, mythology, critique, and iconology."[75]

The role of the literary artist became a bardic one: "We are black magicians, black art/s we make in the black labs of the heart." The role of the poet, educating to blackness and celebrating blackness, put him in the position of a priest vis-à-vis the community. Not only was he to mediate between the existent community and the coming spiritual nation, but through the arts he celebrated the rituals of blackness. He "lives blackly"; the world is to become a "black poem."[76] In Baraka's case, the aesthetic became a part of a totality embodied in the seven principles of Kawaida spirituality.[77] Thus, there came to be a new kind of universality. The old concept of universality was seen as a kind of windmill at which to tilt. The new universality was interpreted in terms of black consciousness reaching out to the nonwhite world and encompassing a metaphysics read into the African spiritualities. Blackness itself became transcendent.

Implicit in these cultural movements, centered in or touching upon Harlem, is a quest for Afro-American cultural identity. No matter who defines the aesthetic, there is a continuing quest for the proper vehicle for Afro-American experience, a continuing search for black identity within America, a continuing return to the black community, and often to the ghetto, for the roots of black identity and experience. Black aesthetics in general, and its quest for identity in particular, are relevant to M.B. Tolson's treatment of Afro-American art and artists in *Harlem Gallery.*

4

Tolson's Harlem Portraits

Harlem fired Melvin Tolson's imagination. During his residence, he tried
to capture Harlem in a sonnet. He showed the sonnet to a fellow student,
a German-American, who complained, "'Harlem is too big, too lusty for
a sonnet. Say we've never had a Negro epic in America.'"[1] Tolson was
sufficiently impressed by the literary life of Harlem to make it the subject
of his master's essay, virtually completed during the year at Columbia
University. Probably around 1934, Tolson returned to the project of a Negro
epic centering on Harlem life, completing a manuscript of roughly
three-hundred pages: "A Gallery of Harlem Portraits."[2]

Although a few poems were published in Calverton's *Modern Quarterly*,
1937-1939, the manuscript was rejected by Maxwell Perkins and by Bennett
Cerf in 1937.[3] One of two other editors to whom the manuscript had been
sent commented: "'The poems carry the accent of authority; the incidents
are interesting and dramatic, and Harlem, in its dramatic and far-flung
constituency transpires as a lively and peculiar event in American life'"
("Odyssey," p. 12). Even though the manuscript went unpublished,[4] Tolson
shared the poems with willing listeners. His son, Melvin, remembers hearing
with delight the poems read aloud during the thirties, and Tolson said that
"professors, bums, preachers, magdalenes, and babbits had read parts of
the Gallery" in places like Duluth, Yazoo, Florida, and Illinois ("Odyssey,"
p. 8). Ultimately, the manuscript, metamorphosed into the *Harlem Gallery*,
reached a wider audience.

The sonnet, now lost, represented Tolson's first attempt to grapple with
the reality of life presented to him in the streets of the black metropolis.
It is evident from Tolson's notes that he was impressed by the throbbing
complexity of life in Harlem — by the variety of persons, by the interaction
of classes, by the different provinces of the black world represented. Such
a subject would be "too big, too lusty" for a single poem and especially
for the traditional sonnet form.

Tolson's second attempt to deal with Harlem in literature was his master's
essay, "The Harlem Group of Negro Writers." In the first chapter, "A
Perspective of Harlem," Tolson placed excerpts from five poets, four black
and one white.[5] Lines from Cullen, Dunbar, Hughes, and Fenton Johnson
stressed different responses to the black man's desire to "sing," from the
dilemma of Cullen — "'To make a poet black, and bid him sing!'" — to
the exaltation of Fenton Johnson — "'We are the children of the sun, /
Rising sun!'" The final word is given to Whitman, who hears America
singing: "'the varied carols I hear . . . / Each singing his . . .'" Tolson
recognized the possibility of the creation of an ethnic literature and saw

a Whitmanesque value in its creation. As Tolson said later in the essay: "Across the milieu of the dark metropolis moved those members of the Harlem group who gave expression to a racial life 'through the medium of art, music or poetry'" (Essay, p. 17).

Tolson made an attempt to characterize the black city from which the literature flowed. He saw Harlem following the diversity of New York City. "Being a city in itself, Harlem has all the aspects of a diversified modern civilization, plus those differentiating customs, dialects, and modes of thought that Negro peoples have brought from all parts of the world" (Essay, p. 8). In the frequently used title, "City of Refuge," Tolson found "an embedded analogy between events in Hebrew history and those in the ethnic experiences of the Negro migrants from the South" (Essay, p. 9). Harlem was then, according to Tolson, not a "slum," "quarter," or "fringe," but a literary and artistic Mecca for Negroes.

Besides the general character of the "Negro city," Tolson outlined specific factors that contributed to the twenty-year-long literary movement. The World War, the cosmopolitanism of New York City, white patrons and writers, the magazines, *Fire* and *Harlem*, the NAACP, and research in black history, such as that conducted by Arthur Schomburg and by Carter Woodson, all helped to quicken the movement. Tolson then described the principal authors of the Renaissance: Cullen, Hughes, McKay, White, Walrond, Fisher, Fauset, Schuyler, Du Bois, J.W. Johnson, and Thurman.

Although Tolson's treatment was objective, some leanings emerge: (1) There seemed to be a bias away from the kind of writing produced by Jessie Fauset; at least, Tolson contrasts the "intellectual solitude" of this "veiled aristocrat" with the popularity of Langston Hughes and noted the different approaches and subject matter of the two authors; (2) Tolson noted adverse reactions of the black bourgeoisie to McKay and Hughes and Schuyler's satirical attack on the customs of the black middle class; (3) He made comments about different poets being considered "black writers" or merely writers. In dealing with Cullen, Tolson saw a connection between race and universality: "He must suffer in some dark Gethsemane in the world of experience, both physical and spiritual; then, and only then, can he sound the depths, the oceanic depths of universal man" (Essay, p. 25). Some typical attitudes of Tolson toward the middle class, race, and universality can be inferred. Tolson reacted against black bourgeois concerns and believed that the black writer could move from "the racial province" to the universal by being faithful to his racial heritage. Nathan Huggins expressed a view similar to Tolson's when he said that a work of art could be a window opening on an "ethnic province" or lead to a "geography of his own humanity."[6] According to Huggins, writers like Bellow, Ellison, Malamud, and Tolson illustrate the latter possibility: "Through their works, the reader is taken through the 'province' into the world at large," a view espoused by Tolson in his master's essay.

In the conclusion, which attempts to evaluate the Harlem Renaissance attitude and methods, Tolson stated that the Renaissance had been "followed by a proletarian literature of Negro life, wider in scope, deeper in significance, and better in stylistic methods" (Essay, p. 120). Asserting that most of the writers of the Harlem Renaissance "portrayed the sensational features of Negro life" for the benefit of white readers, Tolson termed contemporary literature "earthy, unromantic, and sociological; and from it emerges Negro characters that are more graphically individualized" (Essay, p. 121). He ended by citing *New Challenge* magazine as symptomatic of the new direction of black literature, and Zora Hurston, Edward Turpin, Frank Marshall Davis, George Lee, O'Wendell Shaw, and Richard Wright as avatars of the new school of literature. Tolson praised the authors who were more realistic and whose literary products approached proletarian literature.

Tolson's description of literature that is "earthy, unromantic, and sociological" fits the kind of writing of his third attempt to grapple with the reality of Harlem in literary form during the thirties, his *A Gallery of Harlem Portraits*. Influenced by Imagist techniques, Browning's psychology, and Whitman's exuberance,[7] the *Portraits* delved into the harsher aspects of an American black community in order to compose a widely relevant picture of community life. Tolson attempted to reveal the inner lives of the characters as each of the poems moved toward a climax — a dramatic event, a revelation, a statement, or, in many cases, a blueslike cry. While Tolson's method is dramatic, his tone is usually ironic.

Like the cemetery of Spoon River, the gallery is a device for a series of literary portraits. Although a few of these portraits are interconnected, as were some monologues in *Spoon River*, most are cameos of different inhabitants of or visitors to Harlem. The characters represent various ethnic groups: American blacks from all parts of the United States, a few whites, two Chinese and two Africans are detailed. Among classes of society, a few upper-class whites, more of the black bourgeoisie, some of the underworld, and a majority of the black poor are represented. However, as in *Spoon River*, there is not merely a series of isolated character drawings; the characters inhere in, and are vivified by, the common life of Harlem. The typical yet unique New York black community serves as a nexus of the lives of its inhabitants, and as a vehicle for interpretation of their common life.

The milieu of *Portraits* is that of Harlem in the thirties. The present of the poems is the early thirties. Although there are references to the Depression, unemployment, and the Scottsboro case, there is no mention of the 1935 riot. Tolson telescoped the twenties and thirties, much as they may have appeared to him in 1931–1932, with events seen from the perspective of the economically marginal existence lived by most Harlem inhabitants. A wider sense of history, especially black history, is imparted by centenarians like Mother Vibbard and Joshua Granite, "ancient rebel with the mummy face" (*Portraits*, p. 152), who had experienced over a century of American rebellion against various kinds of slavery. The ex-slave, Marzimmu Heffner, adds a sense of the African past.

The locale is specifically Harlem. There is mention of streets like 115th, 116th, and 135th, and of the well-known avenues of Harlem with their social connotations — Seventh, Lenox, Eighth, and Manhattan. Landmarks of the day, such as Abyssinian Baptist Church, a kingdom of Father Divine,

Strivers' Row, Sugar Hill, the Lafayette Theatre, the Tree of Hope, the YWCA, Harlem Hospital,[8] the Harlem Opera House, Liberty Hall, the Savoy Ballroom, Rockland Palace, Plantation Club, and Club Alabam, help convey a sense of place. Reference to landladies and roomers and to empty apartments used by youth groups indicate a characteristic of the Harlem housing situation. Fleeting touches, such as the presence of an organ grinder and his monkey, and allusions to the Black Bottom, the Lindy Hop, the Slow Drag, and the dancing waiters at a club, all help to build the Harlem milieu of the thirties.

Mention of a number of actual historical figures further serves to specify the time and locale. Harlem figures like Richard B. Harrison, Bojangles, Paul Robeson, Langston Hughes, Cab Calloway, Papa Handy, Countee Cullen, Duke Ellington, Marcus Garvey, Father Divine, and Charles Gilpin, evoke the era and the place. References to Flo Ziegfield, Bert Williams, Ulysses Grant, Jack Dempsey, Eugene Debs, Franklin Roosevelt, Jack Johnson, and others lend historical depth to the period, as do allusions to the *Emperor Jones, Negro World,* and *Show Boat.*

Besides this mention of actual persons, fictional characters in *Portraits* resemble historical figures. Abraham Dumas, "The Dean of Negro Letters," is similar in many respects to Du Bois or Locke. Grand Chancellor Knapp Sackville, with his "flashy blue uniform," medal-covered breast, sword, yellow plume, shiny black boots, his title of "Grand Chancellor and Most Exalted Polemarch of the Sons and Daughters of Ethiopia," and speeches on "pride of race" in Liberty Hall (*Portraits,* p. 25), bears a strong resemblance to Marcus Garvey. Peg Leg Snelson combines aspects of the careers of Bojangles and Peg Leg Bates. The name of Chittling Sue evokes the memory of "Pig Foot Mary" who, like Chittling Sue, ended her career as a rich woman owning real estate in Harlem. The white patroness, Miss Felicia Babcock, bears some resemblance to actual whites, like Hughes's patroness who insisted on his primitivism. A few elements of the career of Dr. Harvey Whyte resemble events in the career of Dr. Louis T. Wright. The rise of Mrs. Alpha Devine, scrubwoman, who after "A vision of the Negro Woman Beautiful" (*Portraits,* p. 121), achieved fame and a mansion on the Hudson through the marketing of "Devine Hair Grower," is similar to that of Madame Walker. The Black Moses, barefoot and gigantic, attempting to save souls in a Harlem nightclub, recalls the Barefoot Prophet. Officer John Cushwa may remind one of an actual policeman of the era, while Xavier Van Loon's career parallels in some ways those of Paul Robeson and Roland Hayes, just as Frank Fullison's career corresponds to that of Hubert Harrison.

This is not to suggest that these fictional characters are merely disguised versions of real people. As Tolson said at a later date: "But a flesh-and-blood model is still a model — not a character in a work of art. An artist is not a photographer, a case-historian" ("A Poet's Odyssey," p. 188). For the most part, aspects of careers or striking features of personalities are melded into fictional characters whose psychological makeup is derived chiefly from Tolson: an "imaginary character, (although I knew his prototype)."[9] By suggesting these actual figures, however, Tolson obtained a sense of historical reality and displayed the quality that such figures added to the dimensions of Harlem community life.

More often, characters are not so strikingly reminiscent of historical figures as they are typical of ghetto life and of the inhabitants' attempts to survive. In the introductory poem, "Harlem," Tolson has declared:

> Radicals, prize-fighters, actors and deacons,
> Beggars, politicians, professors and redcaps,
> Bulldikers, Babbitts, racketeers and jig-chasers,
> Harlots, crapshooters, workers, and pink-chasers,
> Artists, dicties, Pullman porters and messiahs . . .
> The Curator has hung the likeness of all
> In *A Gallery of Harlem Portraits*
>
> (*Portraits,* p. 4)

Tolson's intention was to include the panorama of Harlem life in his *Portraits*.

The black bourgeoisie is represented by characters such as Napoleon Hannibal Speare, editor-in-chief of *The Harlem Advocate*, whose paper seems typical of many black papers of the time; Miss Eulaline Briffault, a native Harlemite, who despised "ignorant blacks from the South / And the dirty Jews from the Ghetto" (*Portraits,* p. 6); Mr. Horace Allyn, ready to ask God "'Why in the hell he made me a nigger'" (*Portraits,* p. 70); Mrs. Gertrude Beamish, who is obsessed by "'What will the white folks think?'" (*Portraits,* p. 99); Mrs. Ernest Quirk has a family tree "tall /As the Empire State Buildin" (*Portraits,* p. 75); Mrs. Josephine Wise with her refrain, "'just like a nigger'" (*Portraits,* p. 105); and Mrs. Edith Parker, mulatto widow of a great black criminal lawyer. Also depicted are Frederick Judson whose ideas "were those of the master class: / He scorned both the poor whites and the poor blacks" (*Portraits,* p. 31), and Mr. Alexander Calverton, President of the Harlem Savings Bank, Chairman of the Deacon Board at Mt. Sinai, and self-made man. Dr. Cram Mifflin, "You insulted him if you did not call him 'Doctor' / To distinguish him from the other professors" is another of the class (*Portraits,* p. 71). Although a few other members of the black middle class are not typical of the black bourgeoisie, the general characterization suggests Tolson's contempt for bourgeois affectation and humanity-denying scorn for others.[10] A related type that has become almost a stereotype is the "mouth-Christian" who is revealed to be less than ideally Christian. Deacon Phineas Bloom, Rev. Graves, and, to a lesser extent, Hester Pringle, are characters who present a facade of respectability that covers some sexual irregularity.

Representatives of Harlem's world of entertainment are depicted, from Xavier Van Loon, internationally celebrated actor, to Ivory Frysinger, itinerant piano player, to Ginger Barry, glamorous and notorious entertainer at Club Alabam. There are dancers like Peg Leg Snelson and Winged Feet Cooper. There are singers like the blues queen, Big Bessie, star of the Congo Club, and Black Zuleika, singer-dancer at Sundown Cabaret, killed by a jealous wife, and Stella Sippel, whose songs are broadcast from a Harlem nightclub, leading to her husband's ultimate destruction. Besides orchestra leaders like Gabby Gay and Snakehips Flippen, there are Lovee Long, once the toast of the Riviera and now Harlem songstress, and Maizelle Malloy, now withered and old, once reigning beauty of the Plantation Club.

The underworld is well represented: Diamond Canady, womanizer and gambler; Poker Face Duncan, poolshark; Sparky Zigsmith, holdup man and copkiller; Pearl Triplett, Okay Katie, and Gladys Zimmerman are prostitutes, while Sadie Mulbery and Juarez Mary are women of the underworld. Jazz Boker, dealer in policy and narcotics; Big Shot Lacey, numbers king and Harlem "big shot"; and Duke Higgins, "master of the Subway," a gambling den, represent the criminal element.

Artists and intellectuals are present, as they were in the Harlem community. Francis Keats, "I have known futility, / The desolate servitude of language, / The vanity of trying to put into words / The things I have felt" (*Portraits,* p. 24), lives a nomadic life and finds it difficult to capture feelings in language. Percy Longfellow is not specifically identified as poet, but his responses are poetical and his diction has a kind of lyricism. Having been "enamoured" by many landscapes and many cities, Longfellow returns to Harlem, "mistress of my youth." Sterling, the artist, is shown in his relationship to a woman "whose vanity had cursed him and his art" (*Portraits,* p. 165). Sterling himself is seen as almost ruthlessly honest in exposing their relationship. These three artist observers, Keats, Longfellow, and, to a lesser extent, Sterling, emerge as artists with something of the Ishmael about them.

More fully drawn personalities are those of Abraham Dumas, Xavier Van Loon, and Vergil Ragsdale. Dumas, "An elderly man of catholic tastes and interests, / Nurtured by the culture of two continents" (*Portraits,* p. 10), is described as the "Flaubert of the Harlem Renaissance." After describing his nurturing activities and generally buoyant spirits, the poet Tolson leaves the Dean withdrawn in "his dark tower," a mystic awaiting "a black Whitman . . . a Balzac . . . a Tolstoi" (*Portraits,* p. 10). Xavier Van Loon, entertainer and artist, has risen from impoverished beginnings to fame in New York, London, Paris, Berlin, and Hollywood. He is described finally as one in whose face lay "The tragedy of aboriginal man / Trapped in a desolation" (*Portraits,* p. 192). Vergil Ragsdale, the most carefully described of the artists, is a tragic or, more accurately, a pathetic figure. A dishwasher at Mr. Muranto's café, Vergil is a poet haunted by his yet-to-be-completed "epic of his people," *An African Tragedy.* Tubercular, living miserably, sustained by gin and cocaine, and obsessed with the idea of completing the epic, he is defeated by death and his landlady, who ignorantly burns his manuscript. The character of Ragsdale's vision is contained in "Harlem" as:

"City of the Big Niggers
Graveyard of the Dark Masses,
Soapbox of the Red Apocalypse . . .
I shall be forgotten like you
Beneath the Debris of Oblivion."

(*Portraits,* p. 4)

Each of these men, haunted by an authentic vision, is, in different ways and to different degrees, unfulfilled.

Inauthentic artists also appear. One such artist is Mr. Masters, the "most subtle writer in the Harlem Renaissance," who is attempting to buttress his reputation by writing a novel too exquisitely subtle for understanding. His novel, with its faulty diction, clumsy style, and sex-obsessed protagonist, is "a no-man's land / of mutilated experiences" (*Portraits*, p. 177). Richard Birch is also an artist more interested in career than in artistic inspiration. In contrast to the popular entertainer, Ivory Frysinger, whose religion is "playing and singing for the benefit of others" (*Portraits*, p. 180), and who can touch souls with his music, Richard Birch leaves the audience unmoved because he remains, despite his ambitious mother's urgings and his years of training, a mechanic of the keys with a wooden soul (*Portraits*, p. 171).

Whites are present as they made their presence felt in Harlem of the thirties. There are the southern whites, representatives of the "master class," whose lives have touched on the lives of some black Harlemites. Editor Crum is fond of his black Mammy Suhrie and of the abstract ideal of the "good nigger" he has made of her. He is outraged at being stopped by a black policeman in Harlem and goes home to write editorials on "The Black Peril" and "The Decline of Caucasian Civilization" (*Portraits*, pp. 26–27). Crum, Miss Smithfield, and Colonel Midas Hooker maintain the idealized plantation myth while exploiting the blacks they control. Equally dangerous is the southern-born schoolteacher who acts out her schizophrenic belief in the myth of the Negro beast and in "the Brotherhood of Man" (*Portraits*, p. 175).

Exploitative in a different fashion is Edwin Kennedy, editor of America's best-selling magazine, who sends Ray Rosenfeld to gather material about the latest rage, Harlem. With his imaginative creation buttressed by Warner's exotic illustrations, Rosenfeld disseminates an image of "jungle" Harlem that Harlemites, in their turn, seek to exploit, with both black and white finally conspiring in a cult of escape from civilization. Typical of such whites are the slumming party from Muskogee, Oklahoma, and Elbert Hartman who shows his guests the night life of Harlem. Also caught in her own way in the jungle myth is Miss Felicia Babcock. This white patron, who insists on a stereotype of primitivism for her black protégés, collects African art objects that she does not understand but that validate her claim of Afro-American primitivism.

Evocative of the reality of Harlem life and the white presence therein are examples of white businessmen in Harlem — Ben Rosenbaum, who paints white dolls black for the Negro trade, the Jewish pawnbroker, and Richard Hoover, the disappointed old-line meat dealer.

Although a number of Harlemites harbor memories of abrasive encounters with the southern way of life from which they have fled to the "city of refuge," some Harlemites have less bitter memories of relationships with whites. Uriah Houze remembers an independent old mountain moonshiner who had adopted him as an infant and whom Uriah loved. Ben Shockley remembers his former employer, a "fine old lady of the Old South!" (*Portraits*, p. 227), a noble character who looked forward to a day when the souls as well as the bodies of men would be free. Another white dedicated to freedom is the Communist who explains the laws of unemployment to Steve Wordsworth. Tolson, in these cases, presents individuals who do not succumb to race mythology but who, undeterred by hypocrisy and stereotypic thinking, seek the authentic in human relations.

Members of the working class make up the bulk of the portraits as they made up the bulk of the inhabitants of Harlem. Most of them are not native Harlemites; they come from all parts of the United States, and a few from the West Indies and Africa, to the Negro Mecca. With their past made present through such ancestral figures as Marzimmu, Joshua Granite, and Mother Vibbard, the working poor live in crowded apartments and bring up children under difficult circumstances. They turn to religion for sustenance and social life, or to gin or sexual adventure for relief, go to cabarets and theaters, and persist in dreaming, being disillusioned, and, for the most part, surviving in the face of considerable odds.

The black community's feelings are expressed in the commentary provided by one or another of its members as an action or personality is reflected through that character's eyes. Sister Crispin, the biggest gossip in Harlem, and a lesser gossip like Sister Slemp, convey the conventional opinion of the masses. Miss Briffault is a conduit for middle-class strictures, and century-old Mother Vibbard is a repository of racial wisdom. The yellow journal, *The Harlem Advocate*, also expresses community reaction to its personalities and events in exaggerated form. But the most searching commentary, expressing at times humor, at times pathos, at times tragedy, is that of the ironic and unillusioned voice of the blueslike songs interspersed throughout the poems — the voice of ghetto life and survival.

However, the basic interpretation of the varied lives of characters depicted in *Portraits* is related to the social consciousness of the thirties. In the opening poem, "Harlem," Vergil Ragsdale has an apocalyptic vision of a day he will not live to see — "the quiet Dawn" when black proletarians rise from their tenement houses and overthrow the black bourgeoisie on Strivers' Row and Sugar Hill. The final poems contain more implicit and explicit analyses and images of a corrupt and deteriorating system. In the last poem, the black man, the classic underdog, glimpses freedom at last from his oppressive environment, when "kikes," "dagos," "crackers," and "niggers" stop fighting each other and unite. Between the opening and closing poems are many poems that directly and indirectly reflect Tolson's Marxist views of the nature of the world in which these Harlemites lived. Simply put, Tolson's interpretation at this time of the situation of the black man in America was that the roots of racial exploitation were economic: until the white and black masses realized their exploitation by the "Big Boys" and took steps to unite against their oppression, social ills would continue to multiply.

In the *Portraits*, Tolson sketched a number of characters whose fate was sealed, not because of their innate leanings but because environment had so shaped them. Sometimes these were children of people caught up in the wage struggle, as in the cases of Nig Grinde, street Arab, whose consumptive mother worked a ten-hour day in a factory, and of Pearl Triplett whose mother worked a twelve-hour day in "the white folk's kitchen," and of Senola Hurse's family, lost to Chicago slums because her husband believed "'Money is powah, Honey'" (*Portraits,* p. 16). Whites too are so shaped, as illustrated in the occasion when Slick Gunnar, Public Enemy Number One, is gunned down on a Harlem street and an old black woman asks, "'What made 'im bad?'" (*Portraits,* p. 204).

There are others caught up in the machinery of industrialized civilization. Carrie Green works fourteen hours a day and reaps no reward. Uncle Walt works at a job he detests because he is no longer fit for any other work. There are those who toady to the bosses like Ferenc Glaspell, the "proletarian flunkey of the boss system" (*Portraits,* p. 94), who is obsequious to his superiors but arrogant to his equals. There is a man like Officer Cushwa who has integrity but is unable to oppose the system. And there are misfits who pursue the American dream of democracy only to be disillusioned, like returning veterans Harold Lincoln and Uncle Twitty's son.

But not all are passive victims of capitalist civilization. Peter Osgood, a gadfly and "the biggest fool in Harlem," dispensed truth to unwilling listeners (*Portraits,* p. 65). Another gadfly, the Reverend Isaiah Cloud, puts Christianity and democracy into literal practice, and loses his church as a consequence. Some are visionaries: Uncle Gropper, a tenant farmer, believed in "beauty and truth and fraternity" and had had a vision of the last being first (*Portraits,* p. 117). Some glimpse a vision of solidarity when men are no longer divided by hatred — Tito Crouch during the Depression discovers that the poor white man deserves his sympathy, and Crip McKay is freed from the prison of race hate when, despite shades of Scottsboro, he feels a moment of sorrow for a poor white woman in his railroad boxcar in Arkansas. Others continue to hope, whether because of some sense of worth instilled by black history, as in Michael Ramsey's case, or because of an experience of hope after despair, like Jonah Emerson. One who finally escapes from the tyranny of color and class is Hilmar Enick, who now lives in Moscow where the proletariat has conquered: "Now he is a man, an equal, a comrade / . . . / Building a new civilization / With Brotherhood as the cornerstone" (*Portraits,* p. 199).

More direct social commentary is seen in another set of poems. Many of these are cameos that illustrate, through imagery as well as statement, Tolson's interpretation of the system. Margaret Levy, who left home and husband in order to become "somebody," is seen by that husband as one voice in a vast chorus of "millions and millions / Of overworked, underfed, poorly clad women / Singing the 'Hard Luck Blues' in the Land of Plenty!" (*Portraits,* p. 38). Another image of the deprived in the Land of Plenty is Aunt Tommiezene, an old, destitute woman gazing into the store window at the shoes she needs but cannot afford just as a lady in a Russian sable coat enters the shop. Another vignette of hardship in the Land of Plenty is the chimney sweep, Sootie Joe, whose wealthy customers hear him sing, "*But somebody hasta black hisself / For somebody else to stay white*" (*Portraits,* p. 17).

Besides these cameos of the oppressed, there are portraits of Harlemites who are more articulate about their condition, sometimes using animal imagery to illustrate their points. Noble Fetchit realizes that he does the work while others reap the benefits: "Them that rides in big Cadillacs an' wears fur coats / Don't pick no cotton / An' don't work in no coal mines" (*Portraits,* p. 57). For Uncle Lash, there is no hope in buying black as a remedy for racial ills. He sees that white businesses have not saved the white race but have exploited the masses. Jack Patterson knows exploitation as a matter of class not race: "'Big fish eat up little fish, / An' the color of the fish don't count'" (*Portraits,* p. 127). Grandma Lonigan, who sees in the Depression the extension of poor blacks' condition ("us black folks was borned in a Depression") to the rest of society asserts: "'Chile, hungry dawgs all acts alike'" (*Portraits,* p. 42). Freemon Hawthorne perceives a hint of desperation and coming revolution in the eyes of hungry men as he relays the parable of the desperately hungry rats who picked the cat's bones clean.

Some characters propose remedies or envision apocalyptic endings. Zip Lightner and Big Jim Casey, proletarian heroes, see hope in labor unions where black and white workers unite. Zip Lightner, despite terrorist tactics, organizes white and black sharecroppers in Arkansas.[11] The union brings him to Liberty Hall where he speaks of "De People," hungry but awakening. "De People" ask "'By Gawd, ain't dis a government of de People, / By de People, an' fer de People?'" And Zip foresees "de Jedgment Day": "An' it won't be no thousand years a-gittin' here" (*Portraits,* p. 86). Big Jim Casey, "Jailbird, / Friend of the Workers, / Agitator for a New Republic . . ." a hero inspired by the vision of Debs, will have his funeral in Liberty Hall. Shot during a strike, the dying black, supported by a white miner, gasps out: "'The white and black workers must . . . git . . . together!'" (*Portraits,* pp. 189–90).

These sentiments are echoed in the final poem, "The Underdog," which is not a characterization of any individual but the statement of a "coon," "black bastard," "sambo," "shine," "nigger," "black son of a bitch," who escapes the hatred implicit in these epithets and his own answering hatred — directed at "kikes," "bohunks," "wops," and "crackers" — the reciprocal hatred being instigated by the "great white masters." He also escapes the enclosing vice, superstition, ignorance, illiteracy, disease, crime, and hunger nurtured by segregation. Uniting with the poor and exploited of all races, Sambo threatens a new day: "WE ARE THE UNDERDOGS / ON A HOT TRAIL!" (*Portraits,* pp. 229–30).

After the editors' rejection of *Portraits,* the manuscript remained in Tolson's trunk for twenty years ("Odyssey," p. 195). During this period, Tolson began a renewed education in contemporary poetry. Going beyond the first wave of the moderns — Masters, Sandburg, Frost, and Robinson — Tolson "read and absorbed the techniques of Eliot, Proust, Yeats, Baudelaire, Pasternak, and I believe, all the great moderns. God knows how many little magazines I studied, and how much textual analysis of the New critics" ("A Poet's Odyssey," p. 195). With this background, he reworked *A Gallery of Harlem Portraits* into *Harlem Gallery: Book I, The Curator.*

The movement of Tolson's poetic style is from a plain style with relatively few allusions and relatively simply syntax in *Portraits,* to a style in which the language is compacted, the allusiveness of the verse is stressed, and the parts of the *HG* ode react against or together with each other. The later style was the result of Tolson's long apprenticeship to modern poetics, especially that of Eliot and Crane. There is then a change of style from *Portraits* to *Rendezvous*, and there is another change from *Rendezvous* to *Libretto* and *HG*.

Portraits incorporates free verse techniques and climactic endings in the individual poems. Each poem is generally a vignette with some narrative of each of the characters portrayed. The endings sometimes contain O. Henry types of final statements, and the use of blues lines enlarges meanings as these songs compact the Afro-American experience. Words like "sweet-daddying creeper" are interspersed in the poetry as well as an approach to dialect in the speech of the characters. Names are colorful and sometimes revelatory. There is some approach to distinctive imagery, although the voice of the poet is withdrawn, letting the verse stand or seem to stand as versified reportage. Meanings are clear and references and allusions are to the world of the characters: Harlem of the thirties. The significance of the particular character refers to a wider world of black experience in the fashion of *Spoon River*, with its eclectic portrayal of a microcosmic town.

Tolson's next book, *Rendezvous with America*, shows an experimentation with traditional and nontraditional verse forms. *Rendezvous* is a collection of four long poems and shorter verse. Tolson uses varied metrical forms, including the sonnet in experiments with meters and forms. There is the use of monometer, dimeter, and trimeter as well as the more conventional tetrameter and pentameter. A number of poems depend entirely on short lines or use short lines contrasted with longer lines. There is an experimental range from no rhyme to conventional rhyme patterns, such as quatrains rhyming *a a b b*, *a b a b*, or *a b c b*. The subject here is man — black and white — as revealed by economics, sociology, and psychology. Tolson is essentially hopeful about man despite the failure of modern Americans, especially in the realm of racial justice. He uses natural imagery, including animal imagery, to illustrate these themes.

Although the poems in *Rendezvous* illustrate the traditional metrics of English poetry, a line like "The bones of silence fat no pedigree" is more striking in its compression than the typical *Portraits* line. In *Rendezvous*, the compression of language and the rhetorical stance of Tolson's *Libretto* and *HG* have begun. Such metaphors as those contained in "The Poet" depart from the style of *Portraits* and are forerunners of Tolson's later poetry. Tolson's imagery in *Portraits* occurs most freely in the blues interspersions rather than in the narrative verse itself. The imagery in *Rendezvous* is of the essence of the poetry as illustrated in the above line from "The Poet." The imagery of *Rendezvous*, however, is flatter, less dramatic, and less compacted than the later verse, as illustrated in the following lines: "Who mix laughter with the crack of doom" (*Rend.*, p. 109), "at the crack of doom, potbellies bellylaugh (*HG*, p. 171), and "The rule-or-ruin class, in idols of the tribe / Creates narcissine images of itself" (*Rend.*, p. 99) becomes in *HG*[12]:

The Idols of the tribe,

in voices as puissant as the rutting calls
of a bull crocodile, bellow:
"*We*
have heroes!
Celebrate *them* upon our walls."

In each case the imagery and sense of the earlier poetry is made more
dramatic through more intense, more active poetics as "mixes laughter"
becomes "Potbellies bellylaugh," with imagery reinforced by repetition and
alliteration. In the second example, idols of the tribe is expanded. The animal
imagery is made essential to the expression of the thought and more dramatic
by the direct quotation and the centered placement of words, especially
"*We.*" As the poetics of *Portraits* is flatter and more discursive than
Rendezvous, *Rendezvous* is flatter and more discursive than *HG*.

It is difficult to determine exactly when Tolson read Crane, but Tolson's
wife has said that Hart Crane's poetry had indicated to Tolson that he had
been on the wrong road in poetry.[13] Tolson himself has said that "'The
Bridge' is a way out of the pessimism of 'The Waste Land'" (Notebooks).
In the preface of *Libretto*, Allen Tate placed Tolson "in the direct succession
from Crane." It may be that Tolson studied Crane before *Libretto* but after
Rendezvous, but certainly the condensed language, the startling imagery,
the fascination with words, and the casual rhyme of Crane must have
appealed to Tolson. Certainly Crane's affirmation of man's ability to govern
technology and himself must have struck answering chords in Tolson's
poetry.

As Tolson moved on in his search for a style, he exhibited in "E. & O.
E." and *Libretto* the allusive, tightly wrought, sometimes obscure style of
the academy: "I thought the Establishment, the Academy, would like it"
("A Poet's Odyssey," p. 185).

"E. & O. E." was the first instance of Tolson's new style to be published.
In this poem, the persona makes himself the subject in a poem of chiefly
short lines, occasionally contrasted by a longer line. There are references
to other languages and literatures — American, European, and African —
to the Bible and Shakespeare, to the fauna and flora and customs of other
worlds. Specifically, there are allusions to Greek mythology, Western legend,
Schopenhauer, Gautier, Bodenheim, Salmon, and Herodotus among others.
Metaphors, allusions, and poetic devices exhibit Tolson's change of style.
Discursive links between verses and parts of "E. & O. E." are dropped.
With very few changes, sections of "E. & O. E." were presented as a private
poem of Hideho Heights in *HG*.

The style of "E. & O. E.," and that of the "very literary" *Libretto*, reveals
a honing of language, a freighting of meaning, and a width of reference
requiring an Eliotic set of notes. The later style is achieved and used by
Tolson in *HG*, which he saw as a triumph of his ideal in poetry — "The
S-trinity of Parnassus."[14] The structure in *Libretto* is that of a regular ode
with the various sections entitled with the notes of a musical scale as the
poem moves toward a climax. The subject of the ode is the significance
of the freedom displayed in the founding and history of Liberia: "A moment

for the conscience of mankind." in the final "Do" that sums up the significance of the Liberian experience and previews its future, the verse moves from lines arranged in sestets to centered verse (line 489), and then to prose poetry sections (line 575 to the end). "Do" is thick with fragments of different languages, references to little-known lore, and allusions to African, European, and American thought. *Libretto* represents Tolson's first sustained attempt in the new style, and this style is the direct ancestor of the style used at greater length and with greater mastery in *HG*. From *Portraits* to *HG*, Tolson's poetry involves a gradual transmutation of style so that the relation of *Portraits* to *HG* is such that the earlier poetry is distilled and reconstituted in the later work.

Typical of the change of style are Tolson's expressions of the same idea in *Portraits* and *HG*. In *Portraits,* there is an exchange between Dr. Ernest Quirk and his bourgeois wife:

> I used to remind Dr. Quirk
> That blood will tell.
> He would sneer:
> "You're right, my dear,
> In everybody there is the blood
> Of genius and idiot, saint and blackguard."

> (*Portraits,* p. 74)

In *Harlem Gallery,* Dr. Nkomo says:

> "If
> a Bourbon should shake his family tree
> long enough . . . he
> — beyond a Diogenic doubt —
> would kneel at the mourners' bench,
> dressed in black crepe,
> as cannibal and idiot,
> rapist and ape,
> tumble out."

> (*HG,* p. 62)

Portraits contains poems, almost all entitled with the name of the chief character in the poem, so that well over two hundred characters are described. Except that each poem is a literary portrait, there is no special relevance to the gallery image. In *Harlem Gallery,* the overall structure is that of an ode with each of the twenty-four poems entitled with a letter of the Greek alphabet, so that there is a definite movement from alpha to omega,[15] similar to that in Psalm 119, where each block of verse begins with a different letter of the alphabet in order. Although the *Harlem Gallery* poems entail a description of character, characterization is revealed in a flux of character, interaction, and talk rather than in the automatic presentation of character after character. Tolson intersperses dramatic and discursive poems within the overall framework of the "metaphor and symbol" of the *Harlem Gallery*. What occurs then is not only a change in literary style but a change in the overall structure of the poem since only in the "Upsilon" section are characters, a much smaller number, present in the fashion of the *Portraits.*

There has also been a development of Tolson's literary intention. The intention is still the portrayal of Harlem as a metropolis of the black world. Although the epic intention remains the same, the means to that end has become more elaborate and complex. The *Harlem Gallery* emerges not as the entire epic itself, like *Portraits* in its way, but as the prologue of a pageant of black history. Thus, it sets forth the basic concern of that history and epitomizes its meaning. With the development of his thought, Tolson came to perceive that the whole of the black experience was revealed, not through the primary focus of the economic or sociological, but through that of the arts. Statements like "The artist is the only total *knower*" and "The poet is a sort of barometer in his society" ("A Poet's Odyssey," pp. 190-91), illustrate this opinion. Tolson wished *HG* to reveal the black man in his entirety. What seems apparent is that Tolson, in the development of *HG,* was interested in depicting the black man not merely as part of the universal brotherhood of the oppressed but as the epitome of mankind, the transitional man in a transitional era.

Accordingly, *HG* has fewer specific allusions to Harlem of the thirties than does *Portraits.* The milieu loses its specificity — it refers not only to the twenties and thirties but extends to the early sixties — and tends to become typical, metaphorical, or symbolic. The relationship to actual historical figures is attenuated and, although there are typical figures, they are subordinated to the design that emphasizes artists and intellectuals as focal points of the ode. A gallery, mentioned in "Harlem," is a framing device for literary portraits that we are asked to view as if we were wandering from portrait to portrait in a gallery. In *Harlem Gallery,* the Harlem Gallery is an actual portrait gallery located in Harlem, with Harlemites as painter, curator, consultant, and board of regents. This central image becomes more than a framing device and is projected into a "metaphor and symbol."

In "Alpha," the Harlem Gallery becomes the "metaphor and symbol" of the African pepper bird that awakens African natives and "tells them it's time to start the day's work" ("Key Words," p. 1). The day that The Curator and the poet see coming is characterized as a "people's dusk of dawn." The dusk of dawn has been described by Du Bois as "that subtle sense of coming day which one feels of early mornings even when mist and murk hang low."[16] Curator and poet share an apocalyptic vision of the emergence of blacks and the destruction of the way of life of the "Great White World." Signaling the apocalypse, presaging the new day, is the Harlem Gallery, portraits and poems caroling a different kind of revolution. In "Omega," the Harlem Gallery is said to "chronicle / a people's New World odyssey / from chattel to Esquire!" (*HG,* p. 173). The Harlem Gallery moves beyond an image of physical reality in Harlem to become symbolic of the Afro-American experience.

The Curator, once mentioned but never described in *Portraits,* becomes in *Harlem Gallery* not just a full-blown character but a focal point of *Book*

I, named after him and described as his "autobio-fragment." It is noteworthy that in *Dusk of Dawn* the autobiography of the man Du Bois becomes an "autobiography of a concept of race, elucidated, magnified and doubtless distorted in the thoughts and deeds which were mine."[17] The "autobio-fragment" of The Curator contains a sense of life as it is lived under the aegis of color. As the controlling image of the gallery serves to compose the poem, the central figure of The Curator serves to shape meaning.

The *Harlem Gallery* shares many of the premises of *Portraits* about the economic foundation of oppression. It also deemphasizes political reality to address itself to the concerns of the black man encompassing biological, sociological, and psychological aspects. There is nothing in any way so explicit as the *Portraits's* call for the underdogs of the world to unite. Revolutionary energy is displaced from the world of political activity to the world of creative activity. This displacement is explained somewhat by Tolson's discussion of the ape of God, the creator.[18] According to Tolson, an ape of God is an inspired poet, "a creator who apes or imitates his Creator." The ape of God, like the prophet, is ignored or disdained by those who pursue material goods. As a result, both prophets and ape of God are "crucified on a Cross of Gold." Like the prophet, the ape of God has foreknowledge; and, like the prophet, the ape of God is apocalyptic; he senses before others "the odor of rottenness in a society." The ape of God is also freedom-loving and catholic in taste and interest. Since no man is an isolate, the ape of God is the enemy of social and personal evil. It becomes obvious that the burden of protest, apocalyptic vision, and universality has been shifted from the economic to the artistic plane.

What Tolson did in his final attempt to grapple with the reality of Harlem is to retain the Harlem milieu, characters, and concerns; but as Tolson's own interests, concerns, and tastes developed, he shifted from the "Man with the Hoe," *Spoon River Anthology* approach to one that synthesized the dramatic situation of the black man in Harlem with the idiosyncratic interpretation of his condition, which Tolson had developed through years of study and first hand experience.

5

The Harlem Milieu

In *Portraits*, Tolson included many specifics of Harlem in the twenties and thirties. In *Harlem Gallery*, Tolson moves away from the representational toward the evocative. The era described is not that of the twenties and thirties telescoped but of over four decades of Harlem experience telescoped. The decades include Prohibition, the Depression, World War II, and the postwar period — a time extremely significant in the modern world but especially significant in the development of the black man in America. It was during this period that Harlem acquired the double image of black cultural capital and black ghetto: a definite period of Harlem growth, decline, and possible regeneration occurred from the twenties to the sixties. By choosing the whole era as his period, Tolson is able to evoke first one, then another of the facets of Harlem history. He does so by deft strokes rather than by detail, as the twenties and early thirties are recalled by a description of a Prohibition-era speakeasy, the wartime period by a newsboy's cry that the Desert Fox is dead, the fifties by a reference to "Ike, the painter," and the sixties by mention of an ex-freedom rider. These diverse times are presented in order to illustrate facets of the one time that is always Harlem time.

Tolson is not attempting, as he did in *Portraits*, to build a picture of Harlem through many Harlem settings. His method is evocative rather than representational, and, rather than depict many locations, he selects locations that are reminiscent of permanent aspects of Harlem life and lets them speak for the life itself. He tries to depict the essence of community life in a few settings that may be typical, metaphorical, or symbolic.[1]

There are places mentioned that are not part of the immediate setting through which The Curator moves but that function to give a sense of Harlem life. Illustrative of this use of setting are Tolson's allusions to the Harlem Opera House, an actual Harlem theater that Tolson used to suggest an aspect of Harlem life. The Harlem Opera House was never one of the major black theaters like the Lafayette, but Tolson was undoubtedly fascinated by its name and its former grandeur,[2] and he used it as a fictional type of the Harlem theater, where Gilpin had once performed, later being used for such affairs as Harlem beauty contests. The churches mentioned are also typical, as Mount Zion, Mount Sinai, and the Ethiopian Tabernacle — former ramshackle theater with its "Bishop" Gladstone Coffin — evoke the range of churches from the large institutional churches catering to upper or lower classes to the less formal church with its typical pastor, sermon, and congregation. The subway entrance, where prostitutes and policemen linger, is representational and evocative, as are the Market Place Gallery,[3] the

Haw Haw Club, the Daddy-O Club, and the Bamboo Kraal.

The police station is typical of the ghetto institutions intended to maintain the status quo. The sergeant at the desk, Ghirlandaio,[4] presumably an Italian, has viewed from the perspective of a police station such Harlem goings-on as Hedda Starks's night of misery in a jail cell after a marijuana party and Mr. Starks's apparent suicide. A well-trained crime specialist, Ghirlandaio is as incapable of understanding the importance of the "Harlem Vignettes" as he is unable to unravel the manner of the suicide. The sergeant's general attitude toward Harlem is one of wry, detached amusement at the crime and violence. His attitude, the classic stance of the white outsider and representative of the "Great White World," embodies the alien familiarity of the police station where he works.

The walk-up apartments of John Laugart and The Curator, the tenement room of Mister Starks, and the "broken down flat" of Hideho Heights are typical of many ghetto residences. It is significant that the apartments of these artists and The Curator are not set in Strivers' Row or Sugar Hill but among the ordinary residences of the ghetto. John Laugart's flat is described in most detail. It appears to be an extreme example of ghetto living conditions and of the physical rewards an artist may expect, especially a black artist. The Curator describes Laugart's flat in "Zeta" as a "catacomb Harlem flat," "grotesquely vivisected" (*HG*, p. 37), a reference to the way in which Harlem apartments were cut up into smaller units for greater profit.[5] Inside the flat The Curator is greeted by the sounds of a rat so exaggeratedly huge as to be the "caricature of a rat" and of the "snaggle-toothed" toilet's obscenities. Within the barely furnished flat are an "expendable chair" and "the hazard of a bed." The cliché of the starving artist is altered as the poverty of the artist in Laugart's case is both the fruit of his integrity and the illustration of the shared poverty of his people.

The Angelus Funeral Home, Aunt Grindle's Elite Chitterling Shop,[6] and the Zulu Club are typical of black owned businesses in the ghetto. These are the types of service establishments usually owned or operated by blacks. The black funeral home and the soul-food shop are constants of the ghetto economy; they seldom face competition from white merchants. The club, sometimes black owned but almost always black operated in the ghetto, is also a constant. But these businesses are not presented as typical of ghetto economics; they are presented as typical of the reality of black life in the ghetto.

In "Sigma," the Angelus Funeral Home is presented chiefly through the characters associated with it rather than through a presentation of a funeral parlor in action. Its occupants include Ma'am Shears, owner of the Harlem funeral home and a member of the black bourgeoisie; her companion, Ester Bostic, volatile, calculating, and unsentimental; and Mr. Abelard Littlejohn, the "springbok impresario" of the funeral home and former husband of six women. The relationship between owner and director can be glimpsed in Tolson's images of whale and walrus to describe Ma'am Shears and springbok to describe the prince-nezed Littlejohn. This jumpy man organizes the "performance" of Mister Starks's funeral rites, which "sophists of the black-and-tan / annointers of the black-and-blue" attend in their various capacities (*HG*, p. 134). Since all funerals, being ritual, are to some extent performances, the Harlem funerals — either like A'lelia Walker Robinson's invitation-only funeral and Florence Mills's with its release of blackbirds, or less exalted — were performances in more than one sense. The funeral parlor is finally referred to as the "Dollar Cockpit of Custom and the Van" (*HG*, p. 134). Tolson then presents the funeral home as a stronghold of one type of black "respectability" and display.

In "Eta," Aunt Grindle's Elite Chitterling Shop has a neon sign that can be seen for two Harlem blocks. A jukebox blares the blues in the shop. Dr. Nkomo, who is present behind "an alp of chitterlings, pungent as epigrams" (*HG*, p. 43), calls the jukebox, "That rebel jukebox. Hear the ghetto's dark guffaws / That defy Manhattan's Bible Belt" (*HG*, p. 48). Thus, eating food that has become typical (if not stereotypical) and listening to ethnic music, the inhabitants of the community defy the strictures of white Manhattan: they act out their instinctive refutation of Gertrude Stein's "The Negro suffers from nothingness."[7] The very existence of the chitterling shop, with the dark laughter of its jukebox, is one kind of defiance of the mores of the "Great White World" of Manhattan. Its patrons also evoke a black world stereotyped by whites and scorned by the black bourgeoisie. Mr. and Mrs. Dipsy Muse and a giraffic, dope-sniffing man and his wife act out their uninhibited parts in the action as the Elite Chitterling Shop "pitched and ditched / in the chatter and squawks, in the clatter and guffaws" (*HG*, p. 47).

Tolson's locations help to outline the social geography of Harlem. Theater, church, police station, nightclub, cafeteria, and gallery are all public places involving some fundamental aspect of man's social life. The city is revealed in its locations and institutions for communal participation in entertainment, worship, art, and eating and drinking. Even the police station represents a distinctively urban form of social discipline. With the additional settings of the Angelus Funeral Home and Laugart's apartment, all the basic aspects of life, with the exception of explicit sexual activity, are represented by locations that are not only typical of the city but distinctive of the black ghetto.

The most detailed description of the locations that evoke an image of the black community is that of the Zulu Club, which is not only typical but also metaphorical. On one level, the club is typical of cabarets once so much a part of the Harlem image. Many of the ingredients in the *Harlem Gallery* cabaret scene were incorporated in an extended poem included in *Portraits*, "Big Bessie." The poem was based either on one Harlem nightclub or, more likely, on a composite of many. In the earlier poem, the Congo Club on Upper Lenox Avenue is the setting for a number of realistic vignettes. The "barbaric splendor" of the club is asserted and then detailed with descriptions of walls decorated with a tropical and amorous scene, subdued lights creating eerie shadows in the smoke-filled room, waiters dancing among tables, and a scimitar-shaped platform for the band. Later the MC introduces Big Bessie, who sings blues that are enthusiastically received, causing the "blues intoxicated" patrons to act out their varied responses to her songs.

These ingredients, reminiscent of many cabarets, are reproduced in "Mu," "Nu," and "Xi" in language that is much sharper and more piquant. The Congo Club on Lenox Avenue becomes the Zulu Club on Lenox Avenue. The dimness of the club, the lurid lights, the smoke-filled room, the varied clientele, the performing area with its varicolored lights, the acrobatic dancing,[8] and the enthusiastic crowd reacting with an "*ostinato /* of stamping feet and clapping hands" (*HG,* p. 74), are similar in detail to the Congo Club setting. As Big Bessie had been the focus of attention and action in the Congo Club, Hideho Heights is the focus of attention in the Zulu Club; patrons react "'to a great big poet and a great big man!'" (*HG,* p. 77). On this level, Tolson uses much greater control of language and imagery, and with a surer touch in outlining the flow of incident he is again depicting the nightclub scene.

The way in which Tolson transforms the same ingredients is illustrated by his use of language and imagery. While Gabby Gay and his Red Hot Rhythm Boys "Wailed and blared and quavered mad ecstasies of jazz" in "Big Bessie" (*Portraits,* p. 129), in "Mu," Frog Legs Lux and his Indigo Combo

> spoke with tongues that sent their devotees
> out of this world!

> Black and brown and yellow fingers flashed,
> like mirrored sunrays of a heliograph,
> on clarinet and piano keys, on cornet valves.

(*HG,* p. 71)

In the "Big Bessie" nightclub scene, "The subdued lights spilled eerie shadows / over the shuffling dancers and seated carousers" (*Portraits,* p. 129). In "Mu":

> Lurid lights
> spraying African figures on the walls
> ecstasied maids and waiters,
> pickups and stevedores —
> with delusions of Park Avenue grandeur.

(*HG,* p. 71)

In "Big Bessie," the walls of the Congo Club are "vivid with tropical trees / And voluptuous figures in amorous attitudes" (*Portraits,* p. 129). In "Mu," the wall description is simply included in "spraying African figures on the walls." The "smoke-blurred tables," of "Big Bessie" become in "Mu":

> Cigarette smoke
> — opaque veins in Carrara marble —
> magicked the habitués
> into
> humoresques and grotesques.

(*HG,* p. 71)

Maintaining the essential ingredients of the description with the imagery and especially with the use of verbs, Tolson transformed a description of an action into a form where mood and description nearly coalesce in his second attempt to evoke the ambience of a nightclub. Huot has noted the onomatopoetic effect of lines 90–108 (*HG,* p. 74) and lines 61–180 (*HG,* p. 73), the descriptions of audience response.[9] Further, Tolson's use of such verbs and verb phrases as "spoke with tongues," "flashed," "effervescing," "magicked," "spraying," and "ecstasied," helps evoke the mood of hilarity, of "soul," when "'the cats, the black cats, are gone!'" (*HG,* p. 74).

Tolson reproduced more than a scene; he reproduced a social ritual seen through the eyes of one of its participants, The Curator. Drinking, dancing, and music are part of many ritual activities, but the tone of this ritual is set by the music, jazz. The music is as characteristic of Harlem as the music of Liszt is characteristic of the bourgeois in the solitude of an apartment (*HG,* p. 76). Jazz is communal music; as Hideho explains, "'Jazz is the marijuana of the Blacks'" (*HG,* p. 74). Through play on the word "veld," Tolson evoked the feel of jazz and the African origins suggested in its rhythms. "Basin Street Blues" recalls, in Mardi Gras Zulu and Comus parades and revelry, the faraway American origins of jazz. The Curator, stirred by the music, lets his mind wander back to the "Ancients" of jazz, to:

> Rabelaisian I's of the Boogie-Woogie dynasty
> in barrel houses, at rent parties,
> on riverboats, at wakes:
> The Toothpick, Funky Five, and Tippling Tom!
> Ma Rainy, Countess Willie V., and Aunt Harriet!
> Speckled Red, Skinny Head Pete, and Stormy Weather!
>
> (*HG,* p. 74)

With roots in Africa and America, jazz, as it plays through The Curator's mind, has a long, picturesque history as an integral part of community celebrations.[10]

The Zulu Club scene is an effective device to bring together a variety of characters in a setting that demands their interaction. The lower classes are represented by the "tipsy Lena," the "'willow by a cesspool,'" Dipsy Muse and Wafer Waite. Entertainers — Snakehips Briskie, Frog Legs Lux, Rufino Laughlin, MC — are of course present. Also present are the Zulu Club Wits, "dusky vestiges of the University Wits" (*HG,* p. 82). Vincent Aveline, sports editor, and Black Diamond, "heir presumptive to the Lenox Policy Racket" (*HG,* p. 86), and Dr. Nkomo are also present. There can be seen a range of action and reaction as these various inhabitants of the Harlem ghetto stimulate each other.

Into this atmosphere steps the "poet laureate of Lenox Avenue," "Hideho Heights, / a black Gigas, / ghosted above us" (*HG,* p. 79). The main attraction here is not the singing of Big Bessie but the public recital of a poem, "the racial ballad in the public domain" (*HG,* p. 145). The People's Poet — as he says to a tipsy prostitute, "'Sister, you and I belong to the people'" (*HG,* p. 78) — gives the people an original rendition of the birth of one of their folk heroes, John Henry.[11] The ballad, with its easily accessible metrical pattern, its hyperboles, its imagery, and its wit, is enthusiastically received by all the club's patrons and especially by the Zulu Club Wits who screech their approval. The ballad confirms and celebrates one manifestation of the people's identity; the creative impulse ignited by Hideho's poem touches Frog Legs, who improvises a blues, and The Curator, who responds intensely, unknowingly crushing his cocktail glass. "The Zulu Club patrons whoop and stomp, / clap thighs and backs and knees" (*HG*, p. 81).

The flow of the evening begins at a peak with the Combo, ascends still higher with the ballad of John Henry, descends through discussion to the low point when, having imbibed freely, the Zulu Club Wits become "absent" or "ugly" or "tight." Hideho then "slobbers and sobs, / 'My *people*, / *my* people — / they know not what they do'" (*HG*, p. 92). The whole complex social ritual does not end on the note of hilarity; the jazz-induced high has fled, and the people's poet, having celebrated, drunkenly reveals the underside of his boisterous gaiety.[12]

The total response of the patrons is characterized:

> Bedlam beggars
> at a poet's feast in a people's dusk of dawn counterpoint
> protest and pride
> in honky-tonk rhythms
> hot as an ache in a cold hand warmed.
>
> (*HG*, p. 83)

The laughing, clapping, and whooping of the patrons are thus linked to the continuing theme of a "people's dusk of dawn" heralded by artistic creation. Protest and pride, implicit in the popular ballad, the music, and the patrons' participation in the creative impulse, indicate that revelry goes beyond the social to an ethnic response. The Zulu Club celebration and response are part of a social ritual extended to an ethnic experience.

The ethnic question, foreshadowed in John Henry's coming to Harlem, becomes a continuing theme of a symposium at the Zulu Club. The Zulu Club Wits take up the racial question, first attempted by Joshua Nitze with an anecdote about integration, ending with the stevedore, unable to obtain chitterlings in an integrated Nashville restaurant, replying: "'Night and day, Ma'am, / I've been telling Black Folks / *you* White Folks ain't ready for integration!'" (*HG*, p. 85). The reply to this anecdote by the "Sea-Wolf of Harlem" is a sneering "'Uncle Tom is dead; / but keep a beady eye on his grandson, Dr. Thomas —'" (*HG*, p. 85). The theme is later taken up by Shadrach Martial Kilroy, president of Afroamerican Freedom, Inc., who refers to the white man as the serpent and initiates a discussion with the Sea-Wolf and Dr. Nkomo that moves through images of a frog, a python, and a secretary-bird as figures of the white-black relationship only to end with biblical parodies. The Curator sums up the play of words and images used to define the complex relationship: "Metaphors and symbols in Spirituals and Blues / have been the Negro's manna in the Great White World" (*HG*, p. 91). The social interplay at the Zulu Club has led to verbal play revolving around the ethnic question.

The Zulu Club symposium constitutes a kind of Afro-American male club as the Zulu Club is the setting of discussions — philosophical and otherwise

— self-revelations, and probings of the condition of the black man in America. Although the Zulu Club as a center of action with a beginning, middle, and end, a kind of social ritual, is described in the "Mu," "Nu," and "Xi" sections, it continues to be the social context for intellectual interaction in Tolson's black version of the male club.[13] Such discussions, often with the Zulu Club Wits present to act as stimulant or chorus, contain some of the most significant metaphors in the ode. Set in the Zulu Club, pronouncements about race, society, and self are embedded in a social contest that gives a nexus to the ideas discussed.

Thus, the talk among Dr. Shears, Hideho, and Dr. Nkomo, which reveals Dr. Nkomo's socialist bent, is carried on at a Zulu Club "talk-around," where each of the participants tries to top the others with the aptness of his image. The pyramid of witticisms mounts through images of humanity as a thick mass of bees and Western materialism as "'a steatopygous Jezebel / with falsies on her buttocks'" (*HG*, p. 118) to Hideho's final crowning image of Nkomo as

a St. John who envisions
a brush turkey that makes
a mound of the Old World's decaying vegetables
to generate heat and hatch the eggs of the New.

(*HG*, p. 118)

In the interplay, a vital aspect of Nkomo's philosophy is recalled to the silent applause of the Zulu Club Wits.

Mister Starks relates that his discovery of "the mutuality of minds / that moved independently of each other — " (*HG*, p. 122), the minds of The Curator and Dr. Nkomo, occurs "in the dawn hours / after the Zulu Club habitués / had floundered into Lenox Avenue" (*HG*, p. 121). This setting, when the customary life of the club is withdrawn and only a "neo-janitor" is left of the club's employees, is fitting for the mutual probing that reveals the characters of the African and the Afro-American. In the dawn hours, the skeleton crew, in a social nexus grown tight and narrow (though still merry), probe and reveal themselves and the race question and, by extension, the class question. The peculiar quality of that early-morning hour in a deserted nightclub can be summed up in the lines: "Our crowing laughs and clapping palms / had the scaling motion of clay pigeons from a trap of the *fin de siècle*"(*HG*, p. 124). Basic social relationships are exposed in an appropriately bare social setting as the milk and cream metaphors are played out to the end, and the "oddest hipsters" in Harlem are self-revealed.

The Zulu Club is again the setting of racial discussion and self-revelation when the theme of "*Homo Caucasicus*" and "*Homo Aethiopicus*" is introduced in "Phi." A battle of wits between Dr. Nkomo and Shadrach Kilroy begins with Dr. Nkomo's deflation of Kilroy's assertion of the potency of the black man in the white world. Kilroy is bested in the ensuing dialogue, but the discussion inspires Hideho Heights's creative imagination. Hideho, shaking off the effects of a Zulu Chief he had drunk, rejects Dolph Peeler's image of the pig in the boa's coils as a true image of the black man in the South. As the people's poet. Hideho, in a creation befitting the centennial of the Emancipation Proclamation, presents symbolically what to him is the true racial situation in the image of the sea turtle in the shark's belly. Again, the success of the metaphor is emphasized by the reaction of the Zulu Club Wits and is reemphasized by the bartender, a teetotaler Jamaican who downs a double shot of Zulu Chief. Hideho's symbol thus strikes an answering chord as the Jamaican relates his experience of black-white relations. Hideho then resumes, this time on a note of self-revelation that leads to a discussion of the nature of true art. Philosophical discussion and self-revelation are again rooted in the social context of the nightclub.

As a social nexus, the Zulu Club becomes more than an image; it becomes a metaphor for a complex of relationships poised in the context of a Harlem nightclub. The nightclub represents "a way of life that faces the crack of doom / with wine and wit and wiggle" (*HG*, p. 126). The tragicomic aspect of nightclub hilarity has been revealed from the time of Hideho's sob. This "ghetto laughter" is, according to Tolson, ultimately affirmative.[14] The nightclub is naturally the "sunshiniest place / in the black ghetto —" (*HG*, p. 143). A place where one can literally escape creditors and saviors, it is metaphorically a city of refuge within the black city of refuge:

> for those who have fallen from grace
> for those who are tired of the rat-race
> (the everlasting — *On your mark! Get Set! Go!*)
> in the Land of the Gray Flannel Suit
> and the Home of the Portfolio!
>
> (*HG*, p. 143)

The Zulu Club, with its pain-and-sorrow-defying ritual, becomes a refuge for the physical and spiritual exiles from the "Great White World." It becomes clear that the Zulu Club, through placement and imagery, becomes a kind of metaphor for community life in Harlem. This metaphor is extended as it calls, however ambiguously, on the myth of paradise, since there are references to the Garden of Eden (*HG*, p. 73) and Edenic joys (*HG*, p. 78), and to a "now paradise" (*HG*, p. 143), a play on "paradise enow," a further characterization of the ghetto retreat.[15]

Unlike some of the other settings, the Harlem Gallery has no prototype. There was indeed the federally sponsored Harlem Community Art Center, opened in 1937 at 290 Lenox Avenue, and there was a social nexus of the arts in Harlem as the artists traveled about the community: "This movement from place to place wasn't only a pleasure trip, it was a learning process also, similar, as I have explained, to the importance the impressionists and moderns attached to their meetings in various Parisian cafés."[16] There were various phases of participation in an artistic community, but there does not seem to have been a historical counterpart to the portrait gallery found in *Harlem Gallery*. Tolson himself insisted on the fictional nature of the gallery: "Of course, purely imaginary, although some think it's an actual museum. Had a man write from New York, asking about its location!"[17]

It seems that the genesis of the portrait gallery is related to its imaginative conception in *Portraits* rather than to any actual historical reality. Tolson said: "picture gallery magnetizes me with a potent fascination."[18] The gallery, from its very inception, had a metaphorical quality built into its image.

The Harlem Gallery is first introduced as a "metaphor and symbol," and it retains this character throughout. The gallery, according to Huot, has two meanings: "As the title suggests, the work is a gallery of portraits — character sketches of Harlemites, some very individualistic, some clearly types." (This meaning obviously recalls *A Gallery of Harlem Portraits.*) "In another sense, the title phrase refers literally to a Harlem art gallery, complete with Curator, Board of Regents, and expert consultants."[19] The Harlem Gallery, although referring to an actual building and organization, retains a kind of ambiguity because at the same time the gallery refers to the entire work of art created by Tolson and envisioned by The Curator. In this sense the gallery is not merely a concrete image but a controlling image that must be interpreted at one time metaphorically and at another time symbolically.[20]

In "Iota," the setting of the Harlem Gallery is detailed as the portraits contained in the four wings of the gallery are outlined. The paintings, done in watercolor, oil, tempera, and fresco, depict characters that are artistic on one level, literary on another. Portrayed in the East Wing are the tensions of human experience, the

> paeans and laments of identities
> signed in the thought and felt hinterlands of psyches —
> now impasted and sprayed and fixed
> with waterglass
> on dry plaster.
>
> *(IIG, p. 58)*

Here the subject of the gallery portraits might also be subjects of other artistic disciplines. What is stressed in the East Wing is the artist's re-creation and highlighting of the seemingly contradictory experiences of life — here and there, odd and even, reality and fable, past and present, success and disaster (*HG*, p. 58). In the West Wing, the metaphor used for painting is that of the stage with its dramatis personae, upstage, downstage, and backstage. One can detect overtones of African artistic modes in the moderns. Concerned with "the antique and the newly-made / in our *cis* -Apocalypse" (HG, p. 59), this wing contains a range of faces as varied as any human comedy:

> an upstage of faces as unsoiled as irisated rain
> or repulsive like purulent boils;
> a downstage of faces as madder-bleached as dry bones
> on an alkali plain
> or fissured like agueweeds
> in a marsh's toils;
> a backstage of faces as empty as a mistigris
> or bedeviled like a sea dog's prelithic visage

when the stays lean amiss.

(*HG*, p. 59)

The North Wing's portraits evoke "Negroid diversity — / its Kafiristan gaucherie, / its Attic wit and nerve" (*HG*, p. 60). Thus, the gallery becomes "Harlem's Aganippe / (not America's itching aitchbone) / where characters, flat and round, / project a rhythm, a mood, a scene, a tone" (*HG*, p. 60). The metaphor for painting harks back to the poet as ape of God, for the North Wing contains the ape-cobbler who produces boots for every actor in the Harlem cast. Such poetic garb involves "*Bios* and *Societas* and *X* / as well as the divine" (*HG*, p. 60). In the South Wing are the "dusky Lion Hearts," the varied and varying heroes. These South Wing portraits contrast with each other, as "unsynchronized opposites, / gentlemen and galoots / from Afroamerica" (*HG*, p. 62) are depicted. The heroes, as various as the blue notes heard on a xylophone, as courageous as the seven against Thebes (with the implication of present defeat and ultimate victory), embody the voiceless yearnings of their people in epic art. Although a hero may be challenged as inauthentic, the sum total of the heroes portrayed is "authentic as a people's autography" (*HG*, p. 62).

A comparison of the characters sketched in the *Harlem Gallery* and the portraits displayed in the four wings of the gallery makes plain that there is no literal correspondence between the two. For instance, *Harlem Gallery* contains no character sketches of black heroes, although such heroes might have been included in later books of the epic. The great variety found in the four wings is not reproduced literally. However, the description of the character of the gallery portraits does apply to the character of Tolson's literary portraiture: the emphasis on man — black man — in his totality and his complexity, was surely a working ideal for the *Harlem Gallery*.

In the concluding stanzas of "Iota," artists of various disciplines — Phidias, van Gogh, Aristophanes, Shakespeare, El Greco, Velasquez, Cervantes, Orozco, Dante, and Pissarro — are alluded to as "Olympians wombed in the Vale of Tears" (*HG*, p. 63). Nourished by self and history, these artists, like Balzac, are able to represent the profoundly human. In "Iota," Tolson gave a local habitation to the metaphorical gallery. But even in the process of describing the portraits contained in the four wings, he, through the use of metaphors and allusions to other arts, indicated that the gallery is simultaneously the locus of black portraiture and a metaphor for artistic re-creation. The reader can perceive that for Tolson the gallery represented the only and immemorial way in which Afro-Americans, or any people, can be completely known: through artistic endeavor.

The different uses to which artistic endeavors, especially black artistic endeavor, can be put is illustrated in Tolson's use in "Upsilon" of further images to describe the gallery:

The Harlem Gallery
. . . the creek that connects the island and the mainland . . .
. . . a *g* in Old Anglo-Saxon . . .
. . . an oasis in the Danakil Desert . . .

> . . . and the mascara of dusky middlebrow matrons . . .
>   became the beccafico that excited the top hats,
>   the butt that inebriated the Zulu Club Wits,
>   and the butte that pinked many a butt.

> (*HG,* p. 119)

The Harlem Gallery connects the isolated black man to the mainland of humanity through art. It is a green spot in a parched African desert; that is, another city of refuge in Harlem. It is as rare as the letter *g* in Anglo-Saxon now is. The gallery is a cultural adornment for middle-class matrons. It also becomes an exotic thrill to the elite, an intoxicating drink for the Zulu Club Wits, those dusky bohemians, and an artistic achievement that irritates many who try to take its measure. Tolson then goes on to use the image of a "variegated aviary on / Black Manhattan" for the gallery, with The Curator as Jacobin, so that the Harlem Gallery like the Harlem ghetto itself becomes an enclosure for rare birds. The uses to which art, especially black art, has been put, according to Tolson, are sometimes shallow and sometimes deeply human.

One elaboration of the use of art as mascara can be seen in the gallery's structure. The gallery, like the Zulu Club setting, is a focal point for social interaction, though not for the social ritual of the club. The Harlem Gallery structure dictates a different kind of interplay within the framework of the relationship between the black artist and the black bourgeoisie. The fundamental antagonism between art and the Bulls of Bashan, the arrogant, powerful, materialistic elite, is epitomized in the antagonism between The Curator and the Regents, especially Guy Delaporte III.

The Curator, placed in the uneasy position of encouraging the arts while placating its patrons, carries on a stubborn and tenacious defense of his concept of art. The task is summed up: "'Fetch highbrow stuff for the middlebrows who / don't give a damn and the lowbrows who ain't hip!'" (*HG,* p. 68). The middlebrows, his nominal patrons, are characterized as "eye- / less as knitting needles" and as having "babbitted souls" (*HG,* p. 38). Their attitude toward art is illustrated as Mr. Delaporte and his wife, "oh and yawn and ah their way" (*HG,* p. 64) through the gallery, and Delaporte comments generally, "'I love — God knows I *love* / pictures!'" (*HG,* p. 119). The Regents are too often the millstones that "exhaust summer and winter / in grinding / the spirit of The Curator" (*HG,* p. 171). The Harlem Gallery then becomes The Curator's "*Malakoff*":

> I can imagine his saying to
> anyone
> who advised him to leave,
> "*J'y suis, j'y reste.*"

> (*HG,* p. 121)

The kind of warfare carried on between the two foes is seen in The Curator's attempts to wrest money from the Regents for his own purpose:

> The Regents of the Harlem Gallery

> suffer the carbon monoxide of ignorance
> which — undetected in the
> conference chamber —
> leaves my budget as the
> corpse of a chance.

(HG, p. 40)

Not only must The Curator and Nkomo worry about the Regents' not approving the budget, they are faced more than once with the possibility of losing their jobs. Dr. Nkomo, undeterred by such a possibility, continues his "slips / by design into primitive *objets d'art*" (*HG*, p. 44). On one occasion, after an altercation between Dr. Nkomo and Mr. Guy Delaporte, Dr. Nkomo apologizes in his fashion:

> "I've called the gentleman a liar
> — it's true —
> and I am sorry for it."

(HG, p. 52)

The most dramatic confrontation between the black bourgeois mentality and the artistic occurs in "Kappa." Mr. Delaporte is brought face to face with John Laugart's painting, *Black Bourgeoisie*. The picture, which Tolson said was "perhaps inspired by his [Laugart's] reading the sociological book, *Black Bourgeoisie*, by the Howard University professor, E. Franklin Frazier,"[21] is so penetrating an exposé of the peculiar bourgeois mentality of a large segment of the black middle class that it is described as "retching foulness like Goya's etching, / *She Says Yes to Anyone!*" (*HG*, p. 38). Even Delaporte's "babbitted" soul responds: "Mr. Guy Delaporte III takes his stand, / a wounded Cape buffalo defying everything and Everyman!" (*HG*, p. 65). Dr. Nkomo is pleased by the disturbance: "'Is it not / the black damp of the undisturbed pit / that chokes the vitals — damns the dream to rot?'" (*HG*, p. 66). Dr. Nkomo's final word reasserts the saving potency of the work of art. The Harlem Gallery is then setting and occasion of antagonism between black art lover and black bourgeoisie.

This battle is not primarily a matter of personalities; it is a matter of attitudes. The former and present expatriates, The Curator and Dr. Nkomo, have catholic, iconoclastic approaches to life and art that dismay and alarm the black bourgeoisie. The Regents prefer safe, totemistic art. The argument, with implicit or explicit threats on one side and saving, humanistic wit on the other, is indicative of the larger issues involved, for to Tolson the free mind is linked to the dusk of dawn, and the enclosed mind to a way of life gone rotten. Therefore, the antagonism between Curator and Regents can be seen not only as a concrete reality in the poem but also as a metaphor for The Curator's difficult task of envisioning the Harlem Gallery under threats from bourgeois thinking — black or white.

The gallery becomes a figure of the unfolding work in its symbolic development. In "Alpha," The Curator is awakened by the pepper bird, the Harlem Gallery, the work to be produced. The rest of the canto depicts

The Curator girding himself for the task ahead: the creation of the ode or the envisioning of the Harlem Gallery. In the concluding canto, The Curator, returning finally to the theme, says that he envisions "the Harlem Gallery of my people" (*HG*, p. 171) and has apparently completed with some success the task of creation since:

> for here, in focus, are paintings that chronicle
> a people's New World Odyssey
> from chattel to Esquire!
>
> (*HG*, p. 173)

Evidently, the Harlem Gallery is the poem on one level, and the work of art itself becomes a symbol. The Harlem Gallery in the final stanza is symbolic of the ode, black art, and the black people.

The Harlem Gallery has its symbolic referents. It is impossible to exhaust the symbolic meanings that can be read into the figure, but at least one cluster of meanings can be indicated. The gallery throughout has been used as a symbol of a people's dusk of dawn:

> From nightingales of the old Old World,
> O God, deliver us!
> In the Harlem Gallery, pepper birds
> clarion in the dusk of dawn
> the flats and sharps of pigment-words —
> quake the walls of Mr. Rockefeller's Jericho
> with the new New Order of things,
> as the ambivalence of dark dark laughter rings
> in Harlem's immemorial winter.
>
> (*HG*, p. 57)

The portraits in the gallery and the unfolding creation of the ode, prologue to an epic, presage a "new New Order of things," a renewal beyond that of the establishment of democracy in a revolutionary age. The portraits in the gallery are musical "pigment-words" that have the power to destroy the capitalistic Jericho while the affirmative ghetto laughter "rings / in Harlem's immemorial winter" (*HG*, p. 57). Simplistically, it might be said that art is ushering in the new order of things, but the figure achieves symbolic density when one recalls that the unfolding poem is enacting in its performance the destruction and renewal heralded by the pepper birds as it attempts to destroy, through ghetto laughter, the hypocrisies of the old order and to release the energy of the new.

Black art, sometimes considered an anomaly, becomes central to a vision that sees the structure of Western society as about to undergo radical change, affecting it internally and in its relationship to the darker races. Thus, as Du Bois outlined in *Dusk of Dawn* and elsewhere, the problem of color is not peripheral but central to America and to the world. Change, paradoxically a constant of society and individual according to Tolson, is prepared for and imaged by the sometimes faulty workmanship of the gallery (*HG*, p. 171). In the black ghetto, "flowers of hope" flourish while flowers associated with death grow in the white metropolis as the life of the ghetto and the death of the "Great White World" are imaged.[22]

Further, the Harlem Gallery has reference to the community and people who inspired it. The Harlem Gallery is not meant only to capture the spirit of the people as in *Portraits;* it is meant symbolically to represent the people; that is, not to say what the people are like but to figure what the people are. The Harlem Gallery represents the people not only as they are but as they are to be. The focus of today, surrounded by the peripheral vision of yesterday and tomorrow, acquires the indefinite suggestiveness of the symbol when the work of art itself becomes a symbol. The Harlem Gallery then holds in tension the image of a physical setting in Harlem, a metaphor for artistic creation, and an indefinitely suggestive symbol of the black experience in relation to the "Great White World."

> The moving finger in the Harlem Gallery
> paints dramatis personae in the dusk of dawn,
> between America's epigraph and epitaph.

(HG, p. 171)

6

Characters

M. B. Tolson's characterization in *Harlem Gallery* was the product of a period of evolution. At an early stage, Tolson listed names such as "Wick Gilm," "Milo Church," "Mac May," and "Grindle" — names with the distinctive Tolson flavor. Tolson also listed names allegorically coupled with distinctive traits such as "honesty — Sidney Carter," "integrity — Slabon Carter," "duty — Brown," "fame — Crawford," "hope — Combs," "hate — Freeman," "disillusion — Henry," and "humor — Chrs. Jones."[1] One can see in *Portraits* that characters typical of Harlemites sometimes represent a general trait and are often shaped to illustrate the guiding ideas typical of the country's and Tolson's thirties. In Tolson's earlier consideration of character he seems to have contemplated allegorical, typical, and representational functions for his characters. In *Harlem Gallery*, Tolson built on all of these approaches; he included characters in varying degrees of complexity, from the one-dimensional to those approaching symbolic complexity in historical, typical, and symbolic figures.

Some real persons named in *Harlem Gallery* serve chiefly to evoke a sense of the black experience as it was crystallized in a particular place.[2] The Curator's features are described as: "The Afroamerican's features of *A Man called (sic) White*" (*HG*, p. 125). Tolson explained in "Key Words" that *A Man Called White* is the "autobiography of my old friend who was the whitest man I ever saw, I believe; yet he was a 'Negro'" (p. 6). Tolson used White as a specific illustration of what he regarded as the mythology of race in America. "So the Negroes ask, 'What white man is white?' Shakes his head and laughs, 'God knows!'" ("K.W.," p. 2). Dutch Schultz, another historical character, is featured as the owner of a speakeasy. Although Dutch Schultz was allegedly involved in the Harlem numbers racket, and other gangsters owned such well-known spots as the Cotton Club and Connie's Inn, Tolson used Schultz as an illustration of one type of white control in Harlem: "During Prohibition most speakeasies were controlled by gangsters. . . . Although many of these clubs were in black ghettos with Negro entertainers, Negro customers were not allowed" ("K.W.," p. 6). As black life was impinged upon by the outer reality of white America, in Harlem and elsewhere it is alluded to in these historical references.

The inner life of Harlem and black America is evoked by the names of jazz musicians. In "Mu," The Curator allows his mind to wander back to what Tolson calls the "real *Ancients* of the Jazz World" ("K.W.," p. 4). A second group of jazz musicians, contemporaries of Tolson, were named in "Lambda." King Oliver, Bessie Smith, Jelly Roll Morton, Papa Handy, and Leadbelly are named, as well as Satchmo.[3] Such nationally and internationally known jazz performers as Bessie Smith, Jelly Roll Morton, and Louis Armstrong had appeared in Harlem theaters and ballrooms. Leadbelly had also appeared in New York where he had stayed at the Harlem Y. Papa Handy, with whom Tolson had toured, had offices in New York and appeared at such places as the Manhattan Casino (Rockland Palace). Fats Waller, bandleader and organist at the Lincoln Theatre, is another jazz great mentioned in the ode. These names evoke the sounds of an era and the density of Harlem and black experience figured by the legendary greats of the jazz world.

Some largely one-dimensional participants in the action are not actual historical figures but figures typical of a well-known aspect of Harlem In discussing the early Harlem novel, Eugene Arden noted "the familiar exploitation of Harlem local color" in Thurman's *The Blacker the Berry*.[4] Arden goes on to say: "The very material, in other words, which had once been regarded as destructive in the 'evil city' novels, was now manipulated to suggest a romantic view of the big city."[5] The evil city, with its drinking, gambling, dancing, sex, and world of entertainment, becomes in one tradition a city with its own "exotic" appeal. Into it the young are not corrupted but initiated. A Harlem world with its cast of characters and staple elements enters into literature as one facet of the Harlem community is highlighted. A type had been created, and Tolson utilized this type to establish his own meanings. Thus, in Tolson's Harlem as in some early treatments, there is the underworld element represented by the numbers king, the female speakeasy manager, prostitutes, and others. There are the denizens of the nightclub world, its performers and patrons. Less familiar but also portrayed in early Harlem literature and in *Harlem Gallery* are the black intellectuals, black bohemians, and black middle class.

The cabaret world, a mainstay of some early Harlem literature, is represented by such characters as Frog Legs Lux, Snakehips, and Rufino Laughlin. These essentially one-dimensional characters, reminiscent of the local color featured in much early Harlem literature, reveal Harlem through evocation of time and place rather than through a revelation of its effects on their psyches.

There are other characters whose presentation is still essentially one-dimensional but who, in helping to fix the scene, carry hints of greater complexity. One such character, recalling the exotic Harlem, is Big Mama, a woman on the fringe of the underworld who somehow manages to survive and prosper. "Her conscience was a little clay ball, / baked hard and oiled, / ready for the use of any hand" (*HG*, p. 128). On easy terms with Dutch Schultz, Big Mama sums up her life: "'I was born in Rat Alley. / I live on Fox Avenue. / I shall die in Buzzard Street'" (*HG*, p. 128). Although Big Mama knows the formula for pleasing white patrons, she is equally able to understand the complexities of black people. A character straight from the underworld of speakeasies and big time gamblers, despite her easy conscience and shady past, Big Mama is a figure of one kind of real if tenuous survival.

Hedda Starks, the former Black Orchid, had also been part of the exotic image of Harlem. A former stripteaser of the Bamboo Kraal, she recalls, however imprecisely, the poetic and prose version of Harlem dancers.[6] Hedda, having vamped Mister Starks with "her barbarian bump and sophisticated grind" (*HG*, p. 104), has used the resultant marriage to climb into membership in the black bourgeoisie. However, the publicity attendant upon her affair with Mr. Guy Delaporte has made her position difficult. After her husband's death following the exposure of the affair, Black Orchid is haunted by the ghost of her late husband in her jail cell. Tolson used this exotic type for his own purposes as the striptease figure, the sensational affair, and its effects (a story that would have fit easily into *Portraits*), are used to suggest other meanings through context and interaction. Hedda Starks, the center of her husband's concerns, is ironically not sensationally portrayed.

Known to or about by The Curator are a number of lesser characters who represent types familiar in Harlem but who are presented with a kind of suggestiveness that lifts them somewhat above the merely typical. Dr. Igor Shears, a West Indian later to be buried in Trinidad, is typical of the Harlemite who has "achieved." He is a medical doctor, he has attained a position in the community that allows him to act as patron of the arts, and his wife in her turn has status of her own. He also has the leisure and the means to allow him to pursue his favorite pastime: fishing off the Florida Keys. Shears's inner character is left unknown. The disposition with which he fills his role — cynical, ironic, sophisticated, or, least likely, earnest — is deliberately left undefined as the man hides his inner feelings behind a stoic mask: "yet, the man inside was an enigma to me." (*HG*, p. 115).

Crazy Cain is, in some way, typical. A musician with something flawed in his style, he has been fired from the Harlem Symphony Orchestra by Mister Starks, his mother's husband. There is also something flawed in Cain's "Negro tradition" since he is the great grandson of a mulatto sired as a result of a cottonfield rape. "the noxious tinge / mixed with the blues in his fingers / and the dialect in his veins" (*HG*, p. 116). It is likely that the defect in Cain's musical style may be attributed to the racial mixture. What is clear is that, ignorant of his people's history and his own personal tradition, Cain somehow apprehends that he is the illegitimate son of Mr. Guy Delaporte III. This knowledge is useless, and Crazy Cain, Harlem musician, one result of slavery rape, remains ultimately futile. Cain, as the name implies, is involved in the killing of Mister Starks, but his exact role is left enigmatic (*HG*, p. 109). The outer realities of Cain's story are familiar, but the suggestion of Eliotic resignation bred in the bone enlarges the character.

The Zulu Club Wits, whom Tolson described as "the Bohemian eggheads of the twilight zone of Afro-American culture,"[7] recall the black intellectuals, especially of Harlem's twenties, who add the sophistication of bohemians to that of the "black cats" of Harlem. With intellectual predilections, although usually not professionally employed, this somewhat rootless group finds a social context in the Zulu Club. Wallace Thurman, in *Infants of the Spring*, gave a somber picture of black bohemians of the Renaissance, but Tolson's characterization is shot through with the wit, humor, and hilarity of these lovers, both as wits and as blacks, of metaphors and symbols. One of the group is Joshua Nitze, ex-professor of philosophy; another is Lionel Matheus, the "Sea-Wolf of Harlem," a chronic sneerer; a third is Shadrach Martial Kilroy, advocate of race pride and president of Afroamerican Freedom, Inc. The group indulges in battles of wits, discusses the race question, and, above all, provides an appreciative audience for feats of the creative imagaination. However curiously wrought, the word is the art form they cultivate; race consciousness, the topic to which they most often return. Distinctive as the Wits are, they suggest the peculiar ambivalence, especially acute in the twenties and the thirties, of the black man whose intellectual bent is to some extent unsatisfied and who must opt for the kind of compensatory satisfaction provided by the Zulu Club.

Some Harlem types reflect the Harlem beyond the exotic image. One such character is Vincent Aveline, sports editor of the *Harlem Gazette* and "boon crony" of The Curator. Like so many of these Harlemites, his enthusiasm masks a somber reality. Caught up in the enthusiasm elicited by Hideho's ballad, Aveline seats himself at The Curator's table and groans his tribute to the creative flow of the evening. The Curator idly wonders whether enthusiasm or too much liquor has caused the sports editor to steal a copy of Hideho's "Skid Row Ballads." The evening progresses and Aveline finally reveals that he has discovered his wife's liaison with Guy Delaporte III. The silence of the *omertá* follows this disclosure, and the reader is left with a cameo of the aggrieved husband and the suggestion of a way of life compounded of grief and the stoicism that masks it.

Also suggestive of a way of survival is the Zulu Club's janitor, an ex-chaplain from Alabama Christian College. As a doctor of divinity, who has evidently risked and lost his position at a conservative southern black college because of his role in the freedom rides of the sixties, the "ex-chaplain and neo-janitor" participates in the cream and milk discussion. Having risked a great deal for his integrity, he continues even in the role of janitor to maintain his wit and concern for race under the guise of metaphor:

> "Gentlemen,
> perhaps there is a symbolism
> — a manna for the darker peoples —
> in the rich opacity of cream
> and the poor whiteness of skim milk."

> (*HG*, p. 125)

Another example of a type that Tolson complicated for his own purpose is Black Diamond. Diamond is reminiscent of the Diamond Canady figure in *Portraits* who, like Black Diamond, says: "'I play any game / that you can name, / for any amount / that you can count'" (*HG*, p. 87; *Portraits* p. 7). Black Diamond, heir presumptive to the Lenox Policy Racket, also recalls another Diamond, a Harlem numbers racketeer at 135th Street and Lenox Avenue, said to have accumulated half a million dollars.[8]

In many ways, Tolson's Black Diamond is a typical numbers racketeer. A successful businessman, he has the accoutrements of that success: a glamorous companion, the former Miss Bronze America, informants who furnish him with the lowdown on friend and enemy, a position in the church evidenced by his paying his dues a year in advance, and a life membership in Afroamerican Freedom, Inc. His position, straddling two worlds, is reminiscent of the position occupied by Casper Holstein, numbers king and community leader."His ego lionized / in the first, second, and third person" (HG, p. 87), this "ghetto Robin Hood" is surrounded by hangers-on who react and applaud on cue.[9]

But the tough-talking Black Diamond had another side. He had once been The Curator's art student at Waycross, Georgia, and had painted pictures in Harlem dives and deadends that were presumably emblematic of his people. Searching for an analogy for the cordial but strange relationship between himself and his former pupil, The Curator recalls Seneca and Nero, Aristotle and Alexander. The integrity of the neo-janitor eludes Black Diamond, who has traded fidelity to art for a position supported by the parasitic numbers racket.

Equally successful in business ventures is Mr. Guy Delaporte III, President of Bola Boa Enterprises, Inc. Tolson used that "'wonderfully alliterative name the *Bola boa*'" earlier in the *Libretto*.[10] The snake who gorges, then rests only to gorge again, is an apt image for Delaporte's business, which has long ago destroyed all its competitors. Tolson described Delaporte as "a combination of a Robber Baron and Babbitt, the New Negro of our Free Enterprise. . . . Mr. Delaporte welcomes competition in Business, Sex and Religion. Mr. Delaporte's philosophy is his directive to Negro Business Men: 'Adapt yourself to the environment, move from the environment, or die in the environment.'"[11]

Delaporte has many of the trappings of the black bourgeoisie. He is a symbol of Churchianity (a word both Tolson and Calverton used) at the church of the Sugar Hill elite. The performance of "Sweet Mystery of Life" in "whiskyfied baritone" rather than hymns, Gospel songs, or spirituals, indicates the type of church attended by the Harlem businessman as an act of status. As a Regent of the Harlem Gallery, Delaporte patronizes the arts not from any genuine love of creativity but because such cultural activity is a signature of his obvious success. His success and status are also verified by the Negro press, the casual authenticator of the ambitions of the black middle class, which headlines Delaporte's activities and words. In Tolson's language: "Everytime Guy Delaporte III farts — / the phenomenon is headlined in the Negro press" (HG, p. 120). All of these traits are facets of the world of make-believe in which, according to Frazier, the black bourgeoisie live. As Frazier comments: "The black bourgeoisie suffers from 'nothingness' because when Negroes attain middle-class status, their lives generally lose both content and significance."[12] Beneath the exterior trappings, the nothingness from which Delaporte suffers is highlighted by his failure to control or satisfy his wife, by his own amorous adventures, and by his frustration because "no brand-new-$-world in Harlem gives him pause" (HG, p. 65). Significantly, Delaporte is not included in the Zulu Club scene, which refutes Gertrude Stein's accusation of nothingness.

Although Delaporte, with his obvious hypocrisies, is in some ways a caricature of the black bourgeoisie, he is intended to be taken seriously.

For Delaporte represents in the black community the thinking of the monied class that wishes to dictate the quality of life. Opposed throughout the poem to the free spirit of the artist and to the freedom of the masses from strictures of color, race, and caste is the often humorously portrayed black middle class of Harlem. This class, with its little real power, still recalls the "Brissac jack-boots" and "the alien hob-nails" of very real tyrannies. Delaporte hovers over the Harlem world, not because of his extreme power, but because he internalizes a world of values inimical to its burgeoning life.

Despite Tolson's often wryly humorous treatment of many of his characters, many of these Harlemites evoke a somber reality. To consider only two critics' discussions of Harlem in literature, especially that written by Langston Hughes, both Arthur Davis and Wilfred Cartey see somber overtones in the Harlem portrayals. Discussing the Simple stories, Davis found: "Underneath all of his gaiety and humor there is the basic tragedy of the urban Negro and his circumscribed life."[13] Discussing the Harlem poetry, Davis noted: "This cabaret Harlem, this Jazzonia is a joyous city, but the joyousness is not unmixed; it has a certain strident and hectic quality, and there are overtones of weariness and despair." He concluded: "Whether it is in the dream fantasy world of *The Weary Blues* or in the realistic city of *Montage of a Dream Deferred*, one sees a people searching — and searching in vain — for a way to make Harlem a part of the American dream."[14] Cartey, speaking of Claude McKay's poetry of black Manhattan, finds that "that outer world is stern and hard, inflicting deprivation on Harlem and bringing about the degradation of its people."[15] Even in Hughes's poetry, Cartey saw the somber reality haunting the dream. What these critics have seen in the poetry is a Harlem beneath the Jazzonia. It is this second look at Harlem, seeing beyond the merely exotic elements to the life within, that is represented by many of the Tolson characters built on typical figures. A suggestion of frustrated impulses, of compensation, of survival techniques, and of odd triumphs hints at a Harlem behind the sensational facade.

To focus the inner reality of Harlem, Tolson did not choose any of the more familiar types in literature or in life. That reality is not revealed by the religious devotee, by the hardworking mother, by the hustling youngster, by middle-class aspirants, or by radical doctrinaires. For Tolson the inner reality was not revealed as it had been in *Portraits* by the proletariat. Tolson chose to view the inner life of Harlem through the focus of Harlem artists and art appreciators. The "makers," the artists, became the makers of Tolson's image of Harlem. Tolson's artists are rooted in Harlem and the black community so that these figures are asked to bear the burden of defining a community as well as the nature of art. Thus, characters like Laugart, Starks, Heights, Nkomo, and The Curator move toward symbolic complexity.

Regardless of Tolson's final imaginative working out, most of these characters appear to have had prototypes, although not necessarily Harlem prototypes. The Curator, whose physical appearance is based on that of Walter White, in some ways approximates an ideal of Tolson, perhaps based to some extent on traits of Calverton and Tolson himself. Dr. Nkomo is based on an "African and Africanist" whom Tolson had known at Wiley

College.[16] Hideho Heights's name and manner are based on the public appearance of Cab Calloway and a former debating star of Tolson, Henry Heights. John Laugart also had a prototype: "an imaginary character (although I knew his prototype)."[17] Starks appears not to have a prototype. Based for the most part on individuals whom Tolson had known in one capacity or another, these fictional characters are the subjects of Tolson's most complex characterization as these various acquaintanceships are reconstructed and created anew in Tolson's Harlem.

Significantly, the first character that The Curator meets in Harlem is the painter, John Laugart. Coming after five cantos in which The Curator reflects on various aspects of the arts, "Zeta" depicts, in starkest outlines, what it means to be an artist in contemporary society, specifically in Harlem. Placed where it is, the "Zeta" portraiture reverberates throughout the ode's discussions of art and portrayals of artists. Although individualized, John Laugart is an embodiment of Tolson's "ape of God."

Laugart's physical description emphasizes the stark character of the painter's existence. John Laugart is half-blind, "spoonshaped like an aged parrot-fish" (*HG*, p. 37), has a sheaf of agitated merino hair, and wears odds and ends with an air of dignity. His face is compared to that of a male umbrella bird: "haply black and mute" (*HG*, p. 39), with a drooping lower lip and staring eye; in short, a "Bleak House grotesque." Looking at John Laugart, The Curator sees the "face / of a fantast" (*HG*, p. 38).

Psychologically, Laugart's internal world has the same stark character. Having lived a life difficult even for "a half-blind black son of Hagar" (*HG*, p. 127), Laugart is left with the "thin, cold" vanity that sustains him. The Curator imagines him the "undated voice of a poet crying, / among scattered bones in a stony place, / 'No man cares for my soul!'" (*HG*, p. 38). Reviled, aware of his dependence on liquor, "this castaway talent" can yet affirm his integrity and make the statement that stands out in relief against the background of his bleak surroundings, his comfortless material life, his straitened inner life, his Patmos:

> "It matters not a tinker's dam
> on the hither or thither side of the Acheron
> how many rivers you cross
> if you fail to cross the Rubicon!"
>
> (*HG*, p. 42)

Tolson places this "epitaphic" quotation just before his description of Laugart's death: a stark reality in keeping with the "hogback" road that had been Laugart's life, an ending sealing the inner life with its appropriate outer manifestation. Laugart is robbed and fatally stabbed in his apartment with only a rat for witness.

The stark reality of Laugart's life and death is not intended primarily as an example of the poverty-stricken in Harlem, although he shares aspects of their fates. Laugart's bleak existence is consistently linked to his phenomenal artistic integrity. Seeing the work of art as "'a moment's / antlers of the elaphure in the hunting lodge of time'" (*HG*, p. 112), Laugart dedicates his life to pursuing his artistic vision. Like Tiresias's, Laugart's lack of physical sight is accompanied by second sight. Like the evangelist, this other John has a vision that is apocalyptic in character. Laugart seizes the moment, the social and human reality of his time and place in "Black Bourgeoisie." His kind of artistic insight is linked to the people's dusk of dawn: this "savage and sanative" work, reminiscent of Daumier, Gropper, and Picasso, unveils the foul aspects of middle-class life in terms so explicit that even the unseeing representatives of the class are disturbed. Such ironic art "gives the Gomorrhean blues / to the bulls of Bashan" (*HG*, p. 40).[18]

Laugart then becomes a "Jacob that wrestles Tribus and sunders bonds" (*HG*, p. 40), "Tribus" presumably referring to the idols of the tribe, the mythology created to bolster the ruling class. Laugart sees the work of art as

" . . . an everlasting flower
in kind or unkind hands;
dried out,
it does not lose its form and color
in native or in alien lands."

(*HG*, p. 39)

Believing in the power of the work of art, he becomes praiseworthy: "a radical leaf / created upon an under stem" (*HG*, p. 39), a true artist appearing in a subculture. This man, exiled in his own land, becomes with The Curator, "the Castor and Pollux of St. Elmo's fire, / on Harlem's Coalsack Way" (*HG*, p. 39), the twin lights in Harlem's dark sky. The artist and the curator of art, no matter how straitened the circumstances, continue to be faithful to art, to nurture and disseminate its saving vision.

Against the uncompromising integrity of Laugart, Mister Starks appears to be a compromiser, but in Tolson's complex characterization Starks is a singular figure overwhelmed by the "artistry of circumstances." As Starks's life had been a mixture of pain and humor, The Curator begins his story humorously with an account of his given name.

Tolson evidently took some pleasure in Starks's Christian name, "Mister." He explained in his Notebooks that he had met in Vicksburg a man called Mister who was addressed as Mister Mister Jones. The story is humorously retold in "Rho," and Tolson repeated its explanation in "Key Words": "Negro parents in the South often named their babies Mister, Colonel, General, Doctor, Lawyer, Honorable, Duke, Baron, Queen, Countess and Duchess to keep the good white folk from calling them 'Boy' or Uncle' [*sic*]. . . . Apologizing, he'll say 'Pardon me Judge Smith. I didn't know you were calling me. You see, my name is *Honorable*. My poor old mama who is dead gave me that name in Orange Blossom.' Often, to say this took the courage of Crispus Attucks at the Boston Massacre" (p. 5). Tolson's telling of the story in "Rho" also entailed his delight in the real placenames: Paris, Texas; Broken Bow, Oklahoma; and Onward, Mississippi.[19]

Beginning with this tale, relished by the Zulu Club Wits, The Curator outlines Starks's life. Starks had begun as a "piano-modernist / of the Harlem Renaissance" (*HG*, p. 104), a jazz-pianist in a Prohibition-era speakeasy.

Like the other artists, he had also been an expatriate in Paris where he had frequented the Gaya bar, haven of painters and liberati, and had heard compositions of masters of contemporary music. Returning to Harlem, he had been fascinated by the striptease artist, Black Orchid, whom he married. The discovery of the liaison between Delaporte and Hedda sent Starks into a hell of suffering from which he emerged by his mysterious suicide. This act was, according to The Curator, a Hardyesque *beau geste*. What had remained constant in Starks's varied life, besides his music, was his devotion to Black Orchid. Fascinated by her in her early striptease days, Starks found his life shattered years later by her infidelity. Part of his failure to achieve on the highest level may be laid to the personal entanglements of his life with Hedda.

Something of the character of Mister is illustrated by the cool, witty manner in which he answers Ma'am Shears's attempts to talk him out of his planned suicide: "'Mister, don't try it!' she begged. / 'Try it?' he laughed. 'I'm a Hannibal — not a Napoleon.'" When Ma'am Shears replies "'It's not like Black Folks to commit suicide, '" Starks ripostes: "'Aren't we civilized yet?'" "Ma'am Shears groaned, 'Civilization and suicide?' / 'Soil and plant,' he said. 'Masaryk speaking — in Vienna.'" He then ends the conversation by engaging to meet Dr. and Mrs. Shears and Abelard Littlejohn at "'Archangel Gabriel's hangout / on Elysian Boulevard. / *Au revoir !*'"(*HG*, p. 108). The tone — witty, erudite, and controlled — reveals the man's style and masks his anguish.

More of Starks's character can be gleaned from his compositions: "Pot Belly Papa," "Black Orchid Suite," "Rhapsody in Black and White," and "Harlem Vignettes." Self-defining, Starks had said: "My talent was an Uptown whore; my wit a Downtown pimp" (*HG*, p. 112). Unlike Laugart, Starks had tried to maintain a balance between "want" and "have." To satisfy his need for money, he had made a boogie-woogie record, "Pot Belly Papa," that had sold a million copies. To satisfy his artistic needs, he had written the "Black Orchid Suite," inspired by his wife. His dual role as onetime speakeasy pianist and present-day Harlem Symphony Orchestra leader had some precedent in the career of Ellington, Joplin, J. Rosamond Johnson, and others. But as Starks himself indicates, his divided interest is not solely a matter of catholicity or of the dualism implicit in his Western tails and African baton. Such versatility is in part evidence of a failure of nerve. Starks rationalizes his resultant occasional low spirits by citing the triple handicap of being Negro, Harlemite, and artist — an outcast on three levels. He further rationalizes his shortcomings by ironically stating an accepted view:

> Like all 100-p.c. Negroes,
> I knew a white skin was the open
> sesame to SUCCESS —
> the touchstone of
> Freedom, Justice, Equality.

(*HG*, p. 129)

Starks, however, has created what he feels to be one noteworthy composition, the "Black Orchid Suite," which, unlike "Pot Belly Papa," was unacclaimed. His most earnest composition arising from his deepest inspiration goes unapplauded. Like Laugart's "Black Bourgeoisie," which earned its creator only a bottle of gin, "Charon's grin / and infamy" (*HG*, p. 42), Starks's finest effort fails to strike a responsive chord from its probably bourgeois audience. Even in this less than wholly dedicated artist, there is faithfulness to the task of envisioning his subject and faithfulness to his artistic re-creation of the vision: "the premiere of the *Black Orchid Suite* — / . . . / will forever stir my dust and bones" (*HG*, p. 113). Also like Laugart's masterpiece, Starks's is linked to the dusk of dawn imagery: "sunrise on the summit / between / sunset and sunset — " (*HG*, p. 113).

Something of Starks's attitude toward art can be glimpsed in "Tau," which introduces the "Harlem Vignettes." Exotically done up in a mamba's skin, the manuscript has along its spine a snake's head with a legend in purple-red ink: "'In the sweat of thy face shalt thou make a work of art'" (*HG*, p. 111). Like Yeats in "Adam's Curse," the poet envisions the work of art as one of the most difficult and necessary of labors.[20] Exiled from Eden, the artist must labor to recall the lost vision. The material, "Sanson's images of my own Harlem" constitutes a "few oysters / from a planter's bed — a site located in Harlem / strewn with layers of shells, slag, cinders, gravel" (*HG*, p. 111). Starks's artistic shaping is seen as rescuing what is of true value from the slag heap of Harlem.

When Starks tries to capture the variety of characters in the ghetto, he is epitomizing Tolson's feats in *Harlem Gallery* and *Portraits* as even the title echoes Tolson's titles. "The Vignettes" contains Starks's characterizations of all but one of *Harlem Gallery*'s major characters and some of its minor characters limned by a man of wit, erudition, and penetration. For example, Starks alone is able to see the "charact in the African" that made him a better man than The Curator. Like Tolson's work, the "Vignettes" have been reworked from an earlier imagistic style. Another similarity between Tolson's and his creature's work is that they both project Harlem as a "*comédie larmoyante*." Even though Starks is no black Balzac, his "Vignettes," which will be received with neither great applause nor great condemnation, still contain elements that can prick the conscience of such readers as The Curator.

One can see that Starks's art is rooted in the black community. His "Pot Belly Papa" is written in the idiom of the black man on the street. His symphony, written in another idiom, finds its inspiration in his personal life and in an embodiment of a phase of Harlem life, the combined sophistication and barbarity of the cabaret era. His poems, "Vignettes," written in a modern vein, contain portraits of the "everybodies and somebodies and nobodies / in Harlem's *comédie larmoyante*" (*HG*, p. 112). His "Rhapsody in Black and White," a blues answer to the Tin Pan Alley "Rhapsody in Blue," contains a musical statement about integration based on Aggrey's metaphor of black and white keys on the piano.[21] Whatever their idiom, all of these compositions arise from Starks's experience of black life.

Mister Starks is a complex personality. He evinces the duality seen in the black artist who speaks two languages, works in two idioms. Haunted by visions of excellence, he settles for the attainable. Working within the narrow framework of opportunities available to him as a black man of talent, he yet manages to achieve. Able to perceive the complex relationships, interactions, and psychologies of his fellow Harlemites, he is unable to fathom his wife's inner life. Cool and sophisticated, ever the "highbrow composer," he is unable to banish his anguish and despair over his personal life. Pianist, orchestra leader, composer, and poet, this ape of God is left with the taste of ashes — a figure something less than tragic, somewhat more than pathetic; an ambivalent figure in Harlem's *comédie larmoyante*.

Another two-faceted figure is Hideho Heights, one aspect of whose personality is described: "the Redskin beatnik bard of Lenox Avenue in Harlem."[22] Derived from Calloway and Henry Heights,[23] Hideho has something of the public character of Langston Hughes, whom Tolson called "the chief ballad-singer of proletarian Upper Lenox Avenue, the street of 'the unperfumed drifters and workers.'"[24] Hideho's physical description bolsters his characterization as the "*Coeur de Lion* of the Negro mass" (*HG*, p. 147). He is described as a "great big man" with a "whale of a forefinger," a laugh that quakes pictures on the walls, a ferry-horn voice, bright eyes, a gold-toothed smile, who sports a Daniel Boone rawhide belt. His voice is dramatic; Hideho fleshes out the rhetorical style suitable to the poem he is reciting. His presence is reminiscent of Paul Robeson's, and the rhetorical flourish of his speaking style is complemented by such gestures as his brandishing his flask of bootleg liquor.

Hideho thus plays the part of the heroic bard of the masses, complete with "satyric legends." At the scene in the Zulu Club, in "Xi," poet and people are one. The poet is "no Crusoe"; he and the audience both aim to please. The ballad of John Henry, in language appropriate to the masses, memorializes the heroic qualities inherent in the people and is immediately appreciated by them. Poet, poem, and people are woven into a whole by Hideho's artistry. The Curator likens Hideho's role to that of a "charcoal Piute Messiah / at a ghetto / ghost dance" (*HG*, p. 79). As the people's poet in manner and subject, Heights like Hughes is scorned by the black bourgeoisie who regard him as "a crab louse / in the pubic region of Afroamerica" (*HG*, p. 114). Hideho meets such criticism, as he does more weighty difficulties, with a saving humor and pride. He remains a type of Plato's just man, a poet of whom Plato would approve, a "man square as the *x* in Dixie" (*HG*, p. 113).

There is another facet to the people's poet, however. Hideho has the "damp-dry eyes of the tragic-comic" (*HG*, p. 114). The humor and hilarity occasionally lapse into another mood that is indicative of another disposition. When, undoubtedly drunk, Hideho sobs "My *people*," he sees something other than heroism in the lives of the people. Still self-associated with the people, he touches on the sorrow implicit in their lives. Even The Curator's characterization of Hideho as a charcoal Piute Messiah has its somber overtone. In the ghost dance, the messiah was supposed to rid the land of whites and restore rights to Indians. The dance, in which some of the participants would fall into a trance not totally unlike a jazz high, was an indirect cause of a nineteenth-century Indian outbreak. The partly Indian Hideho's incantations hark back to ritual celebrations whose goal is apocalyptic. Also at odds with the public image is The Curator's hearing, when Heights dramatically takes a swig from his hip-pocket bottle, "a gurgle, a gurgle — a death rattle" (*HG*, p. 69). Further, Hideho, in revealing his private memories, calls up the image of a whore giving birth to a pimp's son on a filthy quilt. Although Hideho interprets the image as a metaphor for artistic creation and miscreation, it seems evident that the image figures at least one root of Hideho's art.

Like the other artists, Hideho values artistic integrity highly. Scorning Uncle Tomism in artist and leader, he insists on integrity as a foundation of artistic production. Although Hideho's language may be mocking, he seriously insists on the special role of the artist: "'Only kings and fortune tellers, / poets and preachers, / are born to be'" (*HG*, p. 79). Beneath the humor, despite contradictory impulses, the people's poet insists on the validity of his role. He insists on the artist's and the man's integrity despite the fact that his outer poise and inner qualms set up real, if human, tensions within the man.

Just as there are apparent contradictions in the poet's personality, there are tensions inherent in the art produced by Hideho. In the ballad of Satchmo composed in the Daddy-O Club, and in the ballad of John Henry's birth recited at the Zulu Club, Heights composes the "racial ballad in the public domain" (*HG*, p. 145). Still in the public domain is the symbolic story of the turtle and the shark, but "E. & O. E." is "the private poem in the modern vein" (*HG*, p. 145). The Curator recognizes the split identity resulting from "the Afroamerican dilemma in the Arts — " (*HG*, p. 146). Since "the Color Line, as well as the Party Line, / splits an artist's identity" (*HG*, p. 147), the dual nature of Hideho's poetry is explained.

The two ballads attempt to immortalize folk heroes, one real and the other fictional. Satchmo, in the tradition of the jazz greats who are themselves legendary, has become a genuine folk hero — "*Wyatt Earp's legend, John Henry's, too, / is a dare and a bet to old Satchmo*" (*HG*, p. 70) — to be sung about with the hyperbole, the cool wit, and the rhyme and rhythm of jive talk. A more traditional ballad celebrates a more traditional hero as John Henry is sung about in a form in which hyperbole mounts on hyperbole to form a glittering tale of the folk hero, and such details as John Henry's choice of food places it squarely in the ethnic tradition. Hideho thus legitimizes the title, "the people's poet," as he celebrates those heroes who write the qualities of the black folk in glittering letters. As in the "Skid Row Ballads," mentioned but unreproduced, it is the black masses who are the poet's concern. The poet's later symbols of the turtle and the shark continue in another vein the celebration of the black folk; this time, blacks in the South.

In "E. & O.E.," Hideho exhibits another idiom as well as another facet of his personality. The subject is not a folk hero but the people's poet himself captured in a subjective rather than objective mode. In *Poetry*, Tolson noted of "E. & O. E.": "The abbreviation is doubtless an *apologia pro vita sua* as well as a bow to custom in Webster's appendix."[25] In the first section quoted, a section Tolson attributed to a "Tartuffean shill" in the original poem, Hideho, in low spirits like Mister, rationalizes the difficulty of the artistic role: "'Why place an empty pail / before a well / of dry bones?'" (*HG*, p. 147). Hideho, after recalling his expatriate youth in Paris, goes on to fashion a newer, more limited, more typically modern version of heroism in art and life as he depicts a man who has seen but never achieved greatness, but has yet attained a measure of integrity.[26] This heroism contrasts with the hyperbole of the earlier balladic incantations as Hideho outlines his own refusal to join in "'Lear's prayer, / or Barabas' curse, / or Job's cry!'" (*HG*, p. 151). Like Laugart always and Starks occasionally, this ape of God refuses to shelter under his own misfortunes, and under difficult circumstances he maintains his identity — his only real boast.[27]

Such artists, expatriates who can view both black and white America from the perspective of one who has been an outsider, are in one sense spiritual exiles among their own people at the same time that they are inspired by their people. They are artists who seek to escape spiritual confinement in a province — ethnic or otherwise — but who nevertheless are rooted in the province. Sustained by their pride and conscious of their shortcomings, artists like Starks and Hideho wear many masks as they perform, now in the dominant Western mode, now in the traditional Afro-American mode, as they perform in popular or esoteric styles.[28] What Tolson said of the black artist in general may be applied to these apes of God, Laugart, Starks, and Hideho:

> in this race, at this time, in this place,
> to be a Negro artist is to be
> a flower of the gods, whose growth
> is dwarfed at an early stage —
> a Brazilian owl moth,
> a giant among his own in an acreage
> dark with the darkman's designs,
> where the milieu moves back downward like the sloth.
>
> (*HG*, p. 153)

7

Personae

On the Harlem scene, Dr. Obi Nkomo fleshes out the abstraction "*Homo Aethiopicus.*" Dr. Nkomo may owe something to an African whom Tolson had met in his youth: a little Bantu scholar with tribal holes in his ears and an Oxford accent who "paraded across the dinner table the dramatic figures of Alexander Pushkin, El-Hadj Omar, Crispus Attucks, Alexandre Duman, Antar, Estevanico, Toussaint L'Ouverture, Menelik, and Frederick Douglass."[1] The figure is certainly derived from a former colleague of Tolson, an "agnostic alien professor" in a "Black Belt Methodist College" (Wiley). Further, aspects of Nkomo's thought correspond to Tolson's, and Tolson's youngest son saw correspondences of attitude between Nkomo and Tolson. Dr. Tolson felt that, like Nkomo, Tolson was to some extent an outsider looking in, an observer, a "person involved in the scene yet not involved in the scene."[2]

Tolson remarked of his *Libretto* that as Pound went to China, he went to Africa.[3] It can be suggested that in *HG*, the African and Africanist Nkomo presents a viable tradition for the Afro-American. Just as black Americans have taken four hundred years for the trek from Africa to Afro-America, Nkomo in his own experience has journeyed from his tribal beginnings to Harlem. In seventy years he has symbolically recapitulated vital aspects of the experience of the black American: "*He absorbs alien ideas as Urdu / Arabic characters*" (*HG*, p. 49).

Certainly Tolson insisted on Nkomo's Africanness. Even his appearance and manner emphasize the African origins. Nkomo extends his ebony forefinger like an assagai blade. He has beanpole legs, charcoal lips, and glistening eyes. In his first appearance, Dr. Nkomo clicks his tongue like a South African tribesman. Later he is described as intoning a rebel Bantu song. He compares himself to Julio Sigafoos, an ex-savage,[4] and he recalls his Zulu childhood with an African folktale.

In the structure of the poem, Dr. Obi Nkomo is carefully placed. Other artists and The Curator have been expatriates; Nkomo remains an expatriate in America. He brings to the poem not just the detached view of a man who comes from another nation but that of a person who comes from a non-Western culture. As African he represents one pole of the Afro-American experience. As colleague of The Curator and "alter-ego / of the Harlem Gallery" (*HG*, p. 43), he is perserver and lover of the arts without himself being an artist. On all counts, as African, expatriate, and critic, Dr. Nkomo is fitted for the role he is to play — that of foil to the many discussants, but chiefly that of the detached, ironic, humane, and absolutely honest observer.

Dr. Nkomo's integrity is also firmly established. His first statement echoes Picasso: "'The lie of the artist is the only lie / for which a mortal or a god should die'" (*HG,* p. 43).[5] In one of his last statements, Nkomo asks what is he who applauds when his self-respect is eaten away (*HG,* p. 153). Throughout the ode, Nkomo's speech never betrays the absolute integrity woven into the fabric of the man. Associated with the iron integrity is a humanistic concern for his fellow human beings: "nobody was a nobody to him" (*HG,* p. 44). His biting irony, the outward manifestation of his attitude toward life, is not intended to offend the person but to reveal the error: "Doctor Nkomo's *All hail to Man* / was a vane on the wing / to winnow the grain / in person, place and thing" (*HG,* p. 44).

Despite these outstanding characteristics, Dr. Nkomo's character as a whole is difficult to define because it is in many respects a unity of opposites. Firmly rooted in the African tradition, Nkomo has forsaken his tribal gods and ultimately the religion of the white man to become "a bastard of Barbarus and Cultura" (*HG,* p. 117). Following the "Christ of the African Veld" to the Statue of Liberty and Wall Street, Nkomo ended his indoctrination into the dominant Western mores by rejecting capitalism. To correspond with his life experience, Nkomo fashions a philosophy of his own from elements of Western thought. He then becomes a Heraclitean, a socialist, and an integrationist. As Nkomo lives this philosophy, it combines a deeply skeptical, unillusioned attitude toward the status quo with a Heraclitean faith in the future and man's potential. As a result of this amalgamation of Western thought and tribal experience, Nkomo is defined by Starks: "His psyche was a half-breed" (*HG,* p. 117). That psychic split seen in the artists Starks and Hideho is depicted graphically in Nkomo, not as two received traditions but as two often contradictory, often dangerous life experiences.

Like some half-breeds, he is detached from both heritages. He observes the Western world where men "rent diving bells to get the bends, / curfew morals, incubate tsetse flies, / stage a barroom brawl of means and ends / in a *cul-de-sac,*" imaged in "Eagles dying of hunger with cocks in their claws!" (*HG,* p. 48). Yet, he is described by The Curator as "A black outsider with all his eggs but one / in the White Man's basket" (*HG,* p. 48). Although alien to the "Great White World," Nkomo has cast his lot with it, presumably not because of submission to its power but because of faith in the ultimate progress of man when the myths of race and class have worn themselves out. Partaking of both traditions, wholly committed to neither, he has trekked the "'dark wayfarer's way between / black Scylla and white Charybdis'" (*HG,* p. 53), has seen and survived the "beasts" in the "disemboweling pits" of Euro-America and in the "death-worming bowels" of Afro-Asia. A living example of his beliefs, this black outsider is dedicated to "multiculture" in a world that has not yet learned to value such an ideal.

But to outline Nkomo's history and beliefs is not to indicate the charm of the man. The images of Dr. Nkomo nested behind "an alp of chitterlings, pungent as epigrams," or Dr. Nkomo greeting the puzzled Harlem matrons with "Aloha," capture something of the uniqueness of his character. Perhaps the most rounded figure in *HG,* and certainly one of the most complex, the old Africanist lives most intensely in his words and metaphors. The metaphors that rise so easily to his lips etch a mind that is witty in a metaphysical sense, that leaps and adventures much as Nkomo had done in his life.

Some of the most striking metaphors can be cited. Nkomo, trying to define himself and fix the identity of a fellow Harlemite, tells the story of the "ghostified cock," which ends with "Mister, *what* are you? / An eagle or a chicken come home to roost?" (*HG*, p. 51). The metaphor of the Bourbon and his family tree answers the question of hereditary worth. Nkomo lets loose metaphor after metaphor, from black damp to crocodile laugh, in his response to Delaporte's outrage at "Black Bourgeoisie" (*HG*, p. 66). To describe black-white relations in a capitalistic society, he uses the metaphor of the python swallowing both the little python and the frog (*HG*, p. 90). The metaphor of Western materialism as a "steatopygous Jezebel / with falsies on her buttocks" (*HG*, p. 118) is apt, Nkomian, and Tolsonian. His playing with the images of milk and cream is typical of the play of his mind as the "*Sit down, servant, please sit down*" (*HG*, p. 124) is indicative of his play of words. The metaphor of black and white, and their ultimate relationship as the bodies of the dead, eaten by vultures, left to rot, with bones swept into the "Sepulchre of Anonymity" (*HG*, p. 157), is chillingly apt. Here is the kind of mentality that composed the African proverbs in the *Libretto*'s "Sol," playing upon the Afro-American dilemma inherent in the Harlem setting.

Nkomo's approach to *HG*'s themes of man and art reflects the experience of a man whose relationship to Western and non-Western worlds has bred the mental attitude of a detached outsider. Most of Dr. Nkomo's pronouncements on man are related to his special interest in race. Characteristically metaphoric, Dr. Nkomo notes that straitened circumstances have a deleterious effect on man:

> "The nicks and cuts under a stallion's tail
> spur him to carry it higher;
> but the incised horsetail of a man
> drains the bones of his I-ness drier."

(*HG*, p. 47)

This generalized remark is applied to the predicament of a Harlemite.

Dr. Nkomo's socialist bent often gives his remarks on race an extension to class; ideas rooted in race are in no way confined to it. The milk-and-cream metaphor can be seen as having an extension from race to class. Dr. Nkomo identifies himself with the homogenized milk that he, opting for a multiculture embracing all races and presumably all classes, drinks. Later, in "Psi," Nkomo provides, in graphic detail, the ultimate relevance of the distinctions, primarily racial but also of class, that divide mankind. Chance may divide men artificially, but the democracy of the grave shows how little meaning such divisions have. Nkomo's belief in integration and socialism is not based on naive optimism but on an experience that has pierced the barriers of race, caste, and class and found them to be vanities.

Although racial distinction may be ultimately vain, such distinction is quite real in the Harlem setting, and Nkomo is very much aware of the fact. Speaking with the detachment of a man inside and outside the situation, Nkomo calls the black American a mixture of many strains in a land where only whites are allowed full civil rights, and Nkomo sees the Afro-American betrayed, left with his hopes depressed and his efforts futile: "'your black dog trapped like an ex-sewage rat, / you go / from the dead end of this to the dead end of that'" (*HG*, p. 136). Yet, recognizing this aspect of the black man's American experience, Nkomo proceeds to say of the black man in general: "Nature is on the square / with the African" (*HG*, p. 156). After having developed the statement, Nkomo asserts that the black man can find in the "Great White World" both "the bitter waters of Marah *and* / the fresh fountains of Elim" (*HG*, p. 156). This remark, coupled with his view of the ultimate futility of discrimination, illustrates a complex attitude in which Nkomo recognizes the value of pluralism while seeing the obstacles to it. Further, in condemning the racial hubris of the ruling majority, he refuses to substitute a countervailing racial hubris for it. For him, race is a possible value among other values, not a ruling arrogance.

As critic, Nkomo both knows and values art. In fact, he sees art as the only possible way of knowing in full. Man, in his tridimensionality — biology, sociology, and psychology — is too complex for definition since a man may be judged a Tartufe or an Iscariot (*HG*, p. 45). Such easy definitions ignore the totality of what a man is, what he may become, and what his relationship is to the complex social and cultural nexus that produced him. Only the imagination of the artist can produce a truly rounded character that reflects the total experience: " . . . Dr. Nkomo contends that only in art can one, through the selectivity of the artist, know a character in the round."[6]

Nkomo accordingly contends that art and life beget incestuously the artist who then draws on life and artistic tradition to produce that heritage of art that "nurtures everywhere / the wingless and the winged man" (*HG*, p. 93). As complementary functions, Nkomo sees the work of art as a pleasure, "a way-of-life's aubade" (*HG*, p. 46), like the dusk of dawn, a way of conquering death (*HG*, p. 48), an explosive force that later quietly works its effects in new life (*HG*, p. 66). Art can therefore be a saving grace to man, whether he be free or symbolically confined. Further, relating this view of art to Harlem, the critic Dr. Nkomo dreams of creating a Harlem character-history in which the uninvolved beholder can "'recompose the unexpected tones in a dusky Everyman / the painter's brush has disassociated against the milieu — / then boned and fleshed and veined again'" (*HG*, p. 170).[7] Art and life for Nkomo are inextricably intertwined.

The character of Nkomo is as sharply defined as his stabbing forefinger and his daring metaphors, and, as erudite mouthpiece for some of Tolson's most deeply considered opinions, he acquires an indefiniteness that is an effect of his function in the ode. He remains both a personality and a consciousness that helps to shape the poem. The least defeated of the major characters, Dr. Obi Nkomo adds wisdom to the complexity of his views and a suggestiveness derived from his African origins as he symbolically figures the dusk of dawn man: "*A whale of a man*, I thought; *a true, / but not a typical, mammal* (*HG*, p. 49).

Another character of symbolic complexity is The Curator, whose voice is heard throughout the ode. The Curator as a character in Harlem is the person who is present, physically or mentally, at all the action. He is the colleague of Nkomo, the cooperator with and patron of Laugart, the friend of Hideho and Starks, an acquaintance of the Zulu Club Wits, the "boon-crony" of Vincent Aveline, the former teacher of Diamond and Fairfax, and the sometime opponent of Delaporte. He is present at eating house and Zulu Club, joining in the rituals enacted there. He is the means of self-revelation, from Laugart's blunt statement to Starks's "Vignettes" to Hideho's private poem. He articulates facets represented in the characters and lives of the *HG* artists. The Curator is a participant in the action, a catalyst to the action, and the framer of those opinions that add context to character and setting. In a sense, the poem takes place in the mind of The Curator.[8]

Why indeed is The Curator the focal point of the ode? First, as octoroon, a "voluntary Negro," he is uniquely qualified to address the questions — "What is Negro?" "What is white?" — implicit in the race mythology of America. His skin is as white, his hair as blond, his eyes as blue as the most Nordic of whites (*HG*, p. 160). Therefore, he is able to be white in Norfolk and black in New York. Of Afro-Irish-Jewish ancestry, The Curator is "both physiologically and psychologically 'The Invisible Man'" whose name we never know.[9] Second, by temperament he is uniquely fitted to view, link, and comment upon the various characters portrayed in the book. A Nestor with at least four decades of experience with artists (and with perhaps just a suggestion of Nestor's futility), he "'is a cosmopolite, a humanist, a connoisseur of the fine arts, with catholicity of taste and interest. He knows intimately lowbrows and middlebrows and highbrows.'"[10] Third, although The Curator, like the alter ego of the Harlem Gallery, Dr. Nkomo, is not himself capable of the production of a work of art, he is especially suited to mediate between artist and art lover, to comment upon the arts, to pursue the links between art and reality, between black arts and black experience:

> I have only pilgrimed —
> to the cross street
> (a godsend in God's acre)
> where
> curator and creator
> meet —

> (*HG*, p. 170)

The Curator, on all three counts, is both participant in and observer of his world.[11]

The Curator's musings help define his identity. As he approaches the task of envisioning the Harlem Gallery, he shows both diffidence and certainty about his role. He sees himself as sometimes "a Roscius as tragedian, / sometimes a Kean as clown" (*HG*, p. 19). On the one hand, he is prepared for his task; on the other hand, he hears a voice questioning the worth of his endeavor. His spirit distressed by the black bourgeoisie and by the scorn of whites, he still girds himself for the task before him, which will involve the unification of "humanness" and "Negroness" in "I-ness" (*HG*, p. 20). Again, in "Beta," he reviews his qualifications for the task, finds himself occasionally lacking the equipment needed to fathom great art, and sees his role as "a minor vocative part" (*HG*, p. 23). Remembering the gifted, unaccommodating generations of artists he has known in varying circumstances, he feels that he is not talented as they were; yet, he affirms of himself that "within the flame is a core / of gas as yet unburnt / and undetected like an uninflected spoor" (*HG*, p. 25).

Although his title makes him and the race "Somebody in the Great White World," [12] the knowledge of his limitations contributes to the attitude with which he views his role. For instance, in his role as The Curator of the Harlem Gallery, he explains that he is an ex-professor of art who, bored by routine, has given up the profession. The Curator is reminded of his former profession by Black Diamond and Richard Fairfax, who have both abandoned their talent: one to be numbers king, the other to sell skin-whiteners — both ultimately betrayals. However, constant tempering of any impulse to hubris is not visible in The Curator's public role as defender of the arts and artist. Hideho regards him as a blackamoor who, thinking too much, is dangerous to the "Great White World" (*HG*, p. 76). Guy Delaporte III considers him to be a perservering Greenland shark. Dr. Nkomo sees him as a dusky Francis I, everlastingly defiant, and Starks observes him defending his "*Malakoff*," the Harlem Gallery, to the end.

The Curator perceives his task as being an interpreter, an

X stopper pausing
between a work of art
and the electromagnet wave causing
the listening ear
to ring and smart.

(*HG*, p. 102)

He sees himself as seeking the how, why, and what of the work of art. In exhibitions, The Curator tries to make this what, how, and why of the work of art available to the public (*HG*, p. 165). The exegesis of a great work of art often requires great patience since the work of art is often so powerful that it must be assimilated little by little; otherwise, its effect would be devastating. Related to the task of making the work of art available is the imperative to decide whether to skim the "milk of culture" for the elite while giving the "'lesser breeds' / a popular latex brand" (*HG*, p. 167).

The Curator, himself a critic, views the critic ambivalently. The merely pedantic critics, with no real love for art, are "weeping monkeys of the Critics' Circus / (colorless as malic acid in a Black Hamburg grape)" (*HG*, p. 29), arguing futilely over useless issues. Such critics refuse to let the artist deal with the truly controversial subjects pertaining to the political and social structure of the world (*HG*, p. 102). Such conventional critics may have an "ism" of their own by which they judge art, but the loving encounter with the work of art is unknown to them. Good critics, however, patiently interpreting genius, become "the fid / that bolsters the topmost mast / of Art" (*HG*, p. 169).

The Curator, a black connoisseur, often discusses art in general; but The Curator's tough view of art can be related to the conditions from which those views arose: the conditions of the black man, especially the black artist, in America. The Curator's opinion of the necessity of art parallels that of Dr. Nkomo and reflects "the mutuality of minds / that moved independently of each other — / like the eyeballs of a chameleon" (*HG*, p. 122). The Curator, like Nkomo, feels that the age is transitional, moving toward a new socioeconomic alignment. In such an age, poised between evacuation and creation, the artist's task is to trumpet the corruption of the old and the coming of the new, not through doctrinaire pronouncements but through his creation of an art that faithfully mirrors the inner reality of his age. Since it is difficult, if not impossible, for men to grasp the reality of their experiences, art provides a means of knowing. The artist, beginning with the reality he experiences, transforms it imaginatively, as the artistic form embodies a way of seizing reality:[13]

> A work of art is a domain
> (mediterranean)
> of *this* race,
> of *that* time,
> of *this* place,
> of *that* psyche,
> with an Al Sirat of its own —
>
> (*HG*, p. 99)

The Curator insists on the freedom of the artist. He sees the scripture of art as esoteric, pluralistic, and contradictory (*HG*, p. 100). Therefore, the ape of God, like his creator, may contrive works of art in various intricate and elaborate modes. In his choice of subject and form, the artist is to free himself from the temptations to please either the vulgar or the elite since "freedom is the oxygen / of the studio and gallery" (*HG*, p. 169). Art is not a single course nor an accepted method but includes in its "Babel city" all varieties and all schools, apostates and apostles. Further, the artist is not to be condemned because he fails to attain the heights; he follows his bent where it may lead. Finally, whether created for the sake of Ars, Cathedra, or the Agora, whether reflective of class, of self, or necessity, whether inspired by "Id or Sinai or Helicon" (*HG*, p. 30), art ultimately mirrors the reality of its age. Thus, although the raison d'être of art remains elusive, art itself for The Curator "is a harbor of colors / (with a hundred mosaic sail) / like Joseph's coat" (*HG*, p. 28).

The artist's task is essentially a lonely and difficult one. He endures the pain of creation " — like Everyman — / alone" (*HG*, p. 30). Although art links the ages, the artist remains solitary in his task:

the artist, like a messiah, is egoistic
and the work of art, like the art of God,
is a rhyme in the Mikado's tongue to all save the hedonistic.

(*HG*, p. 98)

However difficult the task for the artist, The Curator sees the final product as pleasurable to the art lover. The pleasure of art, like happiness, may be unpredictable, but such pleasure draws the artist and the art lover. The artist's

ritual of
light and shadow,
idiom and tone,
symbol and myth,
pleasures the lover of Art alone
in a bourne where no grapes of wrath are sown.

(*HG*, p. 99)

Through such intricacies of form, the art lover is led to pleasure:

unique as the white tiger's
pink paws and blue eyes,
Art
leaves her lover as a Komitas
deciphering intricate Armenian neums,
with a wild surmise.

(*HG*, p. 33)

Such pleasure, strangely soothing to those on life's journey, enables pilgrims to "lave the bruises of the Rain of woes" (*HG*, p. 166).

The Curator discusses what the artist is and what his relationships constitute, but in "Omicron," he reviews the sum of the artist and his affinities. He outlines the artist in relation to tradition, to himself, to the world that produced him, and to the idols of the tribe. In a series of striking metaphors, The Curator sketches in the artist's net loss, net profit, pride, élan, school, grind, temperament, sensibility, and aesthetic distance. The second halves of the metaphors, sometimes in imagery taken from nature, hint at a world hostile to the artist. All in all, the view of the artist that emerges in this series is almost that of an endangered species that somehow manages to survive.

Quite obviously, The Curator's musings are not given in the form in which they occur — the ebb and flow of the ode, its incidents, and interactions. At first, these reflections on art seem to have much to do with the gallery and little to do with Harlem. Called "Philosophy," they are indeed discursive.[14] To a large extent, they represent that mix of philosophy, sociology, economics, psychology, and aesthetics that formed much of Tolson's thought and teaching. Art and the gallery can be related to the experience of life itself, especially to that of the black man in America; but these discourses can also be related to the characterization of The

Curator and to the other artists and intellectuals as well.

These men belong to "the twilight zone of Afroamerican culture." With circumstances conspiring to render them inhabitants of a cultural ghetto (in the first sense of the word), these men and The Curator have somehow escaped, as figured by their expatriation. This escape is mental, and involves not an escape from the people but a return to them with an altered consciousness that has somehow spun out of itself its own freedom — the freedom of the artist. This freedom, as outlined by the characters, is tenuous, hardwon, and hardkept. It provides no shield from the exigencies of life in black America; it provides only a method of living with them. The Curator, seeing and valuing the artistic mode in Harlem and elsewhere, makes an aesthetic construct from the similes, metaphors, and symbols of his discourse, and this "level of talk about the arts" (*HG*, p. 14) is as central to his character as is his participation in the Zulu Club ritual.

The Curator is curiously and humanly flawed. His injunction to "'*taste* the milk of the skimmed / and *sip* the cream of the skimmers'" (*HG*, p. 125) is seen by Nkomo as an "eclipse of faith," and by The Curator as a "failure of nerve" (perhaps recalling that of Starks, and to a lesser extent of Hideho). This inner defeat and knowledge of limitations make his artistic feat all the more remarkable. The artistic feat of The Curator is his lifework of mediation between artist and art lover, and that lifework is the heart of his autobiography. Autobiographical Book I recapitulates the life process through which The Curator has shaped his world and fixed his identity. The Curator's construction of a self under conditions that endanger his "I-ness" is his real work of art:

> I cannot say I have outwitted dread,
> for I am conscious of the noiseless tread
> of the Yazoo tiger's ball-like pads behind me
> in the dark
> as I trudge ahead,
> up and up . . . that Lonesome Road . . . up and up.

(*HG*, p. 164)

Besides such veiled references to race, The Curator also makes more direct statements. Speaking from his own experience, he realizes the possible inhibiting effects of the racial situation upon a black artist. The Curator, in first envisioning his task in the Harlem Gallery, says that mixed with the reveille of the pepper bird in his brain is the "clockbird's / jackass laughter" (*HG*, p. 20). The metaphor encompasses the "scorn of white people for Negroes" so that from the beginning, The Curator's consciousness is imbued with the spirit of his people that calls him to creation and with the inhibiting spirit of whites with nothing but contempt for blacks.[15] This same contempt, and a reaction to it, is alluded to in The Curator's Zulu Club meditation upon Gertrude Stein's "the Negro suffers from nothingness." With such contempt to inhibit him, the black artist becomes a "flower of the gods . . . dwarfed at an early stage." This inhibiting factor makes more difficult the black artist's attempts to escape it by refusing to listen to false pity or to accept proferred substitutions from whites.

With this background, it is possible to understand The Curator's position in the milk-and-cream debate. The Curator claims that in the issue between integration and separation, he prefers the latter:

> "I remain a lactoscopist
> fascinated by
> the opacity of cream,
> the dusk of human nature,
> 'the light between' of the modernistic."

(HG, p. 123)

The Curator remains fascinated by the Afro-American, the twilight man, the transitional man in society and art. Challenged in this view by Nkomo, "'the Nordic's theory of the cream separator / is still a stinking skeleton!'" (*HG*, p. 123), and supported by the janitor, The Curator asserts that in such a transitional age one should "'*taste* the milk of the skimmed / and *sip* the cream of the skimmers.'" The Curator hedges, and such straddling is seen by Nkomo as an act suitable to a hollow man who refuses to dare. The Curator's attitude is complex; just as the Afro-American straddles two worlds, The Curator would advocate a kind of double consciousness, applied to race and class, as a means of accommodation in an oppressive age.

Although identified with his black brothers, The Curator is understandably skeptical about answers to the question, especially obsessive in the South, "What is a Negro?" He finds that a mythology of race has been constructed. The figure of the noble savage is contrasted with the reality of the barracoon. The Black Act of the F. F. V., the theory that one drop of blood makes a man a Negro, is contradicted by the reality of passing. The myth of the white man's abhorrence of race mixing is contradicted by "midnight-to-dawn lecheries, / in cabin and big house" (*HG*, p. 163). The stereotype of the Negro as beast is belied by the fact that the Nordic's physical attributes can be used to place him closer to the ape than the black man. The stereotype that the races are antipodal, with their different attributes immediately visible, is belied by the existence of an octoroon like The Curator. The identity of the Negro, whose definition is vital to the system of racial injustice, remains "occult."

The Curator gives, in metaphoric terms, his own definition of the Afro-American. The scarcely flattering assertion, "The Negro is a dish in the white man's kitchen —" (*HG*, p. 162), is elaborated: "a dish nobody knows" (*HG*, p. 162), tasty and exotic to some and "unsavory and inelegant" to others. After a series of "culinary art symbols," The Curator concludes that the Negro is then an "ethnic amalgam." All attempts to define the Negro, to reach Nigeridentité, are ultimately futile (*HG*, p. 164). Hatred and stereotypical thinking sabotage the enterprise, and ultimately the attempt at definition destroys black Scylla and disappears in the abyss of white Charybdis.[16] For the present, The Curator is content with the statement: "the identity of the Negro is groovy / in all-God's-children-got shoes" (*HG*, p. 171).

The Curator goes beyond mythology and stereotypical thinking in an attempt to fathom the actual situation of the black man in America. The Curator sees black and white yoked together like teeth in a pitch wheel (*HG*, p. 161), and like the oil and the wick that absorbs it (*HG*, p. 152). The black man is cheated of his heritage; the promise of American democracy is denied him, and not even Uncle-Tom antics will avail. However straitened the present, the black man can look forward to a time when the race will come into its own:

> your dreams in the Great White World
> shall be unthrottled
> by pigmented and unpigmented lionhearts,
> for we know *without no*
> every people, by and by, produces its "Chateâu Bottled."

> (*HG*, p. 159)

The Curator's last word on the subject (*HG*, p. 173) is that, despite the straitened present, the black race, and by extension the oppressed, *will* eventually triumph and come to that full flowering of life that has been so consistently denied them. In his opinions on race as on art, The Curator reveals a psyche that is troubled but not tortured, and that, despite its frustrations, is ultimately hopeful.

Finally, The Curator is of primary importance not only because his is the consciousness that dominates the ode but also because his performance in envisioning the ode is the central action of the poem itself as The Curator symbolically figures Tolson's poetic feat.

The poem begins and ends with The Curator's reflections on the performance he is enacting. In "Alpha," the main themes of the poem are seen in The Curator's preparation for his task. The *Harlem Gallery*, the creation he is to accomplish, awakens him in "a people's dusk to dawn." The artistic creation of the poem is a herald of a new order that is destructive of the older, oppressive orders. This particular creation is extended by allusion so that it recalls those artistic revelations of social corruption that enrage the powerful elite. A further extension sees this elite of the powerful and oppressive as the "Great White World" bedeviled by harbingers of Third World challenges to the status quo.

What Tolson has done is to make the specific creation of *HG* symbolic of that creativity inimical to the status quo. Further, he makes The Curator's attempts to escape the inhibiting factors spawned by an oppressive society symbolic of the attempts of the oppressed to claim an identity of their own. Thus, the specific attempts of The Curator to shake off the scorn of "Negrophobes," the whole heritage of impotence and futility read into the Afro-American past, and to assert his "I-ness," are at the same time symbolic of what Tolson saw as the real task of poetry in society in a dusk of dawn age. Simultaneously, the activity of The Curator's creative endeavor, encouraged by an ideal seen in terms of blackness and inhibited by "Negrophobes" in its working out, makes the activity of creation the central concern of the poem.

The poem, having pursued its themes of the nature of man, race, and art, rests not with The Curator's final questionings about race in "Psi" or about art in "Omega" but goes beyond these final concerns to end with the ending of creativity, the accomplished creation of the ode. Again, there are encouraging and inhibiting factors even so near the end of the ode itself, but The Curator finally rests upon his production that he sees as affirming the possibilities for life present in the deathdealing ghetto. Creativity itself has conquered. Not just Melvin Tolson's optimistic beliefs, but The Curator's enactment of those beliefs in the production of the ode is the final assertion in the poem.[17]

The Curator is a complex figure. In one aspect, he is an identifiable character in an identifiable setting. In another aspect, he is a symbolic figure through whose consciousness the poem is viewed. In another aspect, the figure represents that never completely defined area where the consciousness of the protagonist and the consciousness of the poet interact. Despite The Curator's symbolic extension, the figure is rooted in Harlem as the typical black ghetto, for through him Tolson is exploring the seemingly hopeless conditions of negation, frustration, and circumscription so often associated with urban blacks and dealt with in Tolson's own *Portraits.*

The haunted artists and intellectuals of *Portraits* have been given greater depth and focus. The characters portrayed combine in themselves the two aspects of Harlem discussed: Harlem the ghetto and Harlem the cultural center. The ambivalence seen in much of the best Harlem literature, the ambivalence implicit in the thinking of many blacks, is captured in these characters and their changing masks. Art and its freedom are depicted as rooted in the narrow circumstances of the Harlem ghetto. The integrity and artistic daring of these characters are rooted in the straitened lives and split psyches of so many of the artists and intellectuals "dwarfed at an early stage." Tolson, however, made clear that the ambivalent ghetto laughter is ultimately affirmative and, as he saw it, ultimately triumphant, as is The Curator in his envisioning of the ode.

8

Some Thematic Elements

It becomes clear that Tolson evolved his own idea of the Harlem ghetto in *HG*. It has been noted that in his master's essay, Tolson asserted that Harlem was not a "slum," "fringe," or "quarter." In *HG* he did use the term *ghetto* to designate Harlem, and in his notebooks he declared of a later Harlem: "It was not the Harlem I had known during the Harlem Renaissance when it was dubbed the Mecca of the Negro, Nigger Heaven, Black Manhattan, the City of Refuge, the Capital of the Negro World." To Tolson, the ghetto could be an apex of black life and a center of black solidarity for some of its inhabitants; at the same time, as it could be regarded as a cul de sac and Xion wheel for others. What Tolson did was capture the divided reality in a single image that captured both aspects of Harlem life. The contradictions and possible resolution inherent in some of Tolson's main themes can be paralleled by the contradictions of Harlem life.

Tolson's main concerns become more dramatic when related to Harlem, the black city within a city. One such concern of Tolson's was the idea of the black man in white society — a theme vividly presented in the very existence of Harlem. In the thirties, when most Manhattan blacks lived in Harlem, the fact of a black presence in a larger, surrounding white world was evident to the eye. As St. Clair Drake and Horace Cayton noted, it is "in the cities that the problem of the Negro in American life appears in its sharpest and most dramatic forms."[1] Questions of race poised in the Harlem setting develop an added cogency as the questions crystallize problems inherent in the Harlem situation, and the Harlem situation illustrates the questions raised.

Implicit in the Harlem situation is the tension between black and white in American society. Since, however, the nature of the conflict is determined by the fact that whites constitute the controlling majority, images figuring the conflict are those related to various kinds of resistance or nonresistance by the black minority. Since the majority forces tend to work to isolate the individual physically and psychically in the black community rather than combat him actively, "overcrowded and exploited politically and economically, Harlem is the scene and symbol of the Negro's perpetual alienation in the land of his birth."[2] Tolson's animal imagery turns on images of unequal combat in nature. These figures are those of the pig in the coils of a snake, the frog impaled on the python's fangs, and the turtle in the shark's belly. These three images all envision the black man as victim, with varying interpretations of what that condition ultimately means. The last image to be discussed, which falls outside the realm of animal imagery, is the image of black and white keys on the piano, which does not figure

94

a present reality but an ideal. These symbolic representations of the predicament of the Afro-American are not free-floating images but are assigned to various characters in a kind of symposium on the race question.

Tolson saw these discussions as related to the Harlem scene and its movements where (perhaps) for him they were most effectively dramatized: "Peeler's pig in the coils of the boa and H. Heights' sea-turtle and the shark are symols (*sic*) of two attitudes in the Negro race as regards the American dilemma: one defeatist and the other revolutionary. This all started in the 20's with the Negro of the Harlem Renaissance, when Claude McKay wrote his famous sonnet, 'If We Must Die, let us not die like hogs,' and when Marcus Garvey launched his Back-to-Africa Movement in Madison Square Garden. The forerunner of the Black Muslins [*sic*]" (Notebooks).

The image of the pig in the snake's coils was one that Tolson used early. In "A Song for Myself," the image is used:

> The snake
> Entoils
> The pig
> With Coils.
> The pig's
> Skewed wail
> Does not
> Prevail.

(Rend., pp. 49–50)

The application is probably to class as well as race in this poem. In *Libretto,* the image of the bola-boa, although not strictly the same image, figures the predatory white nations as engulfing the black victim. In *HG,* the image is referred to as part of an imaginary poem written by the fictional Dolph Peeler, and the application is primarily to race. The imaginary poem is Peeler's "Ode to the South," in which the cogent image is that of the pig, the black man in the South. The boa, whose coils surround and crush the pig, is the white man. Although the reference is to racial conditions in the South, it is plain that the application is to "many a South of the 'Great White World!'" (*HG,* p. 142). This image then figures the attitude that regards the black American as hapless and helpless victim.

The Zulu Club Wits, continuing this "bunkum session on the Negro" (*HG,* p. 138), call up more figures. Lionel Matheus amplifies the theme of the black man's essential victimhood by shifting metaphors:

> *your* Afroamerican is the frog I saw
> in a newspaper illustration:
> the harder the frog tugged outward,
> the deeper it became impaled
> on the inward-pointing fangs of the snake.

(HG, p. 90)

Kilroy, president of Afroamerican Freedom, Inc., counters this argument with another metaphor:

        you need to see, you son of a Balaam,
              the unerring beak,
              the unnerving eye,
              the untiring wing,
    of Afroamerican Freedom, *Incorporated* —
        the Republic's secretary bird.

(HG, p. 91)

The quality of the discussion is typical of many discussions about the racial situation by blacks through the years. It begins with an identification of the white man as oppressive force; the discussion continues with a skeptic's affirmation of the futility of efforts to correct injustice, to escape from the deathdealing trap. And the trail of metaphors ends with the assertion by the race-conscious president of Afroamerican Freedom, Inc. that his organization, and presumably the efforts of others involved in similar tasks of freeing the black man, will ultimately prevail and foil the white man's oppressive tactics. The animal imagery, as Tolson developed it, strikingly figures the plight of the Afro-American, but the positions that the imagery figures are not strikingly novel. They are instead typical of the kind of discussion conducted by intellectuals like these Wits or the common black man. The tenor of the discussion is important because it mirrors the feelings of the black man about his situation. On the level of feeling, the metaphors are particularly apt for the imagery expresses not merely, or not primarily, an intellectual burden, but chiefly an emotive connotation and in this sense becomes what Tolson called them — symbols of attitudes.

Another participant in the discussion, whose opinion is less common than that of Kilroy or Matheus, is Dr. Nkomo. Playing with the metaphor of the frog impaled on the snake's fangs, Dr. Nkomo gives his view: "'The little python would not let go / the ass of the frog — so the big python swallowed both'" (*HG*, p. 90). This position seems to go back to one that Tolson expressed during the thirties and afterward — the position that race prejudice is a by-product of the capitalist system, that the oppression of both black and white victims encourages race hatred so that both black and white can be further victimized as their eyes are averted from the common enemy.[3] Dr. Nkomo's metaphoric leap represents a level of thinking that goes beyond the labeling of oppressed and oppressor and attempts to ascribe causes.

Hideho Heights, people's poet, also is inspired by the original symbol of the pig in the boa's coils. Calling such an attitude defeatist, he proceeds to "Homerize a theme" (*HG*, p. 139). His metaphor involves the story of the shark and the sea turtle, representing white and black. The shark swallows the sea turtle whole; the "sly reptilean marine" withdraws head and claws into its shell and descends into "pelagic hell."

        "then . . . *then*
          with ravenous jaws
    that can cut sheet steel scrap,

> the sea-turtle gnaws
> . . . and gnaws . . . and gnaws . . .
> his way in a way that appalls —
>
> *his* way to freedom,
> beyond the vomiting dark,
> beyond the stomach walls
> of the shark."

(*HG*, p. 141)

Here again the metaphor captures both the thought and the feeling in symbols beyond paraphrase. The figure of victim turned killer, of the violence of the oppressed who seemingly capitulate to the oppressor, of the sudden, terrifying retribution, carries with it depths of feeling that haunt race relations in America and in microcosmic Harlem, scene of some violence. These interconnected metaphors, attempting to define the indefinable, the complex of thought and feeling inspired by the race question, are presented not as debaters' points but as typical responses to the black-white tensions in America.

Another, ideal view of race relations is presented by Mister Starks in the speakeasy of the twenties. A "new rhythm and melody" haunt Starks as he is inspired by Aggrey's metaphor of integration, "the notes of white keys and black keys / blended in the majestic *tempo di marcia* of Man" (*HG*, p. 130). Recalling "the African's ethnic metaphors / of the narrow upper keys and the broad lower keys" (*HG*, p. 130), Starks names his composition "Rhapsody in Black and White." Starks considers this creation as an answer to Gershwin's "sentimentality" (Notebooks). But Starks also sees his composition as perhaps only an instinctual activity and himself as an artist gambling on God or Caesar like every other artist. The musical version of integration conceived in the half-world of the speakeasy is hedged round with the doubts of its creator. This image of black man in white world, emphasizing possible harmony, is set forward with the tentativeness that many Afro-Americans might feel about such a solution. This figure embodies an ideal that had acquired the familiarity of the cliché, but which embodied a challenge to essential humanity as Tolson gave one resolution to the seemingly inevitable tension between black and white.

Tolson, in this series of figures dealing with the question of the black man enclosed in a white society in a manner analogous to black Harlem in white Manhattan of the thirties, gave several classic answers to the dilemma of the Afro-American. He gave those answers not primarily in a sociological context but in the context of the lives led, and the opinions forged from those lives, by the characters in *HG* as sociological points become aspects of felt lives.

Analogous to the theme of the black man in white society is the motif of the artist in middle-class society. Tolson here shared a perception of tension between artist and middle class not uncommon in modern literature. This perception can be found in the Harlem community as well, since, in varying forms from the twenties on, certain artists, from Hughes and McKay to Imamu Baraka, have commented upon the tension between the black artist and his black middle-class audience. Again Tolson made the debate between artist and the middle class peculiarly his own through development of this theme and the placement of it in the Harlem community.

Tolson had early seen a contradiction between the values of the artist and those of the middle class. In his later development of the "ape of God" concept, the dichotomy between artist and middle class is made plain. According to Tolson, the freedom-loving artist is opposed to the materialistic values of his society. For him, as for Eliot, our civilization can be a Waste Land that the artist, as a kind of prophet, lays bare. The response of materialistic society is to crucify the artist, like the prophet, on a cross of gold. "In our quest for material things, we have ignored the voices of the prophets and the apes of God" (Notebooks). Tolson set up a contradiction between the materialistic values of the civilization and the clearsighted vision of the artist who can sense the "odor of rottenness" in the society. Tolson regarded the middle class as one manifestation of the oppressive, power hungry, materialistic forces in the society. To typify these forces, he referred to them as the "bulls of Bashan," "cruel and bigmouthed oppressors" of the victimized classes and races. There is therefore a kind of constant tension between the values of the artist and the values of the bulls of Bashan.[4]

In "Epsilon," the kind of demand that the powerful class can make upon the artist is outlined:

> The idols of the tribe,
>   in voices puissant as the rutting calls
>   of a bull crocodile, bellow:
>   "We
>   have heroes! Celebrate them upon our walls!"

> *(HG,* p. 34)

As Tolson indicated in earlier writing, "the idols of the tribe" are associated with the narcissistic images of itself developed by the oppressive group that enshrines its mores, its hatreds, its divisiveness in a ruling mythology. To that morass of phobias necessary to retain the ruling group in power, Tolson also gave the names of Sodom or Gomorrah. According to this scheme, the artist is called upon to produce works that authenticate this mythology. Images of blood and class "infix the heart of an Ishmael" (*HG,* p. 34), and through fear and blind choice, the powerful elite can paralyze "even a Michelangelesque imagination" (*HG,* p. 35). Therefore, Tolson and The Curator can say to the bulls of Bashan, "a nod from you is worse than a brief / from the Diable Boiteux" (*HG,* p. 35). An artist who tries to temporize, to serve two masters, will finally be led to the "Belshazzarean table."

Scattered throughout the ode are further references to the demands of the bulls of Bashan and the pressures they exert. The black bourgeoisie make the same demands as the whites for narcissistic images (*HG,* p. 61). The idols of the tribe "make the psyche of the artist lean / inward like an afferent blood vessel" (*HG,* p. 95). The state, when alarmed, may constitute itself an art patron, "and initiates Project CX, / to propagandize

a rubber-stamped pyramid of Art / and to glorify the Cheops at the apex"
(*HG,* p. 169). Derain at Weimar is given as an example of an artist who
capitulated to the demands of the ruling class (*HG,* p. 67). To other forms
of art that do not propagandize the ruling mythology, the reaction of the
class is:

> only half an eye has the other half
> of the Great White World,
> where,
> at the crack of doom,
> potbellies bellylaugh.

(HG, p. 171)

While the bulls of Bashan exert nearly deadly force against the artist,
the artist himself explodes the mythology of race, class, and caste. Like
Calverton, whose "life was an everlasting battle against the idols of the
tribe,"⁵ the ape of God is constantly exploding the mythology and revealing
the reality beneath:

> Sicilian Bull and Sicilian Vespers
> *non obstante,*
>   Art's
>   yen to beard in the den
> deep down under root and stone
> fossick gold and fossil ivory
>   stands out
>   like a whale's
>   backbone.

(HG, p. 36)

The artist is iconoclastic since he perceives that the sacred images may
be embodiments of dead beliefs. One kind of triumph for art is to overcome
finally the bulls of Bashan (*HG,* pp. 98,99).

Since Tolson perceived the artist to be an iconoclast, opposed to the status
quo and bent on revealing society's inner reality, the frequent allusion to
artists who are revolutionaries or satirists or social critics is understandable.
Tolson made reference to the "great laughers," Gogol, Dickens, and Rabelais
— satirists all. In the visual arts he refers to Hogarth, Daumier, Goya, Rivera,
Orozco, Gropper, and Picasso. In different modes these artists point out
the injustice in society through paintings that expose, in scathing attacks,
the hypocrisy or corruption or foulness of contemporary society. As Tolson
saw it, such art is rooted not in mere revulsion but in a counterbalancing
human concern. Tolson's frequent references to the modern school (often
interested in African or other "primitive" art) also indicates his emphasis
on the artist as continually inventive in color, form, and relationships. Thus,
the full array of artists alluded to combines a satiric revelation of society's
corruption with a daring inventiveness and innovative spirit that leap
beyond the conventional. In content and form, these artistic heroes embody
a set of values antagonistic to those of the bourgeoisie.

Although Tolson makes allusion to painters, writers, and musicians, it is understandable that allusions by The Curator in *HG* to the visual arts should be frequent. Here, although there is a range of allusions from caveman art to modern painting, references to the French school of modern painting are most frequent. The artists most frequently alluded to are Picasso and his friends or associates. Since Picasso seems in many ways to have been an avatar of Tolson's "ape of God," a few of the ways in which he embodies Tolson's artistic ideals may be pointed out. Picasso, as one of the circle of writers and painters of a modern school in Paris in the early years of the century, appealed to Tolson's imagaination. He and his group would have seemed like a prototype of the school of artists, the circle of wild horses against the wolves, the image of artists in middle-class society.[6]

The integrity of the man Picasso is evidenced in the quotation: "the lie of the artist is the only lie for which a mortal or a god should die." Although Picasso, in a painting like *Guernica*, revealed the horrors of war, his paintings are not merely savage revelations but are touched with compassion. His work contains both humor and tragedy, and his humor encompasses irony and the saving humor that redeems his monumental works from self-parody. Despite the lonely artistic task and the revolutionary stance, the artist remains humanistic: "he is asserting, by the very act of creating the image, that compassion is possible even at the instant of man's disillusionment."[7]

Picasso's style also appealed to Tolson. Picasso was continuously inventive, going from period to period, from medium to medium, inventing new styles to suit evolving creative needs. Further, in all the complexities of his modern art, some images of Picasso's native Spanish tradition, such as bull, guitar, and shawl, remain. Picasso was also conversant with the entire artistic tradition and his works reveal that knowledge. "His mind is also stocked with the images of art history, and, like classical scholars in the literary field, he is inclined to quote, often aptly and wittily."[8] Finally, *Guernica* is the supreme example of Picasso's ability to make a public statement through the use of images that are sometimes "obscure and private." Picasso was able to combine the larger tradition and the local variation, public statement and private symbol, in a manner unmistakably modern. Picasso's art becomes a kind of hallmark of the genuine artistic effort that escapes the confines of bourgeois society.

In the black community, John Laugart typifies the "ape of God." Like other modern artists, Laugart's lifestyle and art are opposed to the bourgeois values of the society around him. Although the middle class may deride the artist, his art is capable of giving the "Gomorrhean blues / to the bulls of Bashan" (*HG*, p. 40). The black bourgeoisie react to such art as do other middle classes — with a sense of affront, with, indeed, fury. Trapped by convention, these Harlemites confuse their ignominy with glory. Tolson grounded the tension between uncompromising and apocalyptic ape of God and the opposing bulls of Bashan in the Harlem community. Tolson, with symbols of disorder and renewal from the Western tradition, from John at Patmos to Yeats and Wovoka, made his Harlem artist the harbinger of an order destructive to reigning middle-class values.

Related, but not directly parallel, to the black in white society, artist in middle-class society tensions is the dichotomy between being and not being a Negro artist. The implication in the question, "to be or not to be a Negro," has been reverberating in Harlem from Cullen to the Black Arts Movement. For a variety of reasons, the black writer of the twenties and thirties was much concerned with the concept of racial art and its implications. The way in which the black man was to treat the subject of his own black experience became entangled in racial and artistic biases. By the sixties, when a black artist could be assured of his audience, even Baraka's art still embodied the dilemma of the black artist's relation to the Western traditions. As Lloyd Brown has pointed out, while Baraka's assertions rule out the Western component, the "imaginative modes and symbolic structures" of such a work as *The System of Dante's Hell* still rely on the Western tradition that Baraka repudiates.[9] Such duality is a part of the Afro-American dilemma of which Tolson spoke:

> Poor Boy Blue,
> The Great White World
> and the Black Bourgeoisie
> have shoved the Negro artist into
> the white and not-white dichotomy,
> the Afroamerican dilemma in the Arts —
> the dialectic of
> to be or not to be
> a Negro.
>
> (*HG,* p. 146)

Beginning with the salutation, "Poor Boy Blue," a term that, according to Tolson, "Negroes use among themselves in a tragic-comic sense,"[10] Tolson half-ruefully, half-mockingly surveyed the dichotomy in which the black artist is placed. On the one hand, the white audience may expect a sensationalized, exotic treatment of "Negro material." On the other hand, the black middle class may desire an image of the black man that shows that he is essentially similar to whites in all save skin color. Both dominating forces demand an image according to their own needs and therefore place the artist in a difficult position.[11] The necessity for choice is imposed: should the artist attempt to produce art that is overtly or covertly racially didactic or not; should he attempt the universal or remain in the ethnic province? The black artist must face a personal dilemma: is he or is he not a "Negro"?

The prime example of the split personality of the artist is Hideho Heights and "the bifacial" nature of his poetry. An artist who can perform in the Afro-American and in the dominant Western tradition, Hideho exhibits two different personalities in his two modes. In the black tradition he is the assured, bardlike figure defending the racial identity in a manner approved by Afroamerican Freedom, Inc. In the modern tradition, he presents the groping, tentative self, concerned with private matters. Hideho lives the dichotomy and dilemma of the Afro-American artist. It is understood that neither the racial nor the private self is the *real* Hideho, that both are merely aspects of the split self that the racial situation in America engenders.

Hideho's split identity can be seen in the language he uses. He makes allusions to the Bible, to Eliot, and to Shakespeare in his speech. He also talks the talk of the hip urban black as he calls The Curator a "little high yellow Jesus" and peppers his speech and poetry with "black cat," "kicked the bucket," "hoodoo," "groovy blues," and "ask-your-mama."

Starks is another example of an artist who performs on two levels. In fact, Starks incorporates the two traditions in two of his compositions, as the subject matter of the "Black Orchid Suite" and the "Harlem Vignettes." Both arise from his black experience while the form of each arises from the modern idiom. It is clear that Starks meets conflicting demands upon his talent and that the works in the modern idiom conform to a felt need of his psyche. And it is clear that the dichotomy "to be or not to be a Negro" artist is extremely complicated, as complicated as Tolson's question, "What is a Negro?" It is not merely a question of idiom, nor of inspiration, nor of image; it is a question of self-definition under conflicting pressures.

HG itself exemplifies this relationship to two traditions. Although *HG* rests upon its Harlem foundations, its style is evocative of the tradition of modern poetry. Remarking upon this "white and not-white dichotomy," Ronald Lee Cansler has said: "White critics often dismiss the obviously black subject matter and concentrate on the wonderfulness of an Afro-American being able to work in the mainstream of Anglo-American verse, while many black critics apparently feel Tolson was blatantly attempting to please the Academy at the price of his soul."[12] The best-known critics of the later Tolson idiom are Allen Tate, Karl Shapiro, and Sarah Webster Fabio. Allen Tate, in the preface to *Libretto,* claimed: "For the first time, it seems to me, a Negro poet has assimilated completely the full poetic language of his time and, by implication, the language of the Anglo-American poetic tradition."[13] He also found that Tolson's approach made him "not less but more intensely *Negro* in his apprehension of the world than any of his contemporaries, or any that I have read."[14] Shapiro, having noted that Tolson outpounded Pound in *Libretto,* goes on to make about *HG* the much-discussed statement[15] that *"Tolson writes in Negro"* (*HG,* p. 12), which Shapiro calls a "possible American language" (*HG,* p. 13). Both of these poets, in their different ways, find the Tolson idiom an entry into the black American experience. Sarah Webster Fabio rejected the authenticity of Tolson's "Negro" language. "The weight of that vast, bizarre, pseudo literary diction is to be placed back into the American mainstream where it rightfully and wrongmindedly belongs."[16] Tolson's idiom and technique are either, depending on point of view, an entry or barrier to the Afro-American experience. Without arguing the merits of the case, one can see that Tolson faced the dilemma of "to be or not to be a Negro" poet in his own art.

If, for Tolson, "to be or not to be a Negro" was a dialectic, it was probably meant to be resolved in a synthesis of the two apparent opposites. In his Notebooks, Tolson indicated that one should be eclectic in technique, but "the artist must saturate those elements with his own verve, individuality, and imagination, combined with the original in subject and incitement derived from the sphere of race life and environment." He envisioned the poet as imitating the techniques of modern tradition while delving into the "heritage of folk lore and history." One can see from Tolson's comments and his work that he saw as appealing to both traditions such elements of his art as the love of metaphors and symbols shared by the moderns and blacks, and the love of word manipulation to be found in the modern and black traditions. In the same vein, Tolson's technique of juxtaposition was said to be kin to the techniques of Eliot and Pound and to the "associative organization" of the blues.[17]

The Harlem black trying to escape the toils of the "Great White World," the artist trying to escape the strictures of middle-class society, the black artist trying to escape the demands of white and black, represent social realities. But, although these tensions apply primarily to forces in society, in the working out of the ode they apply also to forces impinging upon the individual. As each of these tensions is developed, it becomes clear that it represents conflicting claims on the inner man. The individual feels the imperative to discover his essential self and in each case a powerful outside force or forces seek to impose a definition. In effect, in each of the conflicts, the self, reaching under varying constraints toward self-definition, is faced with a "to be or not to be" dichotomy.

It can be inferred that each of these conflicts — between black and white, between artist and middle class, between conflicting claims on the black artist — however contradictory it may appear, can be imagined into a synthesized unity. It would appear that Tolson saw such choices as logically false[18] but existentially true, and he looked forward to each of the contradictions being worked out, perhaps through pain, surely with difficulty, to a dusk of dawn in which the old contradictions become irrelevant. Tolson attempted to imagine a union of contradictory elements in society and to imagine a unity of the "I-ness," "Negro-ness," and "human-ness" of the individual. Roy Basler goes so far as to say, "He has taken our white-black culture and imagined it into a new thing more representative of the modern human condition than any of his contemporary peers among poets has managed to create."[19] The least that one can say is that, like concentric circles, these themes of conflict arise from the center of the Harlem ghetto, that primary and endlessly suggestive image of the black city within a city.

9

Ghetto Laughter

Tolson was much impressed by the paradox of Harlem. It had been, on the one hand,

> the mecca of the New Negro
> the capitol of the [*sic*] our world of color
> The Jerusalem of Yazoo pilgrims. The Latin Quarters
> of embryo poets and artists. The Grub Street
> of Afro-American image-breakers . . .

(Notebooks)

It was for Tolson, as *HG* exemplifies, in such gathering places as the Chitterling Shop and the Zulu Club, in such characters as Hideho Heights and Dr. Nkomo, in such rites as Heights's recital of his poem and the Zulu Club dialectics, a center of black life and achievement. At the same time, the life that flourishes arises from the strictures of the ghetto, as Harlem and the racial situation limit the expression of its life. Poverty, exploitation, and racism limit the possibilities and shape the psyches of the ghetto residents. From this duality, Tolson fashioned his poem, which is not about the balancing of tragic and comic elements in the ghetto, but about the fashioning of individual and communal identity within the limitations of "this place" and "this time."[1] The synthesis that Tolson anticipated was that of the blues, where disparate elements and modes are held in tension.

In stressing again and again the diversity, the variety of Harlem life, Tolson referred to it as a *comédie larmoyante*.[2] "Harlem is a multiple jack-in-the-box. No Negro novelist has yet pictured Harlem in its diversity — not James Baldwin, not Ralph Ellison, not Richard Wright. It will take a black Balzac to do Harlem's *comédie larmoyante*."[3] This view of Harlem as a *comédie larmoyante* is obliquely related to the concept of ghetto laughter. In discussing the humor in *HG* ("devastating in its demolitions of hypocrisies, snobbishness, half-truths, sophistries"),[4] Tolson equated "dark laughter," *lachen mit yastchekes*, and "*ghetto laughter*." He referred to Stanley Hyman's explanation of *galgenhumor*, "gallows humor." In *The Tangled Bush*, Hyman pointed out that self-destructive humor is "characteristic of all oppressed peoples. Negro humor is so similar that the Negro poet Melvin Tolson characterizes it with the Yiddish phrase *lachen mit yastchekes*, 'laughing with needles stuck in you.'"[5] Such humor, a type of gallows humor, is, according to Hyman, "life-affirming, and greatness of soul consists in cracking a joke with the needles in you, or the noose around your neck, or life almost impossible to endure.'"[6] Tolson thus related the tragicomic sense of his poetry and of black life to the affirmativeness of gallows humor.

Other black writers have touched on the tragicomic aspects of black life — the aspect so characteristic of the blues. Ralph Ellison, for example, described the blues as "an impulse to keep the painful details and episodes of a brutal experience alive in one's aching consciousness, to finger its jagged grain, and to transcend it, not by the consolation of philosophy but by squeezing from it a near-tragic, near-comic lyricism."[7] He goes on to evoke the image of a "a black boy singing lustily as he probes his own grievous wound." The dual aspect of the blueslike ghetto laughter encompasses "the agony of life and the possibility of conquering it through sheer toughness of spirit."[8] An example of the tragicomic attitude expressed in the blues is the song, "They Picked Poor Robin." The song, satirical in form, provoked laughter "even when we ourselves were its object. . . . Our defeats and failures — even our final defeat by death — were loaded upon his back and given ironic significance and thus made more bearable."[9] Thus, Ellison indicated the tragicomic implicit in much of black life. The agony is neither ignored nor indulged in as it is sung through to a resolution that, if not fully triumphant, is at least life-affirming.

From Tolson's Notebooks, one can see that dark laughter was stressed as a response to the strictures of the status quo. The ambivalent laughter of the ghetto not only embodies a personal response to pain but is linked to a communal defiance of the limitations that restrict the black man. Thus, "the ghetto's dark guffaws / that defy Manhattan's Bible Belt!"(*HG*, p. 48) and the "dark dark laughter" of Harlem's "immemorial winter" are associated with the coming of the "new New / Order of things" (*HG*, p. 57). This new order, an affirmative response springing from the confinement of ghetto living, either literally in Harlem or figuratively in black America, is captured in the penultimate stanza of the ode:

> In the black ghetto
> the white heather
> and the white almond grow.
> but the hyacinth
> and asphodel blow
> in the white metropolis!

> (*HG*, p. 173)

The tragicomic becomes a communal and an individual response that presages the race's ultimate role in the "Great White World."

This pattern — established in the content of the ode of the tragicomic, or ambivalence, of the white "flowers of hope" finally springing from the black ghetto — is repeated to some extent in the form of the ode. Of course, the convention of the greater ode itself dictates a progressive movement among its parts as one section, with its imagery and mood, is juxtaposed with other sections with different, often opposing, imagery and mood, and the movement of the whole proceeds to a final unity. The imagery and tone associated with the concreteness of ghetto life (as in the Zulu Club) are juxtaposed with the imagery and tone of The Curator's discursive musings on art and man. The public self with its images plays against the private self and its images. The whole is united by the psychological process of The Curator's making his statement, defining his self, envisioning his ode. However, Tolson's language is the most prominent feature of his artistic performance, and that elaborately constructed language working against and through the concreteness of ghetto life is an embodiment of the "phoenix riddle" that Tolson sees in Harlem.

The quality of Tolson's language has been noted by most of his critics. Some have suggested that Tolson's idosyncratic use of language was part of a conscious or unconscious parody or satire. Thus, Sarah Webster Fabio called his language "pseudo neo-classical Anglo-American diction," and goes on to say: "In certain instances, Tolson's use of the grotesque, overstatement, excesses of diction at each end of the spectrum suggest that his language was very much a part of the parody [of white stereotypes of blacks]."[10] Paul Breman asserted that "Tolson postured for a white audience, and with an ill-concealed grin and a wicked sense of humor gave it just what it wanted: an interesting darkey, using almost comically big words as the best wasp [*sic*] tradition demands of its educated house nigger."[11] Fabio and Breman see Tolson's language as a parody of the white tradition, or of white stereotypes of black tradition. Roy Basler can see the Tolson language partly as satire upon the Anglo-American school of modern poetry: "Tolson's laughing about a technique Tate's masters, Eliot and Pound, had created all too seriously as the hallmark of modern poetry."[12]

What prompts these judgments of possible parodic intention is the very energy of Tolson's performance. According to Tolson's son, his father's genuine joy at word-manipulation existed side-by-side with the ability to look and laugh at such wordplay. Dr. Tolson has pointed out that Tolson satirized intellectual as well as folk poetry, "even the futility of writing poetry." Tolson was able to look ironically even at the tradition that he was using. Further, since Tolson attempted a full rhetorical style, implicit in the very style itself is the possibility of ironic undercutting. In some instances, Tolson allowed such implications to coexist in his verse with the style that provoked it. It would seem that, regardless of the pitfalls of flatulence or pomposity or pseudoliterariness, Tolson deliberately chose for himself the rhetorical scope of *HG*.

Elements of the Tolson style are reminiscent of a modern poetic tradition. Tolson, like the modernists, tried to squeeze all verbiage from his poetry. He juxtaposed the colloquial and the literary. He used irony and wit. His diction included the use of puns. All in all, the complexity and allusiveness, together with the concreteness and precision of modern verse, can be seen in the Tolson style. Tolson's use of internal rhyme, half-rhyme, infrequent rhyme, and, rarely, no rhyme at all, and his use of such linking devices as alliteration, assonance, consonance, and repetition, and his lines with sometimes a trace of regular meter but most often rhythm derived from a freer sense of verse, all hark back to the usage of some modern poets.

Tolson, however, melded these elements from modern tradition into his own ideal of the "S-Trinity of Parnassus" — the linking of sound, sight, and sense in poetry.[13] Since Tolson composed his lines to be read aloud ("Just as sound, / not spelling, / is the white magic of rhyming / in the poet's feat" (*HG*, p. 149), the importance of such devices as internal rhyme, alliteration, and assonance, as well as occasional rhyme, becomes evident. The tone of the orator, the voice of the actor, are sometimes heard in the rhythms of his verse. The centered placement of words on the page is a device that appeals to sight as, generally, the words are so placed as to visually heighten significant phrases or words. *Sense* refers to meaning and to the image's appeal to the senses so that memory and sensual evocation are integrated into the total performance of the ode.[14] Tolson, having worked through the masters of modern poetry, used the devices he found therein as the basis of his peculiar style, a style that can be seen in the characteristic lines:

in the chatter and squawks, in the clatter and guffaws,
as a
Yarmouth yawl yaws
when struck by a rogue-elephant sea.

(*HG*, p. 47)

and

Beneath the sun
as he clutched the bars of a barracoon,
Beneath the moon
of a blind and deaf-mute Sky,
my forebears heard a Camoroon
chief, in the language of the King James Bible, cry,
"O Absalom, my son, my son!"

(*HG*, p. 135)

Tolson's distinctive voice can be heard, for instance, in his use of allusions. For one thing, the allusions in his poems are not exclusively or chiefly literary. The scope is indicated: "He alludes to physics and astronomy; medicine, drugs, astronomy; history and mythology — both classical and ethnic; art of all kinds and ages; birds, fish, marine life, animals — both rare and common, both native and African; plants, trees and shrubs; the Bible; metallurgy; ships, the ocean and sailing; and more."[15] Further, his allusions do not form a pattern of reference to an older tradition conceived as more valid than the present, or to a world larger or smaller than our own, but are intended to extend and complicate the language itself; are, in fact, an element of wordplay.

Tolson was a great manipulator of words, a lover of language. His son recalls "an almost sensual, tactile joy in manipulation of words."[16] Tolson, the teacher who insisted that the dictionary was the one necessary text, the grammarian who wrote for his students a pamphlet on "Forty Uses of the Noun,"[17] brings these kinds of interest in the art of communication to the writing of *HG*.

An example of delight in wordplay is seen in some of the names he invented or combined for the poem: Aunt Grindle's (originally Ladybird's) Elite Chitterling Shop, the Angelus Funeral Home, The Haw-Haw Club, Dipsy Muse, Crazy Cain, Hideho Heights, Wafer Waite, Joshua Nitze, Black Diamond, Shadrach Martial Kilroy, Guy Delaporte III, Bishop Gladstone Coffin, and Bishop Euphorbus Harmsworth. The invented names contain celebration and ironic undercutting of the characters and places named. This same wordplay is evident in Tolson's use of puns, such as "altars" (*HG*, p. 19), "veld" (p. 73), "high-C" (p. 33), "waxed" (p. 118), "by the heels, the land lay" (p. 39), "butt" (p. 119), "merry widow-killer" (p. 108), and "calculus" (p. 116). Tolson also liked to recombine phrases or metaphors, as in "fish of passage" (p. 39), and "chitterlings, pungent as epigrams" (p. 43).[18]

Tolson also liked to include in his performance evocation of different levels of speech. He evokes, but does not exactly represent, the colloquial level in such phrases and words as "blues a-percolating in my head" (p. 69), "out of this world" (p. 71), "whisky-frisky" (p. 78), "High as the ace of trumps" (p. 82), "hi-fied" and "high-*C*ed" (p. 85), "square as the *x* in Dixie" (p 138), "hula-hulaed" (p. 125), "cool, man, cool" (p. 134), "goof" (p. 161), "spiel" (p. 149), "groovy" (p. 171), "egghead" (p. 139), "fatheads" (p. 27), "ace boss" (p. 88), and "dingdong" (p. 89). The colloquial, as this incomplete listing illustrates, is not an occasional patch but is worked into the fabric of Tolson's diction. At the other extreme, formal diction is evoked by such words as "Guy" (p. 21), "olivets" (p. 22), "antipodal" (p. 161), "melismatic" (p. 164), "nonpareil" (p. 165), "roils" (p. 156), "Logos" (p. 156), "cabala" (p. 126), "ondoyant" (p. 147), "lactoscopist" (p. 123), "tribulating" (p. 54), "paeans" (p. 58), "prelithic" (p. 59), "irisated" (p. 59), "satyric" (p. 68), "charivari" (p. 75), " skiascope" (p. 95), "philter" (p. 95), "bourne" (p. 99), "bethel" (p. 26), "opacity" (p. 123), and "hubris" (p. 132). The extremes of diction and the whole middle ground between blend to combine a language that surprises.

Another element of the Tolson performance is his use of verbs, adjectives, and nouns in different grammatical functions. Such verbs and verbal forms as "peacocked" (p. 77), "demosthenized" (p. 77), "lamped" (p. 104), "oraculized" (p. 109), "butterflied" (p. 118), "Homerized" (p. 124), "sweethearting" (p. 124), "right-angled" (p. 138), "out-Marathons" (p. 86), "merry-andrewed" (p. 131), "pilgrimed" (p. 170), "waterlooed" (p. 78), "canyoned" (p. 81), "bellylaughed" (p. 137), "weathercocked" (p. 37), and "obelized" (p. 62) are nouns made into action words. Such adjectives as "tartufish" (p. 22), "peacocky" (p. 158), "Pasternakian" (p. 146), "Lionelbarrymorean" (p. 124), "ask-your-mama"(p. 148), "husk-of-locust" (p. 20), and "blue-devils" (p. 43) derive from nouns and verbs. Tolson necessarily takes fewer liberties in compounding nouns, but "The wherefore and the why" (p. 45) and "tri-dimensionality" (p. 45) are derived from other parts of speech.

Another element of Tolson's performance is his use of similes and metaphors. Tolson's notes indicate that he worked to fashion the complexity of language he achieved: there are pages of notes on metaphors and similes for *HG* that were used or discarded. Although some of his similes depend on startling, generally unremarked similarity between objects, Tolson characteristically yoked startlingly disparate objects at their one point of contact — generally in the word itself — so that the simile generally and the metaphors less frequently act as extended puns in an almost metaphysical sense. As he said: "the miracle of the metaphor smites / disparate realms into a form / tighter than a mailed fist" (*HG*, p. 55). The yoking often adds to the aspect of surprise and innovation in Tolson's language. Some examples of Tolson's usage are "undetected like an uninflected spoor" (p. 25), "Like Caesar's Gaul / like the papal tiara, tripartite" (p. 26), "cry, / like the noise of block tin, / crackles" (p. 31), "flat as an open Gladstone bag" (p. 32), "indicative as uterine souffles" (p. 34), "permanent as terre verte" (p. 41), "impressionistically, / like a Degas weaver" (p. 41), "bare / as the marked-off space / between the feathered areas of a cock" (p. 42), "glance / as sharp as a lance- / olate leaf" (p. 42), "patient as a weaver in haute-lisse tapestry" (p. 45), "vanity scrabbled in vain / like an anchor along the neck-gorge of a sea-floor" (p. 47), "Like a turtle's head, / the session withdrew / into its shell" (p. 52), "Art unites / as the wrist / the hand and arm —" (p. 55), "fame, / dubious as Galon's sight / of a human body dissected" (p. 56), voice "hushed / like the embrace in an accolade" (p. 22), "a *beau geste* as white as a chard" (p. 23), "Mister Starks, / airy as a floating lily pad" (p. 108), and "sunk like a ha-ha-wall" (p. 112).

A backbone of Tolson's performance is his use of the single metaphor, as in "babbitted souls" (p. 38), "Gomorrhean blues" (p. 40), "Cerebean [*sic*] ex-pug" (p. 131), "cross-nailing Second of September" (p. 67), "a democracy of zooids united by a stolon / but separated by a test" (p. 93), "her arms the flukes of a wounded whale" (p. 107), "the sigh of an old she-walrus / after a futile mating bout" (p. 100), and "the black ox treads the wine press of Harlem" (p. 110). Tolson metaphorically yoked character to a "cliché in the *Book of Homilies*" (p. 115), a verbal bouquet to a "geometer's horn angle" (p. 118), moods of The Curator to white and dark stripes surrounding a goshawk's eye (p. 120), man to juice from apples (p. 131), verse of Starks to a smokestack (p. 133), a funeral home to "Dollar Cockpit of Custom and the Van" (p. 134), Negro to "Albert Ryder of many schools" (p. 136), talk to dip of sheep (p. 139), an artistic idea to embryo head down (p. 140), integrity to marble lions that support Alhambra fountain (p. 148), a snore to a mine pump's suction hole (p. 150), The Curator to dusky Lot (p. 152), Negro artist to Brazilian owl moth (p. 153), and the patience of The Curator to that of a cow sucking lime from an antler (p. 165).

Much of the power (and the obscurity) of the ode comes from Tolson's piling metaphor upon metaphor in a sometimes bewildering, often exciting, fashion. Such metaphors as the extended definition of aspects of art (pp. 95–97) are typical of Tolson's usage from the harsh-sounding:

> The grind of the artist
> *is*
> the grind of the gravel in the gizzard
> of the golden eagle

to the quietly impressive:

the esthetic distance of the artist
is
the purple foxglove
that excites
the thermo receptors of the heart
and the light receptors of the brain.

(p. 97)

In this series, Tolson compared the net loss of the artist to the alms of the rich, his net profit to the art-fetish delivered from the flesh, his pride to the leach of green manure, his élan to the rain forest sapling, his school to a circle of wild horses, his temperament to the buffer bar of a Diesel, and his sensibility to the fancier of certain domestic fowls. In this series, the abstract aspect of the artist is yoked to a concrete reality that is itself characteristically developed into a mini-drama.

Extended metaphors, an essential part of Tolson's poetic feat, are too long to be cited here,[19] but it can be noted that in such metaphors Tolson compared the psyche to a crib (p. 23), art to a babel city (p. 26), experience to a revolving stage (p. 26), élan to the artist's spouse (p. 31), the work of art to a mediterranean domain (p. 99), a tavern to a city of refuge (p. 143), and art to the Godavari (p. 166), among others. Tolson also fashioned metaphors that tended to become symbolic images — such as the milk-and-cream metaphors and the metaphors comparing an artist's labor to a woman's giving birth (p. 144), a race to wine (pp. 158–159), and the Negro to a dish (pp. 162–163). Some metaphors are definitely subsumed into their symbolic meaning: the bulls of Bashan, the idols of the tribe, the ape of God, the dusk of dawn, the pepper bird, black Scylla and white Charybdis, the pig in the boa's coils, the secretary bird, the big python, and the turtle in the shark's belly become symbols of continuing themes of Tolson.[20]

The energy of Tolson's performance is visible in the verbal feat of *HG.* Tolson tried to compact his language, to make, as his son observed, every line a great one. Naturally, he failed, sometimes slipping into obscurity or congestion, but the effort is there in every line, and many a sinuous line detaches itself from the context and remains fixed in the memory.

Tolson, through The Curator, declared "Metaphors and symbols in Spirituals and Blues / have been the Negro's manna in the Great White World" (*HG*, p. 91). He also said in his Notebooks: "I have hidden my identity as a Negro poet in Words. Thus I am more militantly a Negro." Tolson evidently felt that his use of words, metaphors, and symbols was expressive of his Negro identity. Therefore, the complicated verbal feat of *HG* can be related in form as well as in content to the Afro-American experience. That Tolson's language can be said to capture the speech of the ordinary ghetto inhabitant is indeed questionable, but it may be said that Tolson's idiosyncratic voice reveals both a "possible American language" and the lyric impulse of the blues. More importantly, the whole poem arising from the Harlem inspiration is itself an analogy or metaphor for that stubborn life that Tolson saw surviving and ultimately triumphing in the Harlems of this world.

Arthur Davis's comment — "If the poem [HG] is to be taken as a serious attempt to depict Harlem (and, by extension, the Negro world), then it is a failure — a brilliant failure, perhaps, but still a failure"[21] — provokes a central question. After an examination of Tolson's performance in HG, and some consideration of its Harlem roots, what comment can be made about the relationship between the two? On the one hand, the Harlem roots, the acutely observed and felt participation in black life in America and in Harlem, undoubtedly contributed to the strengths of HG. Tolson's style and manner are not offset but enhanced by involvement in the concrete, tough, unexotic life of the ghetto. On the other hand, Tolson both succeeded and failed in his attempt to capture the many-sided variety of the Harlem community. He himself noted that neither Ellison nor Wright nor Baldwin has captured Harlem life; and neither has he. Perhaps Harlem life is, finally, unrecapturable. Its kaleidoscopic life, shifting with the decades like the life of the Afro-American, like the substance of America, may be ultimately beyond summing and can only be evoked by an authentic voice here or a keen observer there. But as an *evocation* of Harlem and its life, Tolson surely succeeds, for each one who has inhabited or visited Harlem has his own Harlem to recall. Tolson's Harlem may not be that of the Harlemite who said, "I love this place; this is my turf" (for all Tolson's love and exploration, Harlem was not Tolson's "turf"), but, as one who had an extraordinary capacity to participate in and observe the life of the black man in Harlem and elsewhere, Tolson managed to render an extraordinary vision of the significance of Harlem yesterday and today. And if the single vision is not the complete vision, it is one rendered in a performance as extraordinary, daring, and bold in its mode as any enacted on those Harlem streets.

Notes

Notes to Chapter 1: Introduction

1. Melvin B. Tolson, "A Poet's Odyssey," *Anger, and Beyond*, ed. Herbert Hill, p. 184; henceforth referred to as "A Poet's Odyssey." Biographical information here is based on Joy Flasch, *Melvin B. Tolson*, chapter one.

2. Moxye King, "Fresh Recognition Won by Langston Poet-Prof," *The Daily Oklahoman*, 1 April 1965.

3. Jack Bickham, "A Superbly Successful Human Being," *The Oklahoman Courier*, 29 August 1965.

4. Interview with Dr. Hobart Jarrett, former pupil of Melvin B. Tolson at Wiley College, 8 June 1975.

5. Information included in "Melvin B. Tolson (1900–1966)" in the M. B. Tolson Papers. The "Notebooks and Papers of Melvin B. Tolson" are now in the Manuscript Room, Library of Congress; henceforth referred to as Notebooks. Notebooks and Papers is a miscellany containing notes, letters, notebooks, manuscripts of unpublished works, some drafts of published poetry, and some reviews. See also Flasch, *Tolson*, p. 25.

6. Tolson tried his hand at playwriting, producing adaptations of George Schuyler's *Black No More* and Walter White's *The Fire in the Flint*, as well as other unpublished plays. See Flasch, *Tolson*, p. 27.

7. M. B. Tolson to J. Marie McCleary, 5 March 1942.

8. See Robert J. Huot, "Melvin B. Tolson's *Harlem Gallery*: A Critical Edition with Introduction and Explanatory Notes," Ph.D. diss., University of Utah, 1971, p. 35.

9. Tolson mentions, as objects of study Lowell, Thomas, Williams, Pound, Shapiro, Auden, *Partisan Review, Sewanee Review, Accent, Virginia Quarterly*, Ransom, Tate, Spender, and Burke among others (Notebooks). He was also willing to revise *Libretto* in response to Allen Tate's criticism.

10. Interview, Jarrett.

11. Interview, Dr. Melvin B. Tolson, Jr., 2 June 1975.

12. Notebooks, Tolson's brackets. Further remarks on scholar and poet, *passim*.

13. Tolson, "The Negro Scholar," *Midwest Journal*, Notebooks.

14. Tolson, *Rendezvous with America*, pp. 28–29; henceforth referred to as *Rend.*

15. As has been indicated, Tolson was late in achieving substantial poetic recognition and never achieved any great financial success. In the sixties, Tolson's salary at Langston was approximately $7,000.

16. Interview, Jarrett.

17. Tolson, "Caviar and Cabbage," *Washington Tribune*, 17 February 1940; henceforth referred to as "C. and C."

18. Tolson, in "A Poet's Odyssey," p. 194, and Flasch, in *Tolson*, p. 15, indicate that the years were 1930–1931, but the Columbia University registrar's office lists the dates as 1931–1932, and Tolson himself, in "C. and C." columns (29 June 1940 and 6 May 1944), asserted that he was doing a study of the Renaissance at Columbia, 1931–1932. Further, in "The Odyssey of a Manuscript," Notebooks, p. 6, undated but perhaps written during the thirties, Tolson stated that in 1932 he was "a graduate student in an Eastern University." Work henceforth referred to as "Odyssey."

19. Interview, Jarrett.

20. Tolson, *Libretto for the Republic of Liberia*, pp. 64–65, 287 n; henceforth referred to as *Libretto*.

21. Tolson, "A Man against the Idols of the Tribe," *Modern Quarterly*, p. 30. Reference to Calverton as mentor by Mrs. Ruth Tolson in interview, 24 October 1974.

22. See Flasch, *Tolson*, pp. 29–31. Tolson also spent time with Calverton during Tolson's summer teaching stints at Morgan College. Information contained in letter to the author from Una Corbett, 17 July 1975.

23. Alfred Kazin, *Starting Out in the Thirties*, pp. 62–67.

24. Ibid., p. 63.

25. Richard K. Barksdale to author, 8 January 1975.

26. See views expressed by Oliver Cox, *Caste, Class and Race*. Cox mentions Tolson in the preface to the book.

27. Tolson to Ben and Kate Bell, 28 December 1961.

28. "C. and C." columns (2 January 1939 and 10 February 1940), and Notebooks.

29. Joel Conarroe, *William Carlos Williams'* Paterson, p. 10.

30. Discussions of the city in literature are plentiful, as evidenced by the Modern Language Association's 1977 seminar on the topic. However, see also my "The Idea of the City of God," Ph.D. diss., Columbia University, 1965.

31. Tolson, *A Gallery of Harlem Portraits*, edited, with an afterword, by Robert M. Farnsworth, was published by the University of Missouri Press in 1979.

32. Babette Deutsch, *Poetry in Our Time*, p. 48.

Notes to Chapter 2: Harlem, the Double Image

1. This chapter deals principally with the Harlem community of the early thirties with some attention necessarily paid to the immediately preceding decade and to the later years of the thirties.

2. J. Walker Harrington, "What Tempts Harlem's Palate," *New York Times*, 15 July 1928; *Harlem on My Mind*, ed. Allon Schoener, p. 73.

3. James Weldon Johnson, *Black Manhattan*, p. 3; Clyde Vernon Kiser, *Sea-Island to City*, p. 191; Claude McKay, *Harlem: Negro Metropolis*, p. 16; Roi Ottley, *New World A-Coming*, p. 1; Schoener, *Harlem on My Mind*, p. 1.

4. Even before the concentration of blacks in Harlem and the development of a large black community there, the basis of a separate community had already been laid and something of its distinctive quality had been anticipated in other parts of Manhattan. The populations of small, scattered communities of blacks in Manhattan, under pressure from the Great Migration of 1914–1918, coalesced in Harlem and became not black neighborhoods but a black city with the largest single concentration of urban blacks in this country. For an account of early black life in Manhattan, see Johnson, *Black Manhattan*, and Gilbert Osofsky, *Harlem: The Making of a Ghetto*.

5. *New York City Guide*, Federal Writers Project, Works Progress Administration, p. 257.

6. Myrtle Pollard, "Harlem As Is . . . New York 1936-37," Master's essay, College of the City of New York, 1937, p. 350.

7. Paul Morand, *New York*, p. 270.

8. Stephen Graham, "Harlem," *New York Nights*, p. 247.

9. Wallace Thurman, *The Blacker the Berry*, p. 202, described a typical Harlem theater: "There was as much, if not more, activity in the orchestra and box seats than there was on the stage."

10. Wilbur Young, "Dances Originating in Harlem," in "Research Study Compiled by Workers of the Writers Program of the Works Projects Administration in New York City for 'Negroes of New York,'" 1939, p. 5. Henceforth referred to as "WPA Papers."

11. Ottley, *New World*, p. 63; see also Ira De A. Reid, "Mrs. Bailey Pays the Rent," *Ebony and Topaz*, ed. Charles S. Johnson, p. 146: "There has been an evolution in the eclat of the rent party since it has become 'Harlemized.'"

12. William R. Dixon, "The Music of Harlem," *Harlem: A Community in Transition*, ed. John Henrik Clarke, p. 65.

13. Johnson, *Black Manhattan*, p. 162.

14. Alvin Moss, "Enlargement Points for Chapter I," WPA Papers.

15. Johnson, *Black Manhattan*, p. 232.

16. The public life of the community was chronicled by the black press. There were the New York papers: *Amsterdam News*, *Age*, and *New York News;* there was a New York office of the *Pittsburgh Courier*; and there had been, and continued to be, the radical press, such as *Messenger*, *Challenge*, *The Voice*, *Crusader*, and

Emancipator, all proposing radical solutions to the problems of the day as applied to blacks. Later, there were special interest papers such as *The New Day*, *Spoken Word*, *Voice of Ethiopia*, and *Negro World*. And there were gossip sheets like *Interstate Tattler*.

17. Wesley Curtwright, "The Church Today," WPA Papers, p. 15.

18. Ibid.

19. Odette Harper, "Adam Clayton Powell," WPA Papers, p. 21.

20. Ottley, *New World*, p. 222.

21. *Hunton School Bulletin of Information and Announcement of Courses*, 1933–1934, 1934–1935; "YMCA," Vertical File, Schomburg Collection, n.d.

22. "Announcement," The New York Public Library, Countee Cullen Branch, Vertical File, Schomburg Collection, n.d.

23. Osofsky, *Making of a Ghetto*, p. 181.

24. See comment of W.E.B. Du Bois, "'Krigwa Players Little Negro Theatre,' The Story of a Little Theatre Movement," *Crisis*, p. 136: "The administration of the library has in the last few years changed from an attitude of aloofness from its Negro surroundings, and even resentment, to an attitude which recognizes that this library is serving a hundred thousand Negroes or more. It specializes on books which Negroes want to read; it subscribes to their periodicals and has lectures and art exhibits which attract them."

25. Information found in files of Countee Cullen Branch, The New York Public Library.

26. By 1930, two-thirds of black New York City dwellers lived in the Harlem community, compared to one-half in 1920 and one-third in 1910; Robert Weaver, *The Negro Ghetto*, p. 49.

27. St. Clair Drake and Horace Cayton, *Black Metropolis*, p. 391.

28. Mary White Ovington, *Portraits in Color*, p. 21. Harrison worked with Garvey organizations; however, there have been assertions that some Garvey ideas were borrowed from Harrison and his League. See "Hubert Harrison," WPA Papers.

29. Du Bois, later a harsh critic of Garvey, conceded in 1921 that the "main lines of the Garvey plan are perfectly feasible," and called Garveyism "one of the most interesting spiritual movements of the modern Negro world" despite qualifications; "Marcus Garvey (II)," in *The Seventh Son*, ed. Julius Lester, pp. 181–83.

30. Marcus Garvey, "The Race Wants Strong-minded Statesmen and Staunch Leaders," *The Negro World*, 8 October 1921; Schoener, *Harlem on My Mind*, p. 55.

31. McKay, *Harlem: Negro Metropolis*, pp. 143, 157; Johnson, *Black Manhattan*, p. 258; Ovington, *Portraits in Color*, p. 18: "In retrospect Garvey seems to most white Americans a figure in vaudeville, or, in the poetic words of the New York *World*, 'the eternal child playing "let's pretend."'"

32. Ovington, *Portraits in Color*, p. 31.

33. *New York City Guide*, p. 260.

34. McKay, *Harlem: Negro Metropolis*, p. 49.

35. *New York City Guide*, p. 260.

36. Ibid.

37. Pollard, "Harlem As Is," p. 247.

38. Ottley, *New World*, p. 82.

39. "The Job Ceiling *subordinates* Negroes but does not *segregate* them." Drake and Cayton, *Black Metropolis*, p. 113. Job ceiling refers to the fact that certain better-paying jobs were reserved for whites and that beyond a certain level blacks were not allowed.

40. McKay, *Harlem: Negro Metropolis*, pp. 186–91.

41. [Richard Wright,] "Portrait of Harlem," *New York Panorama*, p. 141.

42. Du Bois in 1934 resigned from the NAACP in a dispute over the organization's continued opposition to segregation in all forms, a position with which he then partially disagreed.

43. Johnson, *Black Manhattan*, p. 136.

44. "New Yorkers constituted more than one-half of the executive and general committees," Seth Scheiner, *Negro Mecca*, p. 202.

45. Nathan Huggins, *Harlem Renaissance*, p. 48.

46. Loften Mitchell, *Black Drama*, p. 100.

47. Tolson contacted the Experimental Theatre in hopes that it would produce one of his plays; "C. and C.," 6 February 1943.

48. Romare Bearden, "The 1930's — An Art Reminiscence," *New York Amsterdam News*, 18 September 1971, p. D24.

49. Ibid., p. D26.

50. These artists devoted themselves to black subjects and some, like Aaron Douglas, showed African influences. Romare Bearden painted popular types of Harlemites and Alston portrayed the Harlem blacks of cabarets and dance halls.

51. "Holstein Set Free by Abductors," *New York Times*, 24 September 1924; Schoener, *Harlem on My Mind*, p. 76.

52. Sadie Hall, "Caspar Holstein," WPA Papers, p. 3.

53. McKay, *Harlem: Negro Metropolis*, p. 102.

54. Ibid., p. 112.

55. Ottley, *New World*, pp. 173–74.

56. Langston Hughes, *The Big Sea*, p. 245.

57. Edward Waldron, "Walter White and the Harlem Renaissance," *CLA Journal*, p. 438.

58. Abram Hill, "The Barefoot Prophet," WPA Papers, p. 3.

59. Ottley, *New World*, p. 64.

60. Wilbur Young, "Exponents of the Dance," WPA Papers, p. 3.

61. Information obtained in interview with James Cannon, longtime Harlem resident and former musician, 15 November 1974.

62. Ottley, *New World*, pp. 220–21.

63. Johnson, *Black Manhattan*, p. 267.

64. Bruce Kellner, *Carl Van Vechten and the Irreverent Decades*, p. 202.

65. Huggins, *Harlem Renaissance*, p. 209. Attesting to the public nature of Cullen's life and career was the *Amsterdam News* headline announcing his marriage to Yolande Du Bois: "Countee Cullen Weds Daughter of Dr. Du Bois. Harlem Folk Throng to Marriage of Negro Poet to Miss Nina Y. Du Bois. He Won Guggenheim Prize. Father of Literary Leader Officiates at Their Nuptials."

66. E. Franklin Frazie Journal of Sociology, p. 88.

67. Robert Weaver, *The Negro Ghetto*, p. 48.

68. Drake and Cayton, *Black Metropolis*, p. 115.

69. McKay, *Harlem: Negro Metropolis*, p. 21.

70. Frazier, *Black Bourgeoisie*, p. 53.

71. Ibid., pp. 35–36.

72. Ibid.

73. James Ford, *Hunger and Terror in Harlem*, p. 18.

74. New York City Mayor's Commission, *The Negro in Harlem*, p. 63.

75. Ibid., p. 53.

76. Ibid., p. 11.

77. McKay, *Harlem: Negro Metropolis*, p. 26.

78. Osofsky, *Making of a Ghetto*, p. 130.

79. Kenneth Clark, *Dark Ghetto*, p. 141.

80. Mayor's Commission, *The Negro in Harlem*, pp. 68–73.

81. Ibid., p. 73.

82. Ibid., p. 81.

83. Kiser, *Sea-Island*, p. 38. "But this so-called partial victory, instead of opening the way for the appointment of Negro physicians and interns in the Municipal hospitals, is turning out to be a policy of systematic racial discrimination." Mayor's Commission, *The Negro in Harlem*, p. 92.

84. Ford, *Hunger*, p. 6.

85. One example of the change in image can be seen in the shuffle of stereotypes in Jack Lait's and Lee Mortimer's *New York Confidential:* "The kindly, grinning, amiable and frequently obsequious Negro was disappearing. In his place came a truculent, class-conscious, race-conscious and union-conscious, embittered man or woman, resenting whites and demanding white wages" (p. 115).

86. Mayor's Commission, *The Negro in Harlem*, subcommittee appendix, p. 1.
87. Ibid., p. 11.
88. Clark, *Dark Ghetto*, p. 119.
89. Langston Hughes, "My Early Days in Harlem," *Harlem: A Community in Transition*, p. 63.
90. Ovington, *Half a Man*, p. 26.
91. See Osofsky, *Making of a Ghetto;* McKay, *Harlem: Negro Metropolis;* Ottley, *New World.*
92. Johnson, *Black Manhattan*, p. 281.
93. [Wright,] "Portrait of Harlem," p. 151.
94. Drake and Cayton, *Black Metropolis*, p. 755.

Notes to Chapter 3: Harlem and the Literary Artist

1. For a discussion of Harlem as cultural capital see Harold Cruse, *The Crisis of the Negro Intellectual*, and "Harlem's Special Place in the 'Theory of Black Cities,' Black and White," in *Black World*, pp. 9-40. Julian Mayfield, for one, disagrees with Cruse's view of Harlem, asserting that Cruse neglects Chicago and other cities; "Childe Harold," *Negro Digest*, pp. 26-27.
2. William Pickens, *The New Negro*, p. 236.
3. Ibid., p. 14.
4. Some of the younger writers and artists attempted on two occasions to produce their own literary magazines, *Fire* and then *Harlem*.
5. Arna Bontemps, "The Awakening: A Memoir," *The Harlem Renaissance Remembered*, ed. Arna Bontemps, p. 1.
6. Mae Gwendolyn Henderson, "Portrait of Wallace Thurman," *Harlem Renaissance Remembered*, p. 158.
7. W. E. B. Du Bois, quoted in "To Encourage Negro Art," *Crisis*, p. 11.
8. See Alain Locke, "Foreword," *The New Negro*, ed. Alain Locke, p. xvii.
9. W. E. B. Du Bois, "American Negro Art," *The Modern Quarterly*, pp. 53-54.
10. Claude McKay, *A Long Way from Home*, p. 321.
11. W. E. B. Du Bois, "Criteria of Negro Art," *The Seventh Son*, II, p. 321.
12. Ibid., p. 319; Locke, "Negro Youth Speaks," *New Negro*, pp. 51, 52.
13. Claude McKay, *Long Way*, p. 322.
14. "Let us hope that the new Negro and the new white man will soon be able to grasp congratulatory hands at the summit." Countee Cullen, "The Dark Tower," *Opportunity*, 5 (April 1927), 118.
15. Langston Hughes, *The Big Sea*, p. 228.
16. E. Franklin Frazier, "Racial Self-Expression." *Ebony and Topaz*, p. 120; W. E. B. Du Bois, "The Looking Glass: Negro Art," *Crisis*, p. 105.
17. At a somewhat later period, Robert Littell, in "Everyone Likes Chocolate," *Vogue*, p. 127, noted "something at once innocent and richly seasoned, childlike and jungle-spiced, which is the gift of the Negro. . . . We go to Harlem not only for amusement, but out of homesickness for a land we have lost."
18. Langston Hughes, "The Negro Artist and the Racial Mountain," *The Black Aesthetic,*, ed. Addison Gayle, Jr., p. 178.
19. Albert C. Barnes, "Negro Art and America," *The New Negro*, pp. 24-25; Carl Van Doren quoted in Arna Bontemps, "The Awakening: A Memoir," *Harlem Renaissance Remembered*, p. 13; Carl Van Vechten, "The Negro in Art: How Shall He Be Portrayed: A Symposium," *Crisis*, p. 219.
20. W.E.B. Du Bois, "American Negro Art," *Modern Quarterly* (October-December 1925), 54.
21. *Crisis*, 31 (March 1926), 29. The series, with its varying replies, continued with interruption through November 1926.
22. Langston Hughes, "The Negro Artist," *Crisis*, p. 278; Georgia D. Johnson, *Crisis*, p. 193; Countee Cullen, "The Dark Tower," *Opportunity*, p. 90.
23. Hughes, *Big Sea*, p. 8.

24. James Weldon Johnson, *Along This Way*, p. 335.
25. McKay, *Long Way*, p. 229.
26. Alain Locke, "The Negro in American Culture," *An Anthology of American Negro Literature*, ed. V.F. Calverton, p. 264.
27. George Schuyler, "The Negro-Art Hokum," *The Nation*, p. 663.
28. Countee Cullen, ed., *Caroling Dusk*, p. 180.
29. Ibid., p. xi. Cullen, quoted in Winifred Rothernell, "Countee Cullen sees Future for the Race," *St. Louis Argus*, 3 February 1928.
30. Cullen noted that his poetry did not always follow this poetic ideal: "'In spite of myself, however, I find that I am activated by a strong sense of race consciousness. This grows upon me, I find, as I grow older, and although I struggle against it, it colors my writing." Cullen, quoted by Darwin Turner, *In a Minor Chord*, p. 70. For full discussion, see "Countee Cullen: The Lost Ariel," pp. 60–88.
31. Letter to Walter White, 7 September 1925, quoted in Edward Waldron, "Walter White and the Harlem Renaissance," *CLA Journal*, p. 451.
32. Hughes, "Negro Artist," *Opportunity*, p. 175.
33. Wallace Thurman, "Negro Poets and Their Poetry," *The Bookman*, p. 559. Thurman further remarks, the "Negro Artists and the Negro," *New Republic*, p. 38: "They seem unable to fathom the innate difference between a dialect farce committed by an Octavus Roy Cohen to increase the gaiety of Babbitts and a dialect interpretation done by a Negro writer to express some abstract something that burns within his people and sears him."
34. James Weldon Johnson, ed., *The Book of American Negro Poetry*, p. 206.
35. Ibid., p. 7.
36. Du Bois, "The Negro College," *The Seventh Son*, II, p. 219.
37. Hughes, *Big Sea*, p. 247.
38. Locke, "Harlem: Dark Weather-Vane," *Survey Graphic*, p. 457.
39. See Johnson, *Along This Way*, pp. 380–81, for a discussion of possibilities of two Harlems.
40. McKay, *Harlem: Negro Metropolis*, p. 254.
41. Wilson Record, *The Negro and the Communist Party*, pp. 109–10.
42. Jerre Mangione, *The Dream and the Deal*, p. 50.
43. Ibid., p. 259.
44. James Weldon Johnson, "Foreword," *Challenge*, p. 2.
45. Richard Wright, "Blueprint for Negro Writing," *New Challenge*, p. 53. Other articles referred to in same issue: Alain Locke, "Spiritual Truancy," pp. 81–85; Eugene Holmes, "Problems Facing the Negro Writer Today," pp. 69–75.
46. Wright, "Blueprint," *New Challenge*, pp. 54, 58, 65, 85; Holmes, "Problems," p. 75.
47. Wright, "Blueprint," *New Challenge,*, p. 54.
48. Marion Minus, coeditor with Richard Wright of *New Challenge*, anticipated some later positions of *New Challenge* writers in an article in the last issue of *Challenge*: "Present Trends of Negro Literature," *Challenge*, p. 11.
49. Allyn Keith, "A Note on Negro Nationalism," *New Challenge*, p. 69.
50. LeRoi Jones, "Philistinism and the Negro Writer," *Anger, and Beyond*, ed. Herbert Hill, p. 56.
51. Wright, "I Tried to Be a Communist," *Atlantic Monthly* (August 1944), pp. 54, 62.
52. Wright, "Blueprint," *New Challenge*, pp. 58,64.
53. Harold Cruse, *The Crisis of the Negro Intellectual*, p. 63.
54. Tolson appeared at the Fisk University Centennial Writers Conference on "The Image of the Negro in American Literature" in April 1966. Although many of the younger writers did not share his views on poetic style, he could be regarded as the "grandfather of the conference." For complete details, see David Llorens,"Seeking a New Image," *Negro Digest*, pp. 60, 62–63.
55. The movement of the discussion from the thirties to the sixties is not intended to suggest that nothing of literary importance occurred in the forties and fifties. Just the names of Harlem-associated writers like James Baldwin and Ralph Ellison would belie that suggestion. For a full discussion of intellectual currents during the forties

and fifties, see Cruse, *Negro Intellectual.*

56. As has been remarked, the Jones/Baraka spiritual quest paralleled a movement of black cultural history. His first exposure was in the Village where he (as well as Corso, O'Hara, C. Olson, W. Burroughs, and E. Davis) was associated with the Black Mountain School group of contemporary poetry. As writer and editor, Jones was concerned with and influenced by the "Anglo-Eliotic" tradition as well as the more meaningful tradition of Williams, Pound, the Imagists, and the Symbolists. Jones, however, already regarding the American establishment as sterile and deathdealing, moved beyond his white contemporaries' rejection of American middle-class society to a rejection of white society on the basis of a philosophy erected on the experience of the Afro-American. For complete discussion, see Theodore Hudson, *From LeRoi Jones to Amiri Baraka.*

57. Kenneth Clark, "Haryou: An Experiment," *Harlem: A Community of Transition,* ed. John H. Clarke, pp. 210–11.

58. Larry Neal, "The Black Arts Movement," *The Drama Review,* p. 32.

59. Hudson, *From LeRoi Jones,* pp. 21, 22.

60. Ibid., pp. 21, 24.

61. Neal, "Black Arts," *The Drama Review,* p. 39.

62. Carolyn Gerald, "The Black Writer and His Role," *Negro Digest,* p. 45.

63. Imamu Amiri Baraka, "City of Harlem," *Home: Social Essays,* p. 93.

64. Baraka, "State/meant," *Home,* p. 251.

65. Ibid.

66. Hudson, *From LeRoi Jones,* p. 43.

67. Larry Neal, "Some Reflections on the Black Aesthetic," *The Black Aesthetic,* p. 31.

68. Hudson, *From LeRoi Jones,* p. 51.

69. James Emmanuel,"Blackness Can: A Quest for Aesthetics," *The Black Aesthetic,* p. 207.

70. Baraka, "The Revolutionary Theatre," *Home,* p. 211.

71. Esther Jackson, "LeRoi Jones (Imamu Amiri Baraka): Form and the Progression of Consciousness," *CLA Journal,* p. 34.

72. Clyde Taylor, "Black Folk Spirit and the Shape of Black Literature," *Black World,* 21 (August 1972), 33.

73. Hudson, *From LeRoi Jones,* p. 137.

74. Baraka, "Revolutionary Theatre," *Home,* p. 212.

75. Neal, "Black Arts," *The Drama Review,* p. 29. Although these techniques result in a distinctive form, one critic has asserted that some of these have their roots in modern poetry: such techniques as "unconventional capitalization, line and word spacing, abbreviations, unclosed parentheses and quotation marks, esoteric images and the like — are actually derivative of E. E. Cummings, T. S. Eliot, Ezra Pound, William Carlos Williams, and Charles Olson à la LeRoi Jones." Bernard Bell, "New Black Poetry: A Double-Edged Sword," *CLA Journal,* p. 43.

76. Melvin Dixon, "Guidelines: Black Theatre: The Aesthetics," *Negro Digest,* p. 42; Neal, "Black Arts," *The Drama Review,* p. 32.

77. Kawaida's seven principles are derived from African spirituality.

Notes to Chapter 4: Tolson's Harlem Portraits

1. Melvin B. Tolson, "Odyssey of a Manuscript," p. 7. There are some references to Harlem in the unpublished "All Aboard" (undated), but the works mentioned here follow the main line of development to *Harlem Gallery.*

2. Reference to *A Gallery of Harlem Portraits* are cited as *Portraits,* with page numbers of the volume published by the University of Missouri Press in 1979.

3. Joy Flasch, *Melvin B. Tolson,* p. 30.

4. Tolson was probably referring to the manuscript when, in "C. and C.," 6 January 1940, he said a manuscript of his was turned down because he would not rewrite to suit an editor: "I will not commit a literary abortion."

5. Tolson, "The Harlem Group of Negro Writers," Master's essay, Columbia University, 1940; hereafter referred to as Essay with page numbers. At one point, Tolson considered beginning the essay with his sonnet.

6. Nathan Huggins, *Harlem Renaissance*, pp. 200–201.

7. Tolson, "A Poet's Odyssey," *Anger, and Beyond*, p. 195; hereafter cited with page numbers.

8. Tolson spoke of a Harlem hospital, and, although there were private hospitals in Harlem, the municipal hospital was Harlem Hospital, and Harlemites customarily thought of this institution.

9. Tolson, "Key Words," Notebooks, p. 3; henceforth referred to as "K. W. " with page numbers.

10. There is, of course, the implication that artists of such scope are necessary to capture the black experience and the Harlem scene.

11. Such activity as organizer parallels one phase of Tolson's career.

12. Tolson, *Harlem Gallery*, p. 61; henceforth cited as *HG*.

13. Interview, Mrs. Ruth B. Tolson, 23 October 1974.

14. Synchronization of "sight, sound, and sense" in poetry. See discussion in chapter nine.

15. Suggested by Dr. Robert Bone, Professor of English, Teacher's College, Columbia University.

16. W.E.B. Du Bois, *Dusk of Dawn*, p. 1.

17. Ibid., p. 2.

18. Tolson, "Ape of God," Notebooks.

Notes to Chapter 5: The Harlem Milieu

1. This kind of movement has been noted by Tolson in his Notebooks: "Start horizontally from fact to metaphor; then the idea moves vertically from metaphor to symbol at the apex of language."

[symbol] C

[metaphor] B   A [historical fact]

2. The theater had been built by Oscar Hammerstein I in 1889 before black people moved to Harlem in numbers (Gilbert Osofsky, *Harlem: The Making of a Ghetto*, p. 77). Tolson was fascinated by such names. In his papers Tolson mentioned names of organizations and businesses beginning with the word "Harlem" that typify the varied aspects of Harlem community life. Among those mentioned is the Harlem Opera House.

3. There was an actual establishment by this name where Langston Hughes and Randy Weston performed at one time. Tolson's name, however, was probably coincidental.

4. The debasement of the name and connotation of the Italian painter to the name of the Italian desk sergeant at a Harlem police station is an example of Tolson's ironic usage. See note 6 below.

5. Tolson's neighborhood in Harlem was subject to this kind of treatment at about the time of his residence there.

6. Aunt Grindle's had been named Aunt "Lady Bird," but Tolson changed the name after Lyndon Johnson had been elevated to the White House ("Key Words," p. 3).

7. Gertrude Stein, *The Autobiography of Alice B. Toklas*, p. 292.

8. Dancing reminiscent of that of entertainer Earl "Snakehips" Tucker. Although Huot regards Snakehips as a "habitué of the Harlem nightspots" (p. 168), thus making his dance spontaneous, it seems likely that Snakehips was a paid entertainer; Robert J. Huot, "Melvin B. Tolson's *Harlem Gallery:* A Critical Edition," Ph.D. diss., University of Utah, 1971.

9. Ibid., p. 169.

10. Tolson was familiar with this tradition. "As a boy, he heard the work songs on Mississippi River steam boats, the legends of the Jesse James country, the blues in St. Louis and Kansas City." "Melvin B. Tolson (1900–1966)," included in the M. B. Tolson papers.

11. Tolson referred to John Henry as the "Beowulf of the Afro-American" (Joy Flasch, *Melvin B. Tolson*, p. 116). His notebooks indicate that he saw the John Henry material as epic. He attempted a version of John Henry as a companion piece to *Libretto* in "John Henry: His Legend."

12. In "Big Bessie," there are the blues lines:

> "*Black folks sing an' clown an' dance*
> *'Cause dey wanta cry.*"

13. There seems to have been something approximating the Zulu Club Wits during Tolson's life. Jack Bickham, "Flowers of Hope," *The Oklahoma Orbit (The Sunday Oklahoman)*, 29 August 1965, p. 9, noted that Tolson named his basement, with its African artifacts, the Zulu Room, where people often gathered for talk. Mr. Oliver Le Grove, in a letter to Tolson, remarked that he wished it had been possible to be with the Zulu Wits and that he would have to content himself with his copy of *HG*. Dudley Randall, in "Melvin B. Tolson: Portrait of the Poet as Raconteur," *Negro Digest*, p. 57, mentions a Zulu Club like that in *HG* and states that chapters "have been formed in various cities across the country." The whole matter is tenuous, but certainly something like the Zulu Club ingredients of talk, food, drink, and companionship did exist.

14. Tolson, "Key Words," p. 7.

15. As such, the Zulu Club is the opposite of the other nightclub described, the speakeasy owned by Dutch Schultz . This underworld retreat is described as Niflheim, guarded by a kind of Cerberus, a place of darkness and cold opposed to the sunshine of the Zulu Club. The speakeasy is also described as a twilight (not dusk of dawn) world whose dissonance is "*directed by a skeleton whose baton is a scythe*" (*HG*, p. 129). This unsavory world, directed by the dregs of white society able to buy and exploit blacks, can be seen as analogous to the corruption of a world in decline as the "sunshiniest place" is analogous to a people's dusk of dawn.

16. Romare Bearden, "The 1930s — An Art Reminiscence," p. D24.

17. Tolson, "Key Words," p. 3.

18. Tolson, "A Poet's Odyssey," p. 194.

19. Huot, "Critical Edition," p. 2.

20. The Harlem Gallery is a controlling image rather than a framing device because of the subject of the ode. The poem in one aspect is about art in society. The image of the Harlem Gallery weaves in and out, never far from the speaker, The Curator, the subject of art, nor the subject of the black man in America. It illustrates and composes the tensions inherent in these subjects.

21. Tolson, "Key Words," p. 3.

22. Although Tolson indicated that the ghetto refers to poor whites and poor blacks, it seems probable that a first reading would involve an association with color, not class distinction (Jack Bickham, "Flowers of Hope," *The Oklahoma Orbit*, p. 8).

Notes to Chapter 6: Characters

1. It is not possible to date these lists exactly since the Notebooks are generally undated.

2. Many of those named were known personally to Tolson.

3. Joy Flasch, *Melvin B. Tolson*, pp. 39, 44, states that Tolson knew Papa Handy. He also knew personally Bessie Smith, Mister Jelly Roll, and Leadbelly.

4. Eugene Arden, "The Early Harlem Novel," *Phylon*, p. 30.

5. Ibid.

6. Evidently, stripteasing as such was not allowed in Harlem clubs although there

had been white stripteasers at the Apollo Theater.

7. Melvin B. Tolson, "A Poet's Odyssey," p. 195.

8. Snelson, no title, WPA Papers.

9. See St. Clair Drake and Horace Cayton, *Black Metropolis*, p. 543, for description of "Upper Shady" in Chicago.

10. Flasch, *Tolson*, p. 86; "Fa," *HG*, lines 125–28, p. 21.

11. Tolson, "Key Words," p. 3.

12. E. Franklin Frazier, *Black Bourgeoisie: The Rise of a New Middle Class in the United States*, p. 195.

13. Arthur Davis, "Jesse B. Semple: Negro American," *Phylon*, p. 28.

14. Arthur Davis, "The Harlem of Langston Hughes' Poetry," *Images of the Negro in American Literature*, ed. Seymour Gross and John Hardy, p. 195.

15. Wilfred Cartey, "Four Shadows of Harlem," *Negro Digest*, p. 24.

16. Tolson, "Key Words," p. 3.

17. Ibid.

18. "John Laugart, like many Negro artists and writers and entertainers, was an expatriot in Paris — Richard Wright, James Baldwin, Brickton. Unlike your Fitzgeralds, they escaped from *both* the black and the white bourgeoisie" (Tolson, "Key Words," p. 3).

19. In Onward, Mississippi, Tolson was moved onward by a white man with a gun (Tolson, "C. and C.," 28 January 1939).

20. In fact, the only work described at any length in *HG* is the work of art.

21. "I have here a picture of a white boy and a black boy playing at the same piano. . . . Obviously, the artist got his idea from Aggrey" (Tolson, "Key Words," p. 7).

22. Tolson, "A Poet's Odyssey," p. 195.

23. Heights was regarded by Tolson as one of his best pupils (Notebooks) and was known for the fiery, dramatic quality of his speeches (interview, Jarrett, 8 June 1975).

24. Tolson, "The Harlem Group of Negro Writers," Master's essay, Columbia University, p. 36.

25. Tolson, "E. & O. E.," *Poetry*, p. 369.

26. "A tension between a heroically sensitive modern mind and hard modern realities . . . seems to me the keynote of modernism" (Notebooks).

27. The lines can also be interpreted as Hideho's inability to attain the epic grandeur of such anguish.

28. "A person in his lifetime may wear not one mask, but many, which are revelations of his complex nature and nurture" (Tolson, "A Poet's Odyssey," p. 187).

Notes to Chapter 7: Personae

1. Melvin B. Tolson, "Odyssey of a Manuscript," p. 2.

2. Interview with Dr. Wiley Tolson, 25 October 1974: "But sometimes I see him as a sort of Nkomo because he sort of stands off and is outside and it may be that particular character may be himself."

3. Tolson, "A Poet's Odyssey," p. 185.

4. According to Tolson's notes, Julio Sigafoos was a feral boy raised by dogs who was captured, schooled, and trained as an astrophysicist: "He was killed, I'm told, chasing a car!" (Tolson, "Key Words," p. 4).

5. This quotation is one that Tolson himself frequently used.

6. Tolson, "A Poet's Odyssey," p. 189.

7. Evidently a Tolson ideal in *HG*.

8. Compare, for example, the personae in "The Waste Land," *Paterson*, and *The Bridge*.

9. Tolson as quoted by Joy Flasch, *Melvin B. Tolson*, p. 100.

10. Ibid.

11. In his Notebooks, Tolson commented: "In autobiographical Book I, The Curator

vivifies (in myth and metaphor and symbol) ideas and places, persons, and things which have given meaning to his life as a man and a collector of works of art. Here, for the first time in major poetry, the Afroamerican artist discovers his identity in the complexities that has [*sic*] made him and his people [variegated heritage]." For the extent to which The Curator represents Tolson, see Robert J. Huot, "Melvin B. Tolson's *Harlem Gallery:* A Critical Edition," Ph.D. diss., University of Utah, 1971, pp. 6–8; Flasch, *Tolson*, p. 99.

12. Tolson, "Key Words," p. 2.

13. It is in character that The Curator's mind runs to such artists as Picasso, Rivera, Hogarth, Dickens, and Gogol, artists who mirrored society in its flawed self.

14. Flasch, *Tolson*, p. 101.

15. Tolson, "Key Words," p. 1; The Curator describes himself as a Pelagian with a black man's reason for denying that a man comes into the world already marked for his destiny (*HG*, p. 164).

16. Flasch suggests that Tolson is referring to the eventual amalgamation of the black race into the white world (Flasch, *Tolson*, p. 130); Huot, "Critical Edition," p. 239, has a different interpretation.

17. An ode is not a dramatic monologue in which we and the author separate ourselves from the character whose voice we hear but a poem in which we regard the persona's musings as presently enacted in his mind as the *HG* creation is in the mind of The Curator.

Notes to Chapter 8: Some Thematic Elements

1. St. Clair Drake and Horace Cayton, *Black Metropolis*, p. 755.

2. Ralph Ellison, "Harlem Is Nowhere," *Shadow and Act*, p. 296.

3. This position, which had more widespread acceptance during later periods, still mirrored one aspect of Tolson's thinking in the sixties.

4. Tolson saw poetry versus "conformity, bureaucracy, routine, stereotype . . . status seeking," characteristics of bourgeois existence (Notebooks).

5. Tolson, "A Man Against the Idols of the Tribe," *Modern Quarterly*, p. 32; see also "The Idols of the Tribe," *Rendezvous*, pp. 97–104.

6. The group was associated with the second decade of the century, especially before World War I; See Andre Salmon, *The Black Venus*, trans. Slater Brown. But Tolson associates the group with the postwar 1920s time of Hughes's and McKay's stays in Paris. Compare to Langston Hughes's *The Big Sea*, p. 155.

7. Keith Sutton, *Picasso*, pp. 7–21.

8. Ibid., p. 21.

9. Lloyd Brown, "Jones (Baraka) and His Literary Heritage in *The System of Dante's Hell*," *Obsidian*, pp. 5–17.

10. Tolson, "Key Words," p. 7.

11. Tolson wrote in his Notebooks that there is no American dilemma: "It is the Negro who faces the dilemma, to fight or not to fight. J. Saunders Redding pictures this in 'On Being Negro in America.' Langston Hughes pictures it in 'The Big Sea.' Dunbar faces it: To write jingles or an epic? To create a stereotype or a hero." Tolson also commented: "Negro poetry has suffered from ethnic didacticism as a result of Negrophobic pressures."

12. Ronald Lee Cansler, "'The White and Not-White Dichotomy' of Melvin B. Tolson's Poetry," *Negro American Literature Forum*, p. 115.

13. Allen Tate, preface to *Libretto*, pp. 10–11.

14. Ibid., p. 11.

15. See Robert J. Huot, "Melvin B. Tolson's *Harlem Gallery:* A Critical Edition," Ph.D. diss., University of Utah, 1971, pp. 24–28; Joy Flasch, *Melvin B. Tolson*, p. 132; Laurence Lieberman, "Poetry Chronicle," *The Hudson Review*, pp. 456–58.

16. Sarah Webster Fabio, "Who Speaks Negro?" *Negro Digest*, p. 55.

17. See Flasch, *Tolson*, p. 86. For a different resolution of the dichotomy, see Tolson's

"A Poet's Odyssey," p. 184: "I like to go about places, hobnob with people, gather rich epithets and proverbs in churches and taverns, in cotton fields and dance halls, in streets and toilets. The rhythm and energy exorcise white magic."

18. Tolson, in notes to "E. & O. E.," stated that to be or not to be is an example of fallacious reasoning; *Poetry*, p. 369.

19. Roy Basler, "The Heart of Blackness — M. B. Tolson's Poetry," *New Letters*, p. 75.

Notes to Chapter 9: Ghetto Laughter

1. In an unpublished novel, Tolson had a character say: "In spite of the poverty, even the cold, as an outsider he was aware that in this street [Lenox Avenue] grew the tough plant of Negro life that chattel and wage slavery had been unable to root out." "All Aboard," p. 111, undated in Notebooks. Joy Flasch, *Melvin B. Tolson*, p. 27, indicated that the novel was composed during the 1950s.

2. Robert J. Huot claimed: "It is a sentimental type of comedy in which the pathos emerges from a realistic presentation of difficulties and sufferings of everyday life, submerging or obliterating the comic effect" ("Melvin B. Tolson's *Harlem Gallery:* A Critical Edition," Ph.D. diss., University of Utah, 1971, p. 195).

3. Melvin B. Tolson, "Miles to Go with Black Ulysses," *Book Week*, p. 12.

4. Tolson, "Key Words," p. 7.

5. Stanley Hyman, *The Tangled Bush*, as quoted in "Key Words," p. 7.

6. Ibid.

7. Ralph Ellison, "Richard Wright's Blues," *Shadow and Act*, p. 78.

8. Ibid., pp. 79, 94.

9. Ralph Ellison, "On Bird, Bird-Watching, and Jazz," *Shadow and Act*, p. 231.

10. Sarah Webster Fabio, "Who Speaks Negro?" *Negro Digest*, p. 55.

11. Paul Breman, "Poetry into the Sixties," *Poetry and Drama: The Black American Writer*, II, ed. C. W. E. Bigsby, p. 101. See also Karl Shapiro "Decolonization of American Literature," *Wilson Library Bulletin*, p. 853: "The forms of the *Libretto* and of *Harlem Gallery* are the Negro satire upon the poetic tradition of the Eliots and the Tates."

12. Roy Basler, "The Heart of Blackness — M.B. Tolson's Poetry," *New Letters*, p. 66.

13. Tolson, "A Poet's Odyssey," p. 192.

14. See Huot, "Critical Edition," p. 20; Flasch, *Tolson*, p. 48.

15. Huot, "Critical Edition," p. 22.

16. Interview, Melvin B. Tolson, Jr., 2 June 1975.

17. Flasch, *Tolson*, p. 33.

18. Tolson also delighted to crowd images and ideas into a single passage, the flow of which is controlled by its grammatical structure as in the if, since, then sentence (*HG*, p. 45), the second stanza (p. 53), and the third stanza (p. 41).

19. Another figure of speech that reinforces the dramatic effect is the synecdoche. In "hobnails" (*HG*, p. 67), "hand" (p. 67), "camel-hair alchemy" (p. 45), "Tongues" (p. 94), "irises" (p. 94), "eye" more than once, "top-hat" (p. 88), "grey eyes and blond ears" (p. 137), "hymens" (p. 163), "Derbies" (p. 128), Tolson used the dramatic part for the more conventional whole.

20. Patterns of imagery, such as those involving food, drink, sailing, and animals, among others, are not discussed here.

21. Arthur Davis, "Melvin B. Tolson," *From the Dark Tower*, p. 173.

Selected Bibliography

A number of items, although published, were found in the Melvin B. Tolson Papers, formerly located at his widow's Washington, D.C., home and transferred in 1975 to the Manuscript Division, Archives of the Library of Congress. References to these items are followed by MBTP (Melvin B. Tolson Papers) and Library of Congress (LC).

Aaron, Daniel. *Writers on the Left — 1912-World War Two: Episodes in American Literary Communism*. New York: Harcourt Brace and World, 1961.

Arden, Eugene. "The Early Harlem Novel." *The Phylon Quarterly*, 20 (First Quarter 1959): 25-31.

Baldwin, James. *Go Tell It on the Mountain*. New York: Dell, 1953.

————. *Nobody Knows My Name: More Notes of a Native Son*. New York: Dial Press, 1961.

————. *Notes of a Native Son*. New York: Dial Press, 1963.

Baraka, Imamu Amiri. "The Black Aesthetic." *Negro Digest* 18 (September 1969): 5-6.

————. *Blues People: Negro Music in White America*. New York: William Morrow, 1963.

————. "The Fire Must Be Permitted to Burn Full Up." *Journal of Black Poetry* 1 (Summer-Fall 1969): 62-65.

————. *Home: Social Essays*. New York: William Morrow, 1966.

————. "Philistinism and the Negro Writer." In *Anger, and Beyond: The Negro Writer in the United States*, edited by Herbert Hill, pp. 51-61. New York: Harper & Row, 1966.

————. "State/meant." *Journal of Black Poetry* 1 (Spring 1967): 14.

Baraka, Imamu Amiri, and Larry Neal, eds. *Black Fire: An Anthology of Afro-American Writing*. New York: William Morrow, 1968.

Barksdale, Richard H. "Distinguished Poet Tells of His Faith in Man." *Atlanta World* 24 April 1966. MBTP.

————. "Symbolism and Irony in McKay's *Home to Harlem*." *CLA Journal* 15 (March 1972): 338-44.

Barksdale, Richard H., and Keneth Kinnamon, eds. "Melvin B. Tolson." In *Black Fire: A Comprehensive Anthology*, pp. 668-70. New York: Macmillan, 1972.

Basler, Roy, "The Heart Of Blackness — M. B. Tolson's Poetry." *New Letters* 39 (March 1973): 63-76.

Bayliss, John, "Ghettoization and Black Literature." In *The Black Writer in Africa and the Americas*, edited by Lloyd Brown, pp. 69-83. Los Angeles: Hennessey and Ingalls, 1973.

Bearden, Romare. "The 1930's — An Art Reminiscence." *New York Amsterdam News* 18 September 1971, pp. D24, D26.

Behan, Brendan. "Down-Town Uptown and in and out of Harlem." In *Brendan Behan's New York*, pp. 77-98. London: Bernard Geis Associates, 1964.

Bell, Bernard W. "New Black Poetry: A Double-Edged Sword." *CLA Journal* 15 (September 1971): 37-43.

Benet, William Rose. "Two Powerful Negro Poets." *Saturday Review* (24 March 1945): 35-36.

Berry, Faith. "Voices for the Jazz Age, Great Migration or Black Bourgeoisie." *Black World* 20 (November 1970): 10–16.

Bickham, Jack. "Flowers of Hope." *Oklahoma Orbit, The Magazine of The Sunday Oklahoman* (29 August 1965): 6, 8, 9.

———. "Langston Poet May Signal New Era." *Sunday Oklahoman* (23 May 1965): 10.

———. "A Superbly Successful Human Being." *Oklahoma Courier* (9 September 1966): 5.

Bodenheim, Maxwell. *Naked on Roller Skates.* New York: Horace Liveright, 1930.

Bontemps, Arna. "The Black Renaissance of the Twenties." *Black World* 20 (November 1970): 5–9.

———. "Famous WPA Authors." *Negro Digest* 8 (June 1950): 43–47.

———. "The Harlem Renaissance." *Saturday Review* (22 March 1947): 12–13.

———. "The New Black Renaissance." *Negro Digest* 11 (November 1961): 52–58.

Bontemps, Arna, ed. *The Harlem Renaissance Remembered.* New York: Dodd, Mead, 1972.

Bontemps, Arna, and Jack Conroy. *Any Place but Here.* New York: Hill and Wang, 1966.

Bontemps, Arna, and others. "Artist in an Age of Revolution: A Symposium." *Arts in Society* 5 (1968): 219–38.

"Books in Brief: *Rendezvous with America.*" *The Christian Century* 61 (20 September 1944): 1078–79.

Breman, Paul. "Poetry into the Sixties." In *Poetry and Drama: The Black American Writer,* II, edited by C. W. E. Bigsby, pp. 99–109. Deland, Fla.: Everett/Edwards, 1969.

Bronz, Stephen H. *Roots of Negro Racial Consciousness: The 1920's: Three Harlem Renaissance Authors.* New York: Libra Publishers, 1964.

Brooks, Gwendolyn. "Books Noted." *Negro Digest* 14 (September 1965): 51–52.

Brown, Claude. "Harlem, My Harlem." In *The Radical Imagination: An Anthology from Dissent,* edited by Irving Howe, pp. 385–90. New York: New American Library, 1967.

———. *Manchild in the Promised Land.* New York: New American Library, 1965.

Brown, Lloyd. "Jones (Baraka) and His Literary Heritage in *The System of Dante's Hell.*" *Obsidian* 1 (Spring 1975): 5–17.

Burke, Arthur. "Book Review: Lyrico-Dramatic." *The Crisis* 52 (February 1945): 61.

Calverton, V[ictor] F[rancis]. "The Advance of the Negro." *Opportunity* 4 (February 1926): 54–55.

———. *An Anthology of American Negro Literature.* New York: Modern Library, 1929.

———. *The Awakening of America.* New York: John Day, 1939.

———. "The Compulsive Basis of Sociological Thought." *American Journal of Sociology* 36 (March 1931): 689–720.

———. *The Liberation of American Literature.* New York: Charles Scribner's, 1932.

———. *The Newer Spirit: A Sociological Criticism of Literature.* New York: Boni and Liveright, 1925.

Cansler, Ronald L. "'The White and Not-White Dichotomy' of Melvin B. Tolson's Poetry." *Negro American Literature Forum* 7 (Winter 1973):

115–18.

Cartey, Wilfred. "Four Shadows of Harlem." *Negro Digest* 18 (August 1969): 22–25, 83–92.

Cendrars, Blaise. *African Saga.* New York: Payson and Clarke, 1927.

Challenge and *New Challenge.* 1934–1937; reprint Westport, Conn.: Negro Universities Press, 1970.

Chapman, Abraham. "Black Poetry Today." *Arts in Society* 5 (1968): 401–8.

Chesnutt, Charles. "The Negro in Art: How Shall He Be Portrayed: A Symposium." *Crisis* 33 (November 1926): 28–29.

Ciardi, John. "Recent Verse." *The Nation* 178 (27 February 1954): 183.

City University of New York in Cooperation with Harlem Cultural Council and New York Urban League. *The Evolution of Afro-American Artists 1800–1950.* New York: Exhibition Presented at CUNY, 1967.

Clark, Kenneth B. *Dark Ghetto: Dilemmas of Social Power.* New York: Harper & Row, 1965.

Clarke, John Hendrik, ed. *Harlem: A Community in Transition.* 2d ed. New York: The Citadel Press, 1969.

———. "The Neglected Dimensions of the Harlem Renaissance." *Black World* 20 (November 1970): 118–29.

Collier, Eugenia. "The Four-Way Dilemma of Claude McKay." *CLA Journal,* 15 (March 1972): 345–53.

———. "Heritage from Harlem." *Black World* 20 (November 1970): 52–59.

Conarroe, Joel. *William Carlos Williams'* Paterson: *Language and Landscape.* Philadelphia: University of Pennsylvania Press, 1970.

Conroy, Jack. *The Disinherited.* 1934; reprint New York: Hill and Wang, 1963.

———. "Tolson: A Poet to Appreciate." *Chicago Sun-Times* 18 July 1965. MBTP.

Cook, Mercer, and Stephen Henderson. *The Militant Black Writer in Africa and the United States.* Madison: University of Wisconsin Press. 1969.

Cox, Oliver Cromwell. *Caste, Class, and Race: A Study in Social Dynamics.* New York: Doubleday, 1948.

Crane, Hart. *The Complete Poems and Selected Letters and Prose of Hart Crane.* Edited by Brom Weber. New York: Doubleday, 1966.

Cruse, Harold. "Black and White: Chapter One: Outline of the Next Stage." *Black World* 20 (January 1971): 19–41, 66–71.

———."Part II: Black and White: Outlines of the Next Stage." *Black World* 20 (March 1971): 5–31.

———. "Part III: The Special Significance of Harlem—Its Place in the 'Theory of Black Cities': Black and White: Outlines of the Next Stage." *Black World* 20 (May 1971): 9–40.

———. *The Crisis of the Negro Intellectual.* New York: William Morrow, 1967.

———. "Harold Cruse Looks Back on Black Art and Politics in Harlem." *Negro Digest* 18 (November 1968): 19–25, 56–59.

Cullen, Countee, ed. *Carolling Dusk: An Anthology of Verse by Negro Poets.* New York: Harper and Brothers, 1927.

———. *Color.* 1925; reprint The Arno Press and the New York Times, 1969.

———. "The Dark Tower." *Opportunity* 4 (December 1926)-6 (September 1928).

———. "The Negro in Art: How Shall He Be Portrayed: A Symposium." *Crisis* 32 (August 1926): 193–94.

———. *One Way to Heaven.* New York: Harper and Brothers, 1932.

Davis, Arthur. "The Alien and Exile Theme in Countee Cullen's Racial Poems." *The Phylon Quarterly* 14 (Fourth Quarter 1953): 390–400.

——. *From the Dark Tower: Afro-American Writers 1900 to 1960.* Washington, D.C.: Howard University Press, 1974.

——. "The Harlem of Langston Hughes' Poetry." In *Images of the Negro,* edited by Seymour Gross and John Hardy, pp. 194–203. Chicago: University of Chicago Press, 1966.

——. "Jesse B. Semple: Negro American." *The Phylon Quarterly* 15 (First Quarter 1954): 21–28.

De Carava, Roy, and Langston Hughes. *The Sweet Flypaper of Life.* New York: Hill and Wang, 1967.

Delancey, Rose Mary. "Tolson Hailed as a Great Poet." *Fort Wayne News-Sentinel* (24 April 1965): 4-A.

Deutsch, Babette. *Poetry in Our Time: A Critical Survey of Poetry in the English-Speaking World 1900 to 1960.* 2d ed. New York: Doubleday, 1963.

Dixon, Melvin. "Guidelines: Black Theatre: The Aesthetics." *Negro Digest* 18 (July 1969): 41–44.

Dodson, Owen. "Countee Cullen." *Phylon* 7 (First Quarter 1946): 19–20.

Drachler, Jacob, ed. *African Heritage: Intimate Views of the Black Africans from Life, Lore, and Literature.* New York: Crowell-Collier Press, 1963.

Drake, St. Clair, and Horace Cayton. *Black Metropolis: A Study of Negro Life in a Northern City.* 2 vols. New York: Harper & Row, 1962.

Du Bois, W[illiam] E[dward] B[urghardt]. "American Negro Art." *Modern Quarterly* 3 (October–December 1925): 53–56.

——. "The Browny Reader." *Crisis* 36 (July 1929): 234, 248–50.

——. "The Browny Reader: Two Novels." *Crisis* 35 (June 1928): 202.

——. "The Crisis Book Club." *Crisis* 27 (January 1924): 106.

——. *Dusk of Dawn: An Essay Toward an Autobiography of a Race Concept.* 1940, reprint New York: Shocken Books, 1970.

——. "Krigwa: Crisis Prizes in Literature and Art, 1926." *Crisis* 33 (December 1926): 70–71.

——. "'Krigwa Players Little Negro Theatre,' The Story of a Little Theatre Movement." *Crisis* 32 (July 1926): 134–36.

——. "The Looking Glass: Negro Art." *Crisis* 33 (December 1926): 104–5.

——. "The Negro in Art: How Shall He Be Portrayed: A Symposium." *Crisis* 32 (June 1926): 71–73.

——. "Postscript." *Crisis* 39 (October 1932): 331.

——. "Proposed Rules of the Competition." *Crisis* 38 (May 1931): 157–58.

——. *The Seventh Son: The Thought and Writing of W. E. B. DuBois.* Ed. Julius Lester. 2 vols. New York: Vintage Books, 1971.

——. "To Encourage Negro Art." *Crisis* 29 (November 1924): 11.

Du Bois, W.E.B., and Alain Locke. "The Younger Literary Movement." *Crisis* 27 (February 1924): 161–63.

Dunbar, Paul Lawrence. *The Sport of the Gods.* 1902; reprint London: Collier, Macmillan, 1970.

Elder, Lonne. *Ceremonies in Dark Old Men.* New York: Farrar, Straus and Giroux, 1969.

Ellison, Ralph. *Invisible Man.* New York: Signet Books, 1952.

——. *Shadow and Act.* New York: Random House, 1964.

Ellison, Ralph, and Stanley Edgar Hyman. "The Negro Writer in America, An Exchange." *Partisan Review* 25 (Spring 1958): 197–211, 212–22.

Emanuel, James A., and Theodore L. Gross, eds. "M. B. Tolson." In *Dark Symphony,* pp. 471–72. New York: The Free Press, 1968.

"An Evening with the Poet, M. B. Tolson." *Langston University Gazette* (June 1965): 3. MBTP.

Fabio, Sarah Webster. "Who Speaks Negro?" *Negro Digest* 16 (December 1966): 54–58.

———. "Who Speaks Negro? Who Is Black?" *Negro Digest* 17 (September/October 1968) 33–37.

Fabre, Michel. *The Unfinished Quest of Richard Wright.* Translated by Isabel Barzun. New York: William Morrow, 1973.

Farrison, W. Edward. "Langston Hughes: Poet of the Negro Renaissance." *CLA Journal* 15 (June 1972): 401–10.

Fauset, Jessie. *The Chinaberry Tree: A Novel of American Life.* 1931; reprint New York: Negro Universities Press, 1969.

Federal Writers Project of Works Progress Administration in New York City. "Negro Harlem." *New York City Guide: A Comprehensive Guide,* pp. 257–65. New York: Random House, 1939.

Felderson, Lewis H. "The New Breed of Black Writers and Their Jaundiced View of Tradition." *CLA Journal* 15 (September 1971): 18–24.

Fire. 1926; reprint Westport, Conn.: Negro Universities Press, 1970.

Fischer, Russell G. "*Invisible Man* as History." *CLA Journal* 17 (March 1974): 338–67.

Fisher, Rudolph. "Blades of Steel." In *Readings from Negro Authors for Schools and Colleges,* edited by Otelia Cromwell and others, pp. 90–91. New York: Harcourt, Brace, 1931.

———. "The City of Refuge." In *The Best Short Stories of 1925,* pp. 66–75. New York: Small and Maynard, 1925.

———. *The Conjure-Man Dies: A Mystery Tale of Dark Harlem.* New York: Covici, Friede, 1932.

———. *The Walls of Jericho.* New York: Alfred A. Knopf, 1928.

Flasch, Joy. "Greatness Defined." *Saturday Review* (4 September 1965): 39.

———. "Humor and Satire in the Poetry of M. B. Tolson." *Satire Newsletter* 7 (Fall 1969): 29–36.

———. "M. B. Polson [*sic*]: A Great American Poet." *Oklahoma Librarian* 18 (Ocotober 1968): 116–18.

———. *Melvin B. Tolson.* New York: Twayne, 1972.

Ford, James W. *Hunger and Terror in Harlem.* New York: Harlem Section Communist Party, 1935.

Frazier, E. Franklin. *Black Bourgeoisie: The Rise of a New Middle Class in the United States.* Glencoe, Ill.: The Free Press. 1957.

———. "Negro Harlem: An Ecological Study." *American Journal of Sociology* 43 (July 1937): 72–88.

"Fresh Recognition Won by Langston Poet-Prof." *Daily Oklahoman* 1 April 1965. MBTP.

Fuller, Hoyt. "An Address by Hoyt Fuller." *Journal of Negro History* 57 (January 1972): 83–98.

———. "A Survey: Black Writers' Views on Literary Lions and Values." *Negro Digest* 17 (January 1968); 10–45, 84–89.

Fussiner, Howard R. "A Mature Voice Speaks." *Phylon* 15 (First Quarter 1954): 96–97.

Gayle, Addison, Jr., ed. *The Black Aesthetic.* New York: Doubleday, 1970.

———. "The Harlem Renaissance: Towards a Black Aesthetic." *Midcontinent American Studies Journal* 11 (Fall 1970): 78–87.

———. "The Politics of Revolution: Afro-American Literature." *Black World* 21 (June 1972): 4–12.

Gerald, Carolyn. "The Black Writer and His Poetry: Shaping An Image for Ourselves." *Negro Digest* 18 (January 1969): 42–48.

Glaser, William. *A Harlem Almanac.* New York: Columbia University Bureau of Applied Social Research, 1964.

Graham, Stephen. "Harlem." In *New York Nights,* pp. 242–67. New York: George H. Doran, 1927.

Grey, Edgar M. "The Sleeping Giant — The Harlem Negro." *New York Amsterdam News* (10 November 1926): 15.

Hascler, James L. "The Negro Poet's Objectives: Propaganda vs. Art." *Langston University Gazette* (March 1958). MBTP.

Hatcher, Harlan. *Creating the Modern American Novel.* New York: Farrar and Rinehart, 1935.

Hayden, Robert, ed. "M. B. Tolson." In *Kaleidoscope: Poems by American Negro Poets,* pp. 56–57. New York: Harcourt, Brace and World, 1967.

Herskovits, Melville. *The American Negro: A Study in Racial Crossing.* New York: Alfred A. Knopf, 1928.

Hill, Herbert. *Anger, and Beyond: The Negro Writer in the United States.* New York: Harper & Row, 1966.

———. "In Memory of M. B. Tolson . . . 1900–1966." *Tuesday* (November 1966): 26.

———. "The Negro Writer and the Creative Imagination." *Arts in Society* 5 (1968): 245–55.

Hudson, Theodore R. *From LeRoi Jones to Amiri Baraka: The Literary Works.* Durham, N.C.: Duke University Press, 1973.

Huggins, Nathan. *Harlem Renaissance.* New York: Oxford University Press, 1973.

Hughes, Langston. *The Best of Simple.* New York: Hill and Wang, 1969.

———. *The Big Sea.* New York: Alfred A. Knopf, 1940.

———. *Fields of Wonder.* New York: Alfred A. Knopf, 1947.

———. *Fine Clothes to the Jew.* New York: Alfred A. Knopf, 1927.

———. *Five Plays.* Edited by Webster Smalley. Bloomington: Indiana University Press, 1963.

———. "Harlem Literati in the Twenties." *Saturday Review* (22 June 1940): 13–14.

———. "Here to Yonder." *Chicago Defender* (15 December 1945).

———. *I Wonder as I Wander: An Autobiographical Journey.* New York: Rinehart, 1956.

———. *Montage of a Dream Deferred.* New York: Henry Holt, 1951.

———. "The Negro Artist and the Racial Mountain." In *The Black Aesthetic,* edited by Addison Gayle, Jr., pp. 692–94. New York: Doubleday, 1970.

———. "The Negro in Art: How Shall He Be Portrayed: A Symposium." *Crisis* 31 (April 1926): 278.

———. *Shakespeare in Harlem.* New York: Alfred A. Knopf, 1942.

———. *Something in Common and Other Stories.* New York: Hill and Wang, 1963.

———. "The Twenties: Harlem and Its Negritude." *African Forum* 1 (Spring 1966): 11–20.

———. *The Weary Blues.* New York: Alfred A. Knopf, 1935.

Huot, Robert J. "Melvin B. Tolson's *Harlem Gallery:* A Critical Edition with Introduction and Explanatory Notes." Ph.D. dissertation, University of Utah, 1971.

Hurston, Zora Neale. *Dust Tracks on a Road: An Autobiography.* New York:

J. B. Lippincott, 1942.

Jackman, Marvin. "The Black Revolutionary Poet." *Journal of Black Poetry* 1 (Spring 1967): 17.

Jackson, Esther M. "LeRoi Jones (Imamu Amiri Baraka): Form and the Progression of Consciousness." *CLA Journal* 17 (September 1973): 33–56.

Jacobsen, Josephine. "Books in Review." *The Baltimore Evening Sun* (2 November 1965): A-20. MBTP.

Johnson, Charles S., ed. *Ebony and Topaz: A Collectanea. Opportunity: Journal of Negro Life.* New York: National Urban League, 1927.

Johnson, Georgia Douglas. "The Negro in Art: How Shall He Be Portrayed: A Symposium." *Crisis* 32 (August 1926): 193.

Johnson, James Weldon. *Along This Way: The Autobiography of James Weldon Johnson.* New York: The Viking Press, 1933.

———. *The Autobiography of an Ex-Coloured Man.* 1912; reprint New York: Hill and Wang, 1968.

———. *Black Manhattan.* New York: Alfred A. Knopf, 1930.

———. *The Book of American Negro Poetry.* Rev. ed. 1931; reprint New York: Harcourt, Brace and World, 1959.

———. "Negro Authors and White Publishers." *Crisis* 36 (July 1929): 228–29.

———. "Romance and Tragedy in Harlem — A Review." *Opportunity* 3 (October 1926): 316–17, 330.

K., J. "Unprejudiced Poems." Raleigh, N.C., *The News and Observer* (8 October 1944): 15.

Kazin, Alfred. *Starting Out in the Thirties.* Boston: Little, Brown, 1965.

Kellner, Bruce. *Carl Van Vechten and the Irreverent Decades.* Norman: University of Oklahoma Press, 1968.

Kent, George E. "Patterns of the Harlem Renaissance." *Black World* 21 (June 1972): 13–24, 76–80.

———. "The Soulful Way of Claude McKay." *Black World* 20 (November 1970): 37–51.

Killens, John Oliver. "Another Time When Black Was Beautiful." *Black World* 20 (November 1970): 20–36.

———. "The Black Writer and the Revolution." *Arts in Society* 5 (1968): 397–99.

Kinnamon, Keneth. *The Emergence of Richard Wright: A Study in Literature and Society.* Urbana: University of Illinois Press, 1972.

Kiser, Clyde Vernon. *Sea Island to City: A Study of St. Helena Islanders in Harlem and Other Urban Centers.* New York: Columbia University Press, 1932.

Knopf, Alfred. "The Negro in Art: How Shall He Be Portrayed: A Symposium." *Crisis* 31 (April 1926): 280.

Lait, Jack, and Lee Mortimer. "Black Ghetto." In *New York Confidential,* pp. 104–25. Chicago: Ziff-Davis, 1948.

"Langston Hears Poet's 'Odyssey.'" *The Daily Oklahoman* (9 April 1965): 16.

Larsen, Nella. *Quicksand.* 1928; reprint New York: Negro Universities Press, 1969.

"Lauded Oklahoma Poet Working Hard after Battle with Cancer." *Daily Oklahoman* (4 February 1965): 33.

Lee, Don L. "Black Poetry: Which Direction." *Negro Digest* 17 (September/ October 1968): 27–32.

———. "On *Kaleidoscope* and Robert Hayden." *Negro Digest* 17 (January 1968): 51–52, 90–94.

"Liberia Honors Poet Laureate from Oklahoma." *Daily Oklahoman* (24 November 1965): 10.

Liebermann, Laurence. "Poetry Chronicle." *The Hudson Review* 18 (Autumn 1965): 455–60.

"Life in Harlem: View from the Back Street." *New York Times* (4 September 1966): 5, section 4.

Littell, Robert. "Everyone Likes Chocolate." *Vogue* 66 (1 November 1936): 127–28.

Littlejohn, David. "M. B. Tolson." In *Black on White: A Critical Survey of Writing by American Negroes*, pp. 81–83. New York: Grossman, 1966.

Llorens, David. "Black Don Lee." *Ebony* 24 (March 1969): 72–80.

———. "Seeking a New Image: Writers Converge at Fisk University." *Negro Digest* 15 (June 1966): 54–68.

Locke, Alain. "American Literary Tradition and the Negro." *Modern Quarterly* 3 (May–July 1926): 215–22.

———. "From *Native Son* to *Invisible Man:* A Review of the Literature of the Negro for 1952." *Phylon* 14 (First Quarter 1953): 34–44.

———. "Harlem. Dark Weather-Vane." *Survey Graphic* (August 1930). 457–62, 493–95.

———. *The New Negro.* 1925; reprint New York: Atheneum, 1970.

Lowe, Ramona. "Poem 'Rendezvous with America' Wins Fame for Melvin Tolson." *Chicago Defender* (24 February 1945).

McCall, Dan. "The Quicksilver Sparrow of M. B. Tolson." *American Quarterly* 18 (Fall 1966): 538–42.

———. "Tolson 65." *Negro Digest* 15 (September 1966): 66.

McDougald, J. I. "The Federal Government and the Negro Theatre." *Opportunity* 14 (May 1936): 135–37.

McKay, Claude. *Harlem: Negro Metropolis.* New York: E. P. Dutton, 1940.

———. *Harlem Shadows. The Poems of Claude McKay.* New York. Harcourt, Brace, 1922.

———. *Home to Harlem.* 1928; reprint New York: Pocket Books, 1965.

———. *A Long Way from Home.* 1937; reprint Arno Press and the New York Times, 1969.

Major, Clarence. "Black Criteria." *Journal of Black Poetry* 1 (Spring 1967): 15–16.

Mangione, Jerre. *The Dream and the Deal: The Federal Writers Project, 1935–1943.* Boston: Little, Brown, 1972.

Martin, Charles. "The Harlem Negro." *AME Quarterly Review* 26 (October/November/December 1916): 1–8.

Masters, Edgar Lee. *Spoon River Anthology.* 2d ed. Toronto: Macmillan, 1944.

Mayfield, Julian. "Childe Harold." *Negro Digest* 18 (November 1968): 26–27.

Milner, Virginia Scott. "A 'Great Poet' Unknown in Our Own Midwest." *The Kansas City Star* (25 July 1965): 50.

Mitchell, Loften. *Black Drama: The Story of the American Negro in the Theatre.* New York: Hawthorn Books, 1967.

———. "Harlem, My Harlem." *Black World* 20 (November 1970): 91–97.

Morand, Paul. *New York.* New York: Henry Holt, 1930.

Munro, C. Lynn. "LeRoi Jones: A Man in Transition." *CLA Journal* 17 (September 1973): 57–78.

Neal, Larry. "The Black Arts Movement." *The Drama Review* 12 (Summer 1968): 29–39.

"New Light on the Invisible." *Times Literary Supplement* (25 November

1965): 1046–49.

New York City Housing Authority. *Harlem, 1934: A Study of Real Property and Negro Population.* New York: Polygraphic Company of America, 1934.

Newsome, Effie Lee. "Book Review: Melvin B. Tolson, *Rendezvous with America.*" *The Negro College Quarterly* 2 (December 1944): 171–72.

Olney, James. *Metaphors of Self: The Meaning of Autobiography.* Princeton: Princeton University Press, 1972.

"One Harlem Poet Who Writes Language of the 'Blacks.'" *Muhammad Speaks* (13 August 1965). MBTP.

Oringeriff, Nora Bell. "Langston Honors Retiring Professor." *Sunday Oklahoman* (11 April 1965). MBTP.

Osofsky, Gilbert. *Harlem: The Making of a Ghetto: Negro New York, 1890–1930.* New York: Harper & Row, 1966.

Ottley, Roi. "*New World A-Coming.*" 1943; reprint New York: Arno Press and the New York Times, 1968.

Ottley, Roi, and William Weatherby. *The Negro in New York: An Informal Social History, 1626–1940.* New York: Praeger, 1967.

Ovington, Mary White. *Half A' Man: The Status of the Negro in New York.* 1911; reprint New York: Hill and Wang, 1969.

———. *Portraits in Color.* New York: Viking Press, 1927.

Petry, Ann. *The Street.* Boston: Houghton Mifflin, 1946.

Pickens, William. *The New Negro: His Political, Civil and Mental States and Related Essays.* New York: Neale, 1916.

"Poets Thieves by Listening, Tolson Says." *Daily Oklahoman* (15 February 1966). MBTP.

Pollard, Myrtle. "Harlem As Is . . . New York 1936–1937." Master's thesis, College of the City of New York, 1936.

Porter, James A. "Afro-American Art at Floodtide." *Arts in Society* 5 (1968): 257–70.

Pound, Ezra. *The Cantos of Ezra Pound.* New York: New Directions, 1970.

Price, Libby, "A.-S. Faculty Hears Tolson." Oklahoma State University *O' Collegian* (16 February 1966). MBTP.

———. "Honors Paid to Langston's Great Poet, Melvin Tolson." *Stillwater Daily-News Press* (11 April 1965). MBTP.

Ramsaran, J. A. "The 'Twice-Born' Artists' Silent Revolution." *Black World* 20 (May 1971): 58–68.

Randall, Dudley. "Melvin B. Tolson: Portrait of a Poet as Raconteur." *Negro Digest* 15 (January 1966): 54–57.

———. "Rev. of La Poésie Négro Américaine." *Negro Digest* 15 (September 1966): 93. MBTP.

Record, Wilson. *The Negro and the Communist Party.* Chapel Hill, N.C.: University of North Carolina Press, 1951.

Redding, Saunders. "Negro Writing in America." *The New Leader* 43 (16 May 1960): 8–10.

Richardson, Jack. "The Black Arts." *The New York Review of Books* 11 (19 December 1968): 10–13.

Riley, Clayton. "The Death Horse Rides Our Harlems: The Theatre of Black Reality." *Black World* 20 (April 1971): 37–38.

Rodman, Selden. "On Vistas Undreamt." *New York Times Book Review* (24 January 1954): 10.

Salmon, Andre. *The Black Venus.* Translated by Slater Brown. New York: Macauley, 1929.

Scheiner, Seth M. *Negro Mecca: A History of the Negro in New York City,*

1865–1920. New York: New York University Press, 1965.

Schoener, Allon, ed. *Harlem on My Mind: Cultural Capital of Black America: 1900–1968*. New York: Random House, 1969.

Schuyler, George. "The Negro-Art Hokum." *The Nation* 122 (16 June 1926): 662–63.

Seamster, Cynthia. "Laureate Poet Explains Principles at Banquet." *The Daily O' Collegian* (16 February 1966). MBTP.

Shapiro, Karl. "Decolonization of American Literature." *Wilson Library Bulletin* (June 1965): 843–54.

———. "A Foot in the Door: Performing a Primary Rite for Our Literature." *Book Week, The Washington Post* (10 January 1965): 1. Reprinted with omission of one paragraph as introduction to *Harlem Gallery*.

Shelton, Austin J. "The Ideology of Blackness and Beauty in America and Africa." *Présence Africaine* 79 (Third Quarter 1971): 126–36.

Sherwood, John. "'Architect of Poetry': Harlem Poet's Epic Out 30 Years Later." Washington, D.C., *The Evening Star* (31 March 1965): E-2.

Spector, Robert D. "The Poet's Voice in the Crowd." *Saturday Review* (7 August 1965): 29.

Spingarn, J[oel] E. "The Negro in Art: How Shall He Be Portrayed: A Symposium." *Crisis* 31 (April 1926): 278–79.

"State Poet Recalls Robert Frost." *Daily Oklahoman* (10 February 1963). MBTP.

Stein, Gertrude. *The Autobiography of Alice B. Toklas*. New York: Harcourt, Brace, 1933.

Sternsher, Bernard, ed. *The Negro in Depression and War, Prelude to Revolution, 1930–1945*. Chicago: Quadrangle Books, 1969.

Stribling, T[homas] S. "Noted Southern Writer Discovers Real Harlem." *The New York World* (11 March 1928): 7M.

Sutton, Keith. *Picasso*. New York: Marboro Books, 1962.

Swados, Harvey, ed. *The American Writer and the Great Depression*. New York: Bobbs-Merrill, 1966.

Taylor, Clyde. "Black Folk Spirit and the Shape of Black Literature." *Black World* 21 (August 1972): 31–40.

Thompson, Dolphin G. "Tolson's Gallery Brings Poetry Home." *Negro History Bulletin* 29 (December 1965): 69–70.

Thurman, Wallace. *The Blacker the Berry: A Novel of Negro Life*. 1929; reprint New York: Arno Press and the New York Times, 1969.

———. *Infants of the Spring*. 1932; reprint Freeport, N.Y.: Books for Libraries Press, 1972.

———. "Negro Artists and the Negro." *New Republic* 52 (31 August 1927): 37–39.

———. "Negro Artists and the Negro World." *Chicago Bee* (8 October 1927). Vertical File, Schomburg Collection.

———. "Negro Poets and Their Poetry." *The Bookman* 67 (July 1928): 555–61.

Tillman, Nathaniel. "The Poet Speaks." *Phylon* 5 (First Quarter 1944): 389–91.

"Tolson Draws Praise." *Dallas Times Herald* (17 January 1965). MBTP.

Tolson, M[elvin] B[eaunorus]. "Abraham Lincoln of Rock Spring Farm." In *Soon, One Morning: New Writings by American Negroes: 1940–1962*, edited by Herbert Hill, pp. 572–77. New York: Alfred A. Knopf, 1969.

———. "African China." *Voices* 140 (Winter 1950): 35–38.

———. *A Gallery of Harlem Portraits*. Edited by Robert M. Farnsworth.

Columbia: University of Missouri Press, 1979.

———. "Alpha," "Beta," "Gamma," "Delta," "Epsilon," "Zeta," "Eta." *Prairie Schooner* 35 (Fall 1961): 243–64.

———. "Caviar and Cabbage." *The Washington Tribune* 20 November 1937 to 27 May 1944.

———. "Claude McKay's Art." *Poetry* 83 (February 1954): 287–90.

———. "The Contributor's Column." *Atlantic Monthly* 168 (September 1941).

———. "Dr. Harvey Whyte." *Modern Monthly* 10 (August 1937): 10.

———. "E. & O. E." *Poetry* 78 (September 1951): 330–44, 369–72.

———. "Hamuel Gutterman." *Modern Monthly* 10 (April 1937): 7.

———. *Harlem Gallery: Book I, The Curator.* New York: Twayne, 1965.

———. "Jacob Nollen." *Modern Monthly* 10 (May 1937): 10.

———. "Kikes, Bohunks, Crackers, Dagos, Niggers." *Modern Quarterly* 11 (Fall 1939): 18–19.

———. "Langston Hughes' Goodbye Christ a Challenge and Warning — Tolson." *Pittsburgh Courier* (4 February 1933): 10.

———. *Libretto for the Republic of Liberia* London: Collier-Macmillan, 1970.

———. "A Man against the Idols of the Tribe." *Modern Quarterly* 11 (Fall 1940): 29–32.

———. "The Man from Halicarnassus." *Poetry* 81 (October 1952): 75–77.

———. "Miles to Go with Black Ulysses." *Bookweek, New York Herald Tribune* (20 February 1966): 2, 12.

———. "The Negro Scholar." *Midwest Journal.* MBTP.

———. "Notes on the Trombone of the West." *Voices* 140 (Winter 1950): 50–52.

———. "A Poet's Odyssey." In *Anger, and Beyond: The Negro Writer in the United States,* edited by Herbert Hill, pp. 181–95. New York: Harper & Row, 1966.

———. *Rendezvous with America.* New York: Dodd, Mead, 1944.

———. "Richard Wright: Native Son." *Modern Quarterly* 11 (Winter 1939): 19–24.

———. "The Tragedy of the Yarr Karr." *The* [Wiley College] *Wild Cat* (1926): 193–98. Reprinted, Appendix A, in Joy Flasch, "Melvin B. Tolson: A Critical Biography." Ph.D. dissertation, Oklahoma State University, 1969, pp. 246–50.

———. "Uncle Walt." *Modern Monthly* 10 (March 1938): 10.

———. "Vergil Ragsdale." *Modern Quarterly* 11 (Winter 1939): 48.

———. "Will the Real Moses Please Stand Up?" *Book Week, New York Herald Tribune* (30 May 1965): 5, 8.

"Tolson Speaks on Negro History in Convocation." *The Fisk University Forum* (26 February 1956). MBTP.

Toomer, Jean. "Earth Being." *The Black Scholar* 2 (January 1971): 3–14.

———. "A New Force for Co-operation." *The Adelphi* 11 (October 1934): 25–31.

Tulip, James. "Afroamerican Poet — M. B. Tolson." *Poetry Australia* 10 (June 1966): 37–39.

Turner, Darwin. *In a Minor Chord:Three Afro-American Writers and Their Search for Identity.* Carbondale: Southern Illinois University Press, 1971.

Turner, Lorenzo D. "Words for a Vast Music." *Poetry* 86 (June 1955): 174–76.

"Two Powerful Negro Poets." *Saturday Review* (24 March 1965): 35–36.

Turpin, Waters. *These Low Grounds.* New York: Harper, 1937.

Van Doren, Carl. "The Negro Renaissance." *Century* 3 (March 1926): 635–37.

Van Doren, Mark. "Home to Harlem." *Nation* 126 (28 March 1928): 351.

Van Vechten, Carl. "The Negro in Art: How Shall He Be Portrayed: A Symposium." *Crisis* 31 (March 1926): 219–20.

———. *Nigger Heaven*. New York: Alfred A. Knopf, 1927.

Vietorisz, Thomas, and Bennett Harrison. *The Economic Development of Harlem*. New York: Praeger, 1970.

Wakin, Edward. *At the Edge of Harlem: Portrait of a Middle-Class Negro Family*. New York: William Morrow, 1965.

Walcott, Ronald. "Ellison, Gordone and Tolson: Some Notes on the Blues, Style and Space." *Black World* 22 (December 1972): 4–29.

Waldron, Edward E. "Walter White and the Harlem Renaissance: Letters from 1924–1927." *CLA Journal* 16 (June 1973): 438–57.

Walker, Margaret. "New Adventures into Poetry." MBTP.

Weaver, Robert. *The Negro Ghetto*. New York: Russell and Russell, 1967.

West, Dorothy. "Elephant's Dance: A Memoir of Wallace Thurman." *Black World* 20 (November 1970): 77–85.

White, Chappell. "Anderson 'Variations' Shows Writer's Skill." *The Atlanta Journal* (27 May 1970): 8-c.

White, Walter. "The Negro in Art: How Shall He Be Portrayed: A Symposium." *Crisis* 31 (April 1926): 279–80.

———. "The Negro Renaissance." *Palms* 4 (October 1926): 3–7.

Williams, John A. "The Harlem Renaissance: Its Artists, Its Impact, Its Meaning." *Black World* 20 (November 1970): 17–18.

Williams, William Carlos. *Paterson*. New York: New Directions, 1963.

Wilson, Charles M. *Liberia*. New York: William Sloane Associates, 1947.

Wright, Richard. "The Ethics of Living Jim Crow: An Autobiographical Sketch." *American Stuff: An Anthology of WPA Writers*. New York: Viking Press, 1937.

———. "I Tried to Be a Communist." *Atlantic Monthly* 174 (August 1944): 61–70.

———. "I Tried to Be a Communist." *Atlantic Monthly* 174 (September 1944): 48–56.

———. "Portrait of Harlem." *New York Panorama: A Comprehensive View of the Metropolis*. New York: Random House, 1938.

Zweig, Michael. *Black Capitalism and the Ownership of Property in Harlem*. Stony Brook, N.Y.: Economic Research Bureau, State University of New York, 1970.

Unpublished Works

Hill, Abram. "On Strivers Row: A Comedy about Sophisticated Harlem." Typescript, 193? Schomburg Collection.

New York City Mayor's Commission on Conditions in Harlem. "The Negro in Harlem: A Report on Social and Economic Conditions." New York; Typescript, Schomburg Collection. Original, Municipal Archives and Record Center.

"Report of Subcommittee Which Investigated the Disturbance of March 19th" 29 May 1935. Schomburg Collection.

Tolson, M[elvin] B[eaunorus]. "All Aboard." MBTP, LC.

———. "The Apes of God." Notebooks. MBTP.

———. "Beyond the Zaretto." MBTP.

————. "Bivouac on the Santa Fe." MBTP.

————. "Black No More." 1947?

————. "Dark Laughter." Tuskege. MBTP, LC.

————. "The Fence War." MBTP, LC.

————. "Fire in the Flint." Performed 28 June 1952, Municipal Auditorium in Oklahoma City.

————. "The Foreground of Negro Poetry." MBTP, LC.

————. *A Gallery of Harlem Portraits*, MBTP.

————. "The Harlem Group of Negro Writers." Master's essay, Columbia University, 1940.

————. "John Henry in Harlem." 1941. MBTP, LC.

————. "Key Words." MBTP.

————. "The Lion and the Jackal." MBTP.

————. Miscellaneous Notes, Similes, Metaphors, Notes, and Essays. MBTP.

————. "The Moses of Beale Street." MBTP, LC.

————. "Notes on Negritude." MBTP, LC.

————. "Notes on Robert Frost." MBTP, LC.

————. "The Odyssey of a Manuscript." MBTP.

————. Poems: Drafts. n.d. MBTP, LC.

————. "Southern Front." 6 November 1937. MBTP, LC.

————. "Transfiguration Springs" from "Upper Boulders in the Sun." MBTP.

Federal Theatre Project, Federal Writers Project. Wallace Thurman, Countee Cullen, Zora Neale Hurston, Claude McKay, Harlem, Schomburg Collection, New York Public Library, Countee Cullen Branch, YMCA (Harlem Branch). Vertical File. Schomburg Collection.

Writers Program, New York City. "Negroes of New York." "The Negro in Manhattan: Research Study Compiled by Workers of the Writers Program of the Work Projects Administration in New York City for "Negroes of New York." New York: Typescript, 1939. Schomburg Collection.

Interview with Mrs. Regina Andrews, 1975.

Interview with Mr. Edward Boatner, 1975.

Interview with James Cannon, 15 November 1974.

Interview with Dr. Hobart Jarrett, Professor of English, Brooklyn College, CUNY, 28 May 1975.

Interview with Dr. Arthur Tolson, Professor of History, Southern University, Baton Rouge, 26 October 1974.

Interview with Dr. Melvin B. Tolson, Jr., Professor of Modern Language, University of Oklahoma, 2 June 1975.

Interview with Mrs. Ruth Tolson and Miss Ruth Tolson, widow and daughter of Melvin B. Tolson, 23 October 1974.

Interview with Dr. Wiley Tolson, 25 October 1974.

Lecture by Joy Flasch. "Melvin Beaunorus Tolson: The Man." Black Heritage Week, Oklahoma State University. MBPT, LC.

Richard K. Barksdale, Professor of English, University of Illinois–Urbana, to author, 8 January 1975.

William Stanley Braithwaite to M. B. Tolson, 24 January 1954; 17 May 1956. MBTP.

V.F. Calverton to M. B. Tolson, 17 October 1939. MBTP.

Mary Chamberlain to M. B. Tolson, 4 February 1944. MBTP.

John Ciardi to Richard Brown, Assistant Director, Breadloaf Writers Conference, Middlebury College, 27 February 1954. MBTP.

Nina Corbett to M. B. Tolson, 24 September 1965. MBTP.

Una Corbett to author, 17 July 1975. MBTP.

Ralph Ellison to Mrs. Melvin B. Tolson, 1 September 1966. MBTP.

Nathaniel Hare to M. B. Tolson, 12 May 1958. MBTP.

Abram Hill to M. B. Tolson, 24 June 1953. MBTP.

W. C. Handy to M. B. Tolson, 13 January 1954. MBTP.

Langston Hughes to M. B. Tolson, 1944–1966. MBTP.

Oliver La Grove to M. B. Tolson, n.d. MBTP.

R. Henri Heights III to M. B. Tolson, 9 September 1944. MBTP.

Maxwell Perkins to M. B. Tolson, 28 November 1938. MBTP.

Dudley Randall to M. B. Tolson, 6 June 1965; 9 June 1966. MBTP.

Samuel Sillen to M. B. Tolson, 21 November 1946. MBTP.

Jacob Steinberg to M. B. Tolson, 20 January 1954; 2 April 1954. MBTP.

Tolson to Ben and Kate Bell, 28 December 1961. MBTP.

Tolson to Dr. Johnnie Marie McCleary, 5 March 1942.

Tolson to Carl Murphy, President Afro-American Newspapers, 26 January 1954. MBTP.

Tolson to the Press of James A. Decker, 15 February 1949. MBTP.

Tolson to Allen Tate, 4 March 1950; 28 November 1950. MBTP.

Oral History. "The Reminiscences of William S. Braithwaite." Oral History Research Office, Columbia University, 1959, #345.

Oral History. "George S. Schuyler." Oral History Research Offices, Columbia University, 1962, #431.

Record of "Meetings — 1931." 135th Street Branch Library. Countee Cullen Branch Files.

Index

A

Abyssinian Baptist Church, 14,19,
  21,42
"Adam's Curse," 78
AFL, 23
African Legion, 16
African Orthodox Church, 16
African Tragedy, An, 45
Aggrey's metaphor of integration,
  78,97
"Alpha," 53,66,92
Alston, Charles, 19
American Academy of Arts and
  Letters, 2
American Federation of Musicians,
  23
American Negro Exposition,
  National Poetry Contest, 1
Amsterdam News, 21
Andrews, Regina, 15
Anger, and Beyond, 3,6
Antar (Antarah Ibn Shaddao),
  82
"Ape of God," 54,75,98–100
Arden, Eugene, 70
Aristophanes, 64
Armstrong, Louis, 13,69
Atlanta University, 32
Atlantic Monthly, 1
Attaway, William, 34
Attucks, Crispus, 82

B

Back-to-Africa movement, 95
Bacon, Francis, 5
Bailey, Bill, 21
Baldwin, James, 104,111
Balzac, Honoré, 45,64,78,104
Bamboo Kraal, 56,70
Bannarn, Henry, 19
Baraka, Imamu Amiri, 36,37–39,
  97,101. *See also* Jones, LeRoi
Barefoot Prophet, 21,43. *See also*
  Martin, Elder Claybourne
Barksdale, Richard H., 7
Barnes, Albert, 30
Barthé, Richmond, 19
Basler, Roy, 103,106
Bates, Peg Leg, 21,43
Baudelaire, Charles, 10,49

Bearden, Romare, 19
Bellow, Saul, 41
Bennett, Gwendolyn, 15,27
Bentley, Gladys, 13,29
Bess Hokim award, 1
"Beta," 87
Bible, 51,101
Black Act of the F. F. V., 91
Black Arts Movement, 37,38,101
Black Arts Repertoire Theatre/School
  (BART/S), 36,37
Black Bourgeoisie, 66
Black Cross Nurses, 16
Black Mass, 37
Black Muslims, 95
Black No More, 15
Black Star Line, 16
Blacker the Berry, The, 70
Bledsoe, Jules, 22
Boas, Franz, 7,15
Bodenheim, Maxwell, 51
Boni Publishers, 25
Bontemps, Arna, 15,28,34,35
Breadloaf (Vermont), 2
Breman, Paul, 106
Bridge, The, 3,8,9,11,51
Bronzeville (Chicago), 25
Brotherhood of Sleeping Car
  Porters, 23
Brown, Lloyd, 101
Brown, Sterling, 7,33,35
Browning, Robert, 42
Buck and Bubbles, 21
Bulls of Bashan, 76,98–100
Burleigh, Harry T., 15

C

"C. and C.," 7,8
Calloway, Cab, 12,43,75,79
Calverton, V. F., 7–8,40,73,99
Campbell Rose McClendon Players, 19
Cansler, Ronald Lee, 102
Cantos, 8
Capone, Al, 6
Carter, Elmer, 15
Cartey, Wilfred, 74
Cause of African Redemption, 6
Cayton, Horace, 22,26,94
Century, The, 25,27
Cerf, Bennett, 40
Cervantes, Miguel, 64

Challenge, 33
Christy, Arthur, 7
"City of Refuge," 41
Civic Club, 27
Clark, Kenneth, 24,36
Club Alabam, 43,44
Cohen, Octavus Roy, 31
Color, 22
Columbia University, 6,7,8
Commandment Keepers, 14
Communist League of Struggle for
  Negro Rights, 33
Communist party, 33,35
Congo Club, 58
Conjure Man Dies, 19
Connie's Inn, 12,69
Conroy, Jack, 35
Cotton Club, 12,13,69
Cox, Oliver, 4,8
Crane, Hart, 2,3,8,9,11,50,51
Crazy Horse, 38
Crisis, 4,18,27
Crosswaith, Frank, 14
Cruse, Harold, 35,36
Cullen, Countee, 6,15,20,22,
  28,29,30,31,32,33,34,40,
  41,43,101
Cullen, Rev. Frederick, 22
Cuney, Waring, 33,34
Curator, The, 56,61,74,86–
  93,98

D

Daddy-O Club, 56
Daily Worker, 34
Dante, 64
"Dark Symphony," 1
Daumier, Honoré, 76,99
Davis, Arthur, 74,111
Davis, Benjamin, 33,35
Davis, Frank Marshall, 42
Debs, Eugene, 43
Delaporte, Guy, III, 65,73–74
Dempsey, Jack, 43
Derain, André, 99
Dickens, Charles, 9,99
Disinherited, The, 35
Divine, Father, 16–17,42,43
Divinites, 14,17
Dixon, Dean, 15
Dodson, Owen, 34,35
Douglas, Aaron, 15,19,20
Douglass, Frederick, 18,82
Drake, St. Claire, 22,26,94
Du Bois, W. E. B., 15,16,18,19,
  27,28,32,41,43,53,54,67
Dumas, Alexandre, 82
Dunbar Garden Players, 19

Dunbar, Paul Lawrence, 3,40
Dusk of dawn, 53,67
Dusk of Dawn, 54,67
Dutchman, 37

E

"E. & O. E.," 1,51,80
Eastman, Max, 7
El Greco, 64
Eliot, T. S., 2,3,8,10,49,50,
  51,98,101,103,106
Elks, 20
Ellington, Duke, 12,29,43,77
Ellison, Ralph, 7,33,41,104,
  105,111
Emperor Jones, 43
"Epsilon," 98
Estevanico, 82
"Eta," 57
Ethiopian Tabernacle, 55
Experimental Death Unit #1, 37

F

Fabio, Sarah Webster, 102,106
Fanon, Franz, 37
Fauset, Jessie, 15,28,32,41
Federal Art Project, 19
Federal One projects, 33
Federal Theatre Project (Negro
  Unit), 19
Federal Writers Project, 33,63
Fire, 41
Fire in the Flint, 20
Fisher, Rudolph, 6,15,20,21,27,
  32,41
Fisk University, 32
Flaubert, Gustave, 45
Flight, 20
Ford, James, 33
Four Quartets, 8
Frazier, E. Franklin, 22,29,31,
  66,73
Freedomways, 36
Frost, Robert, 7,49

G

Gale, Moe, 25
Gale, Zona, 7
Gallery of Harlem Portraits, A, 2,
  10,40,42,43,47,49,55,63,
  68,69,72,74,78,93
Gant, Willie, 13
Garvey, Marcus, 6,14,15,16,17,
  20,43,95
Garveyism, 16. *See also* Garvey,
  Marcus
Gautier, Théophile, 51

Gershwin, George, 97
Gilpin, Charles, 20,43,55
God Sends Sunday, 15
Gogol, Nikolai V., 99
Goya, Francisco, 66,99
Granite, Joshua, 42
Grant, St. John, 14
Grant, Ulysses, 43
Greek mythology, 51
Gropper, William, 76,99
Guernica, 100
Guggenheim Foundation, 20,22,25

H

Haiti, 19
Hall of Literature (Chicago), 1
Hamid, Sufi Abdul, 14,16,17–18
Hamilton Lodge, 13
Handy, W. C. "Papa," 15,43,69,70
Harlem, life in the '20s and '30s,
    16–47
"Harlem," 2,44,47,53
Harlem Advocate, The, 44,47
Harlem Artists Guild, 19
Harlem Community Art Center, 62
Harlem Community Players, 19
Harlem Experimental Theatre, 19
Harlem Gallery, 53,62–68,86
Harlem Gallery, 1,2,8,10,39,40,
    50–55,57,58,62,64,65,66,67,
    68,69,70,73,78,82,84,86,
    87,90,92,94,95,97,98,99,
    102,104,106,110,111
"Harlem Group of Negro Writers,
    The," 40
Harlem Hospital, 24,43
Harlem (magazine), 41
Harlem Opera House, 43,55
Harlem Players, 15
Harlem Renaissance, 27–32,37,
    40–41
Harlem riots of 1935, 24–25,32,42
Harlem String Trio, 14
Harlem Suitcase Theatre, 19
"Harlem: The Mecca of the New
    Negro," 27
"Harlem Vignettes," 78
Harlem Writers' Guild, 36
Harlem Youth Opportunities
    Unlimited (HARYOU), 36
Harmon Foundation, 25
Harper's, 25,27
Harper Publishers, 25
Harris, Abraham, 7
Harris, James E., 15
Harris, Jessie Fauset. *See* Fauset,
    Jessie
Harrison, Hubert, 14,16,43

Harrison, Richard B., 43
Haw Haw Club, 56
Hayden, Palmer, 19
Hayes, Roland, 43
Haynes, George, 15
Heffner, Marzimmu, 42
Heights, Henry, 79
Heights, Hideho, 51,56,58–62,
    72,74,79–81,83,90,96,101–2,
    104,107
Henry, John, 59,60,79,80
Herodotus, 51
Herskovitz, Melville J., 7,15
Hill, Abram, 33
Hogarth, William, 99
Holstein, Casper, 19–20,25,73
Hook, Sidney, 7
Hotel Dumas, 17
Houseman, John, 19
Howard University, 32
Huggins, Nathan, 18,41
Hughes, Langston, 6,19,20,21,
    22,25,27,30,31,32,33,35,
    40,41,43,74,79,97
Hunton School, 15
Hurston, Zora Neale, 20,27,32,
    34,42
Huot, Robert, 59,63
Hyman, Stanley, 104

I

Idols of the tribe, 5,98
"If We Must Die," 95
"I-ness," 87
Infants of the Spring, 32,71
International Club (Columbia
    University), 15
International House, 8
"Iota," 63,64
Irish literature, 28

J

Jackman, Harold, 22
Jarrett, Hobart, 2–3,4
J-E-L-L-O, 37
John Reed Club, 33
Johnson, Charles S., 6,15,18,28,
    29,32
Johnson, Fenton, 40
Johnson, Georgia Douglas, 27,30
Johnson, Jack, 43
Johnson, James P., 13
Johnson, James Weldon, 12,15,18,
    20,23,25,28,30,32,33–34,41
Johnson, J. Rosamund, 77
Johnson, Lyndon, 2
Johnson, Malvin Gray, 19

Johnson, William H., 19
Jones, Eugene Kinckle, 18
Jones, LeRoi, 35,36–37. *See also*
  Baraka, Imamu Amiri
Joplin, Scott, 77
Jubilee Singers, 15
Juilliard School, 14

K

"Kappa," 66
Kazin, Alfred, 7–8
Kawaida spirituality, 39
Keats, John, 31
Kelly, William E., 15
"Key Words," 69,76
Kiser, Clyde, 12,14
Knopf, Alfred A., 21,25
Krigwa Players, 19
Krum Elbow Estate, 17

L

Lafayette Theatre, 13,19,43,55
Langston College, 1
Larsen, Nella, 27
Laugart, John, 56,74–76,100
Leadbelly (Ledbetter, Huddie), 70
Lee, George, 42
Leslie, Lew, 25
Liberia, 16
Liberty Hall, 16,43
Libretto for the Republic of
  Liberia, 1,50,51,52,73,82,
  84,95,102
Lincoln Theatre, 70
Lincoln University, 6
Liszt, Franz, 59
Locke, Alain, 7,15,28,
  31,33,35,43
Log Cabin Theatre, 3
Longfellow, Henry W., 3
L'Ouverture, Toussaint, 82
Lumumba, Patrice, 38
Lunceford, Jimmie, 12
Lyons, Eugene, 7

M

Macbeth, 19
McKay, Claude, 12,16,19,21,22,
  25,28,29,30,31,32,33,
  34,41,74,95,97
Malamud, Bernard, 41
Malcolm X Shabazz, 36
Man Called White, A, 69
Manhattan Casino, 70
Market Place Gallery, 55
Martin, Elder Claybourne, 21,43
Marxism, 7–8,35–36

Masters, Edgar Lee, 7,10,49
Menelik, II, 82
Millay, Edna St. Vincent, 31
Miller, Kelly, 15
Mills, Florence, 20
Mitchell, Loften, 19
Modern Quarterly, 40
Monroe, Harriet, 7
Moore, Johnny, 36
Moore, Richard B., 14
Morton, Jelly Roll, 13,69
Moss, Carlton, 15,33
Moton, R. R., 15
Mount Sinai Church, 55
Mount Zion Church, 55
"Mu," 58,61,69
Muhammed's Mosque No. 7, 36

N

Nation, 28
National Association for the
  Advancement of Colored People
  (NAACP), 1,4,18,20,29,34,
  41
Native Son, 35
Neal, Larry, 37
Negro Art Theatre, 19
Negro Digest, 38
"Negro in Art: How Should He Be
  Portrayed, The," 30
Negro World, 16,43
New Book of American Negro Poetry,
  15
New Challenge, 34,35,42
New Negro movement, 20
New Negro, The, 28,29
New York City Guide, 33
New York Coordinating Committee for
  the Employment of Negroes, 21
New York Panorama, 33
New York Public Library, 15
New York Times, 12
Niagara movement, 18
Nigger Heaven, 13,20
Nkomo, Obi, 52,59–61,74,82–85,
  86,88,96,104
Notebooks, 102,105,110
Novum Organum, 5
"Nu," 58,61
Nugent, Bruce, 20
Nugent, Richard, 33

O

O. Henry, 50
"Ode to the South," 95
"Odyssey," 7
Office of Economic Opportunity
  (OEO), 36

Offord, Carl, 33
Oliver, King, 69
Omar, El-Hadj, 82
"Omega," 53,93
"Omicron," 89
Opportunity, 20,27,30
Orozco, José, 64,99
Ottley, Roi, 12,17,33
Ovington, Mary White, 15,18,25
Oxford University, 3

P

Pasternak, Boris, 49
Paterson, 8,9,11
Patterson, Charles, 36
Pepper bird, 53,66,67
Perkins, Maxwell, 40
"Phi," 61
Phidias, 64
Picasso, Pablo, 76,83,99–101
Pissarro, Camille, 64
Plantation Club, 43
Plato, 9,79
"Poet, The," 50
Poetry: A Magazine of Verse, 1,80
"Poet's Odyssey, A," 6,8
Poston, Ted, 33
Pound, Ezra, 3,8,82,103,106
Powell, Adam Clayton, Jr., 15,21
Price-Patton, Sari, 20
Proust, Marcel, 49
"Psi," 84,93
Pushkin, Alexander, 82

R

Rabelais, François, 99
Randolph, A. Phillip, 14,21
Redding, J. Saunders, 28
Reed, Clarence, 36
Reid, Arthur, 14
Reid, Ira DeA., 15
Rendezvous with America, 1,11,50, 51
Revolutionary Theatre, 38
"Rhapsody in Blue," 78
"Rho," 76
Rivera, Diego, 99
Robeson, Paul, 43,79
Robinson, Bill "Bojangles," 21, 29,43
Robinson, Edwin Arlington, 7,49
Robinson, L. A'Lelia Walker, 20,57
Rockefeller Foundation, 6,25
Rockland Palace, 17,43
Rogers, J. A., 15,33

Roosevelt, Franklin, 43
Rose, Ernestine, 15
Run Together, Chillun, 19

S

Salem Methodist Episcopal Church, 22
Salmon, Andre, 51
Sandburg, Carl, 7,49
Savage, Augusta, 15,19
Savoy, The, 13,19,43
Schoener, Allon, 12
Schomburg, Arthur, 15,41
Schomburg Collection, 15
Schopenhauer, Arthur, 51
Schultz, Dutch, 20,69,70
Schuyler, George, 7,15,31,41
Scottsboro case, 6,42,48
Scribner's Magazine, 28
Seabury Investigation, 20
Second Part of the Night Club, 13
Shakespeare, William, 51,64,101
Shapiro, Karl, 102
Shaw, O'Wendell, 42
Show Boat, 43
Sigafoos, Julio, 82
"Sigma," 56
Sixth World Congress of the Comintern, 33
Small's Paradise, 12–13
Smith, Bessie, 13,69
Smith, Willie "The Lion," 13
"Sol," 84
"Song for Myself, A," 95
Southern Association of Dramatics and Speech Arts, 3
Spelman award, 25
Spenser, Edmund, 3
Spingarn, Joel, 7
Spirit House, 37
Spoon River Anthology, 10,42,50, 54
Stalin, Joseph, 33
Starks, Hedda (Black Orchid), 70–71,77
Starks, Mister, 56,70,74,76–79, 83,90,102
Stein, Gertrude, 57,73,90
Still, Will Grant, 15
Stinette, Mac, 22
Strivers' Row, 43,47,56
Sufi. *See* Hamid, Sufi Abdul
Sugar Cane, The, 13
Sugar Hill, 24,43,47,56,73
Survey Graphic, 25,28,32
System of Dante's Hell, The, 101

T

Tammany Hall, 21,25
Tangled Bush, The, 104
Tate, Allen, 51,102,106
"Tau," 78
Taylor, Clyde, 38
Tennyson, Alfred, Lord, 3
Thomas, Norman, 7
Thorndike, Edward, 7
Thurman, Wallace, 6,15,27,28,
    31,32,41,70,71
Tolson, Melvin B., 1–11,40,47,
    50–55,68–69,75,94–100,102,
    106–10
Tolson, Melvin B., Jr. (son), 40,
    106,107
Tolson, Ruth (wife), 51
Tolstoi, Leo, 45
Toomer, Jean, 20,27
Tree of Hope, 43
Tubman, William, 1
Tucker, Earl "Snakehips," 13,21
Turf Club, 20
Turpin, Edward, 42
Tuskegee Institute, 2

U

Ubangi Club, 12
"Underdog, The," 49
United Front, 33
United Negro Improvement Associa-
    tion, 16
"Upsilon," 53,64
Urban League, 18

V

Van Doren, Carl, 15,21,30
Van Vechten, Carl, 13,20,22,30
Velasquez, Diego, 64
Vesey, Denmark, 38
Vibbard, Mother, 42,47
Viking Press, 25

W

Walker, Madame C. J., 20,43

Waller, Fats, 13,70
Walrond, Eric, 27,41
Ward, Ted, 19
Washington, Booker T., 16
Washington Tribune, 1
"Waste Land, The," 8,10,51
Waters, Ethel, 29
Weaver, Robert, 22
Welles, Orson, 19
West, Dorothy, 34
White, Walter, 7,18,20–21,27,
    41,74
Whitman, Walt, 11,40,42,45
Whittall (Gertrude Clarke) Poetry
    and Literature Fund, 2
Wiley College, 1,4,6,74,82
Wilkins, Roy, 18
Williams, Bert, 43
Williams, William Carlos, 3,8,9,
    10,11
Wilson, Frank, 15
Witter Bynner award, 22
Woodson, Carter, 15,41
World Tomorrow, 28
Wovoka, 100
WPA, 18,19,23
Wright, Dr. Louis T., 43
Wright, Richard, 7,25,33,34–35,
    38,42,104,111

X

"Xi," 58,61

Y

Yeats, William Butler, 49,78,100
Yerby, Frank, 34
YMCA, 14,15,43
Yoruba religion, 36

Z

"Zeta," 56,75
Ziegfield, Florenz, 43
Zulu Club, The, 58–62,65,
    71–72,80